Stolen Legacy

also available **The Mis-education** *and* **The Willie Lynch letter**

by

George G.M. James and Carter G. Woodson

ISBN: 978-1-63182-062-5

Stolen Legacy

also available **The Mis-education** *and* **The Willie Lynch letter**

All Rights reserved. No part of this book maybe reproduced without written permission from the publishers, except by a reviewer who may quote brief passages in a review to be printed in a newspaper or magazine.

Printed January, 2014

Published and Distributed By:

Lushena Books
607 Country Club Drive, Unit E
Bensenville, IL 60106
www.lushenabks.com

ISBN: 978-1-63182-062-5

Printed in the United States of America

PREFACE

HEREIN are recorded not opinions but the reflections of one who for forty years has participated in the education of the black, brown, yellow and white races in both hemispheres and in tropical and temperate regions. Such experience, too, has been with students in all grades from the kindergarten to the university. The author, moreover, has traveled around the world to observe not only modern school systems in various countries but to study the special systems set up by private agencies and governments to educate the natives in their colonies and dependencies. Some of these observations, too, have been checked against more recent studies on a later tour.

Discussing herein the mistakes made in the education of the Negro, the writer frankly admits that he has committed some of these errors himself. In several chapters, moreover, he specifically points out wherein he himself has strayed from the path of wisdom. This book, then, is not intended as a broadside against any particular person or class, but it is given as a corrective for methods which have not produced satisfactory results.

The author does not support the once popular view that in matters of education Negroes are rightfully subjected to the will of others on the presumption that these poor people are not large taxpayers and must be content with charitable contributions to their uplift. The author takes the position that the consumer pays the tax, and as such every individual of the social order should be given unlimited opportunity make the most of himself. Such opportunity, too, should not be determined from without by forces set to direct the proscribed element in a way to redound solely to the good of others but should be determined by the make-up of the Negro himself and by what his environment requires of him.

This new program of uplift, the author contends, should not be decided upon by the trial and error method in the application of devices used in dealing with others in a different situation and at another epoch. Only by careful study of the Negro himself and the life which he is forced to lead can we arrive at the proper procedure in this crisis. The mere imparting of information is not education. Above all things, the effort must result in making a man think and do for himself just as the Jews have done in spite of universal persecution.

In thus estimating the results obtained from the so-called education of the Negro the author does not go to the census figures to show the progress of the race. It may be of no importance to the race to be able to boast today of many times as many "educated" members as it had in 1865. If they are of the wrong kind the increase in numbers will be a disadvantage rather than an advantage. The only question which concerns us here is whether these "educated" persons are actually equipped to face the ordeal before them or unconsciously contribute to their own undoing by perpetuating the regime of the oppressor.

Herein, however, lies no argument for the oft-heard contention that education for the white man should mean one thing and for the Negro a different thing. The element of race does not enter here. It is merely a matter of exercising common sense in approaching people through their environment in order to deal with conditions as they are rather than as you would like to see them or imagine that they are. There may be a difference in method of attack, but the principle remains the same.

"Highly educated" Negroes denounce persons who advocate for the Negro a sort of education different in some respects from that now given the white man. Negroes who have been so long inconvenienced and denied opportunities for development are naturally afraid of anything that sounds like discrimination. They are anxious to have everything the white man has even if it is harmful. The possibility of originality in the Negro, therefore, is discounted one hundred per cent to maintain a nominal equality. If the whites decide to take up Mormonism the Negroes must follow their lead. If the whites neglect such a study, then the Negroes must do likewise.

The author, however, does not have such an attitude. He considers the educational system as it has developed both in Europe and America an antiquated process which does not hit the mark even in the case of the needs of the white man himself. If the white man wants to hold on to it, let him do so; but the Negro, so far as he is able, should develop and carry out a program of his own.

The so-called modern education, with all its defects, however, does others so much more good than it does the Negro, because it has been worked out in conformity to the needs of those who have enslaved and oppressed weaker peoples. For example, the philosophy and ethics resulting from our educational system have justified slavery, peonage, segregation, and lynching. The oppressor has the right to exploit, to handicap, and to kill the oppressed. Negroes daily educated in the tenets of such a religion of the strong have accepted the status of the weak as divinely ordained, and during the last three generations of their nominal freedom they have done practically nothing to change it. Their pouting and resolutions indulged in by a few of the race have been of little avail.

No systematic effort toward change has been possible, for, taught the same economics, history, philosophy, literature and religion which have established the present code of morals, the Negro's mind has been brought under the control of his oppressor. The problem of holding the Negro down, therefore, is easily solved. When you control a man's thinking you do not have to worry about his actions. You do not have to tell him not to stand here or go yonder. He will find his "proper place" and will stay in it. You do not need to send him to the back door. He will go without being told. In fact, if there is no back door, he will cut one for his special benefit. His education makes it necessary.

The same educational process which inspires and stimulates the oppressor with the thought that he is everything and has accomplished everything worth while, depresses and crushes at the same time the spark of genius in the Negro by making him feel that his race does not amount to much and never will measure up to the standards of other peoples. The Negro thus educated is a hopeless liability of the race.

The difficulty is that the "educated Negro" is compelled to live and move among his own people whom he has been taught to despise. As a rule, therefore, the "educated Negro" prefers to buy his food from a white grocer because he has been taught that the Negro is not clean. It does not matter how often a Negro washes his hands, then, he cannot clean them, and it does not matter how often a white man uses his hands he cannot soil them. The educated Negro, moreover, is disinclined to take part in Negro business, because he has been taught in economics that Negroes cannot operate in this particular sphere. The "educated Negro" gets less and less pleasure out of the Negro church, not on account of its primitiveness and increasing corruption, but because of his preference for the seats of "righteousness" controlled by his oppressor. This has been his education, and nothing else can be expected of him.

If the "educated Negro" could go off and be white he might be happy, but only a mulatto now and then can do this. The large majority of this class, then, must go through life denouncing white people because they are trying to run away from the blacks and decrying the blacks because they are not white.

CHAPTER I

THE SEAT OF THE TROUBLE

THE "educated Negroes" have the attitude of contempt toward their own people because in their own as well as in their mixed schools Negroes are taught to admire the Hebrew, the Greek, the Latin and the Teuton and to despise the African. Of the hundreds of Negro high schools recently examined by an expert in the United States Bureau of Education only eighteen offer a course taking up the history of the Negro, and in most of the Negro colleges and universities where the Negro is thought of, the race is studied only as a problem or dismissed as of little consequence. For example, an officer of a Negro university, thinking that an additional course on the Negro should be given there, called upon a Negro Doctor of Philosophy of the faculty to offer such work. He promptly informed the officer that he knew nothing about the Negro. He did not go to school to waste his time that way. He went to be educated in a system which dismisses the Negro as a nonentity.

At a Negro summer school two years ago, a white instructor gave a course on the Negro, using for his text a work which teaches that whites are superior to the blacks. When asked by one of the students why he used such a textbook the instructor replied that he wanted them to get that point of view. Even schools for Negroes, then, are places where they must be convinced of their inferiority.

The thought of the inferiority of the Negro is drilled into him in almost every class he enters and in almost every book he studies. If he happens to leave school after he masters the fundamentals, before he finishes high school or reaches college, he will naturally escape some of this bias and may recover in time to be of service to his people.

Practically all of the successful Negroes in this country are of the uneducated type or of that of Negroes who have had no formal education at all. The large majority of the Negroes who have put on the finishing touches of our best colleges are all but worthless in the development of their people. If after leaving school they have the opportunity to give out to Negroes what traducers of the race would like to have it learn such persons may thereby earn a living at teaching or preaching what they have been taught but they never become a constructive force in the development of the race. The so-called school, then, becomes a questionable factor in the life of this despised people.

As another has well said, to handicap a student by teaching him that his black face is a curse and that his struggle to change his condition is hopeless is the worst sort of lynching. It kills one's aspirations and dooms him to vagabondage and crime. It is strange, then, that the friends of truth and the promoters of freedom have not risen up against the present propaganda in the schools and crushed it. This crusade is much more important than the anti-lynching movement, because there would be no lynching if it did not start in the schoolroom. Why not exploit, enslave, or exterminate a class that everybody is taught to regard as inferior?

To be more explicit we may go to the seat of the trouble. Our most widely known scholars have been trained in universities outside of the South. Northern and Western institutions, however, have had no time to deal with matters which concern the Negro especially. They must direct their attention to the problems of the majority of their constituents, and too often they have stimulated their prejudices by referring to the Negro as unworthy of consideration. Most of what these universities have offered as language, mathematics, and science may have served a good purpose, but much of what they have taught as economics, history, literature, religion and philosophy is propaganda and cant that involved a waste of time and misdirected the Negroes thus trained.

And even in the certitude of science or mathematics it has been unfortunate that the approach to the Negro has been borrowed from a "foreign" method. For example, the teaching of arithmetic in the fifth grade in a backward county in Mississippi should mean one thing in the Negro school and a decidedly different thing in the white school. The Negro children, as a rule, come from the homes of tenants and peons who have to migrate annually from plantation to plantation, looking for light which they have never seen. The children from the homes of white planters and merchants live permanently in the midst of calculations, family budgets, and the like, which enable them sometimes to learn more by contact than the Negro can acquire in school. Instead of teaching such Negro children less arithmetic, they should be taught much more of it than the white children, for the latter attend a graded school consolidated by free transportation when the Negroes go to one-room rented hovels to be taught without equipment and by incompetent teachers educated scarcely beyond the eighth grade.

In schools of theology Negroes are taught the interpretation of the Bible worked out by those who have justified segregation and winked at the economic debasement of the Negro sometimes almost to the point of starvation. Deriving their sense of right from this teaching, graduates of such schools can have no message to grip the people whom they have been ill trained to serve. Most of such mis-educated ministers, therefore, preach to benches while illiterate Negro preachers do the best they can in supplying the spiritual needs of the masses.

In the schools of business administration Negroes are trained exclusively in the psychology and economics of Wall Street and are, therefore, made to despise the opportunities to run ice wagons, push banana carts, and sell peanuts among their own people. Foreigners, who have not studied economics but have studied Negroes, take up this business and grow rich.

In schools of journalism Negroes are being taught how to edit such metropolitan dailies as the Chicago Tribune and the New York Times, which would hardly hire a Negro as a janitor; and when these graduates come to the Negro weeklies for employment they are not prepared to function in such establishments, which, to be successful, must be built upon accurate knowledge of the psychology and philosophy of the Negro.

When a Negro has finished his education in our schools, then, he has been equipped to begin the life of an Americanized or Europeanized white man, but before he steps from the threshold of his alma mater he is told by his teachers that he must go back to his own people from whom he has been estranged by a vision of ideals which in his disillusionment he will realize that he cannot attain. He goes forth to play his part in life, but he must be both social and bisocial at the same time. While he is a part of the body politic, he is in addition to this a member of a particular race to which he must restrict himself in all matters social. While serving his country he must serve within a special group. While being a good American, he must above all things be a "good Negro"; and to perform this definite function he must learn to stay in a "Negro's place."

For the arduous task of serving a race thus handicapped, however, the Negro graduate has had little or no training at all. The people whom he has been ordered to serve have been belittled by his teachers to the extent that he can hardly find delight in undertaking what his education has led him to think is impossible. Considering his race as blank in achievement, then, he sets out to stimulate their imitation of others The performance is kept up a while; but, like any other effort at meaningless imitation, it results in failure.

Facing this undesirable result, the highly educated Negro often grows sour. He becomes too pessimistic to be a constructive force and usually develops into a chronic fault-finder or a complainant at the bar of public opinion. Often when he sees that the fault lies at the door of the white oppressor whom he is afraid to attack, he turns upon the pioneering Negro who is at work doing the best he can to extricate himself from an uncomfortable predicament.

In this effort to imitate, however, these "educated people" are sincere. They hope to make the Negro conform quickly to the standard of the whites and thus remove the pretext for the barriers between the races. They do not realize, however, that even if the Negroes do successfully imitate the whites, nothing new has thereby been accomplished. You simply have a larger number of persons doing what others have been doing. The unusual gifts of the race have not thereby been developed, and an unwilling world, therefore, continues to wonder what the Negro is good for.

These "educated" people, however, decry any such thing as race consciousness; and in some respects they are right. They do not like to hear such expressions as "Negro literature," "Negro poetry," "African art," or "thinking black"; and, roughly speaking, we must concede that such things do not exist. These things did not figure in the courses which they pursued in school, and why should they? "Aren't we all Americans? Then, whatever is American is as much the heritage of the Negro as of any other group in this country."

The "highly educated" contend, moreover, that when the Negro emphasizes these things he invites racial discrimination by recognizing such differentness of the races. The thought that the Negro is one thing and the white man another is the stock-in-trade argument of the Caucasian to justify segregation. Why, then, should the Negro blame the white man for doing what he himself does?

These "highly educated" Negroes, however, fail to see that it is not the Negro who takes this position. The white man forces him to it, and to extricate himself therefrom the Negro leader must so deal with the situation as to develop in the segregated group the power with which they can elevate themselves. The differentness of races, moreover, is no evidence of superiority or of inferiority. This merely indicates that each race has certain gifts which the others do not possess. It is by the development of these gifts that every race must justify its right to exist.

CHAPTER II

HOW WE MISSED THE MARK

How we have arrived at the present state of affairs can be understood only by studying the forces effective in the development of Negro education since it was systematically undertaken immediately after Emancipation. To point out merely the defects as they appear today will be of little benefit to the present and future generations. These things must be viewed in their historic setting. The conditions of today have been determined by what has taken place in the past, and in a careful study of this history we may see more clearly the great theatre of events in which the Negro has played a part. We may understand better what his rôle has been and how well he has functioned in it.

The idea of educating the Negroes after the Civil War was largely a prompting of philanthropy. Their white neighbors failed to assume this responsibility. These black people had been liberated as a result of a sectional conflict out of which their former owners had emerged as victims. From this class, then, the freedmen could not expect much sympathy or cooperation in the effort to prepare themselves to figure as citizens of a modern republic.

From functionaries of the United States Government itself and from those who participated in the conquest of the secessionists early came the plan of teaching these freedmen the simple duties of life as worked out by the Freedmen's Bureau and philanthropic agencies. When systematized this effort became a program for the organization of churches and schools and the direction of them along lines which had been considered most conducive to the progress of people otherwise circumstanced. Here and there some variation was made in this program in view of the fact that the status of the freedmen in no way paralleled that of their friends and teachers, but such thought was not general. When the Negroes in some way would learn to perform the duties which other elements of the population had prepared themselves to discharge they would be duly qualified, it was believed, to function as citizens of the country.

In as much as most Negroes lived in the agricultural South, moreover, and only a few of them at first acquired small farms there was little in their life which any one of thought could not have easily understood. The poverty which afflicted them for a generation after Emancipation held them down to the lowest order of society, nominally free but economically enslaved. The participation of the freedmen in government for a few years during the period known as the Reconstruction had little bearing on their situation except that they did join with the uneducated poor whites in bringing about certain much-desired social reforms, especially in giving the South its first plan of democratic education in providing for a school system at public expense.

Neither this inadequately supported school system nor the struggling higher institutions of a classical order established about the same time, however, connected the Negroes very closely with life as it was. These institutions were concerned rather with life as they hoped to make it. When the Negro found himself deprived of influence in politics, therefore, and at the same time unprepared to participate in the higher functions in the industrial development which this country began to undergo, it soon became evident to him that he was losing ground in the basic things of life. He was spending his time studying about the things which had been or might be, but he was learning little to help him to do better the tasks at hand. Since the Negroes believed that the causes of this untoward condition lay without the race, migration was attempted, and emigration to Africa was again urged. At this psychological moment came the wave of industrial education which swept the country by storm. The educational authorities in the cities and States throughout the Black Belt began to change the course of study to make the training of the Negro conform to this policy.

The missionary teachers from the North in defense of their idea of more liberal training, however, fearlessly attacked this new educational policy; and the Negroes participating in the same dispute arrayed themselves respectively on one side or the other. For a generation thereafter the quarrel as to whether the Negro should be given a classical or a practical education was the dominant topic in Negro schools and churches throughout the United States. Labor was the most important thing of life, it was argued; practical education counted in reaching that end; and the Negro worker must be taught to solve this problem of efficiency before directing attention to other things.

Others more narrow-minded than the advocates of industrial education, seized upon the idea, feeling that, although the Negro must have some semblance of education, it would be a fine stroke to be able to make a distinction between the training given the Negro and that provided for the whites. Inasmuch as the industrial educational idea rapidly gained ground, too, many Negroes for political purposes began to espouse it; and schools and colleges hoping thereby to obtain money worked out accordingly makeshift provisions for such instruction, although they could not satisfactorily offer it. A few real industrial schools actually equipped themselves for this work and turned out a number of graduates with such preparation.

Unfortunately, however, the affair developed into a sort of battle of words, for in spite of all they said and did the majority of the Negroes, those who did make some effort to obtain an education, did not actually receive either the industrial or the classical education. Negroes attended industrial schools, took such training as was prescribed, and received their diplomas; but few of them developed adequate efficiency to be able to do what they were supposedly trained to do. The schools in which they were educated could not provide for all the experience with machinery which white apprentices trained in factories had. Such industrial education as these Negroes received, then, was merely to master a technique already discarded in progressive centres; and even in less complicated operations of industry these schools had no such facilities as to parallel the numerous processes of factories conducted on the plan of the division of labor. Except what value such training might have in the development of the mind by making practical applications of mathematics and science, then, it was a failure.

The majority of Negro graduates of industrial schools, therefore, have gone into other avenues, and too often into those for which they have had no preparation whatever. Some few who actually prepared for the industrial sphere by self-improvement likewise sought other occupations for the reason that Negroes were generally barred from higher pursuits by trades unions; and, being unable to develop captans of industry to increase the demand for persons in these lines, the Negroes have not opened up many such opportunities for themselves.

During these years, too, the schools for the classical education for Negroes have not done any better. They have proceeded on the basis that every ambitious person needs a liberal education when as a matter of fact this does not necessarily follow. The Negro trained in the advanced phases of literature, philosophy, and politics has been unable to develop far in using his knowledge because of having to function in the lower spheres of the social order. Advanced knowledge of science, mathematics and languages, moreover, has not been much more useful except for mental discipline because of the dearth of opportunity to apply such knowledge among people who were largely common laborers in towns or peons on the plantations. The extent to which such higher education has been successful in leading the Negro to think, which above all is the chief purpose of education, has merely made him more of a malcontent when he can sense the drift of things and appreciate the impossibility of success in visioning conditions as they really are.

It is very clear, therefore, that we do not have in the life of the Negro today a large number of persons who have been benefited by either of the systems about which we have quarreled so long. The number of Negro mechanics and artisans have comparatively declined during the last two generations. The Negroes do not proportionately represent as many skilled laborers as they did before the Civil War. If the practical education which the Negroes received helped to improve the situation so that it is today no worse than what it is, certainly it did not solve the problem as was expected of it.

On the other hand, in spite of much classical education of the Negroes we do not find in the race a large supply of thinkers and philosophers. One excuse is that scholarship among Negroes has been vitiated by the necessity for all of them to combat segregation and fight to retain standing ground in the struggle of the races. Comparatively few American Negroes have produced creditable literature, and still fewer have made any large contribution to philosophy or science. They have not risen to the heights of black men farther removed from the influences of slavery and segregation. For this reason we do not find among American Negroes a Pushkin, a Gomez, a Geoffrey, a Captein or a Dumas. Even men like Roland Hayes and Henry O. Tanner have risen to the higher levels by getting out of this country to relieve themselves of our stifling traditions and to recover from their education.

CHAPTER III

HOW WE DRIFTED AWAY FROM THE TRUTH

How, then, did the education of the Negro take such a trend? The people who maintained schools for the education of certain Negroes before the Civil War were certainly sincere; and so were the missionary workers who went South to enlighten the freedmen after the results of that conflict had given the Negroes a new status. These earnest workers, however, had more enthusiasm than knowledge. They did not understand the task before them. This undertaking, too, was more of an effort toward social uplift than actual education. Their aim was to transform the Negroes, not to develop them. The freedmen who were to be enlightened were given little thought, for the best friends of the race, ill-taught themselves, followed the traditional curricula of the times which did not take the Negro into consideration except to condemn or pity him.

In geography the races were described in conformity with the program of the usual propaganda to engender in whites a race hate of the Negro, and in the Negroes contempt for themselves. A poet of distinction was selected to illustrate the physical features of the white race, a bedecked chief of a tribe those of the red a proud warrior the brown, a prince the yellow, and a savage with a ring in his nose the black The Negro, of course, stood at the foot of the social ladder.

The description of the various parts of the world was worked out according to the same Plan. The parts inhabited by the Caucasian were treated in detail. Less attention was given to the yellow people, still less to the red, very little to the brown, and practically none to the black race. Those people who are far removed from the physical characteristics of the Caucasians or who do not materially assist them in the domination or exploitation of others were not mentioned except to be belittled or decried.

From the teaching of science the Negro was likewise eliminated. The beginnings of science in various parts of the

Orient were mentioned, but the Africans' early advancement in this field was omitted. Students were not told that ancient Africans of the interior knew sufficient science to concoct poisons for arrowheads, to mix durable colors for paintings, to extract metals from nature and refine them for development in the industrial arts. Very little was said about the chemistry in the method of Egyptian embalming which was the product of the mixed breeds of Northern Africa, now known in the modern world as "colored people."

In the study of language in school pupils were made to scoff at the Negro dialect as some peculiar possession of the Negro which they should despise rather than directed to study the background of this language as a broken-down African tongue—in short to understand their own linguistic history, which is certainly more important for them than the study of French Phonetics or Historical Spanish Grammar. To the African language as such no attention was given except in case of the preparation of traders, missionaries and public functionaries to exploit the natives. This number of persons thus trained, of course, constituted a small fraction hardly deserving attention.

From literature the African was excluded altogether. He was not supposed to have expressed any thought worth knowing. The philosophy in the African proverbs and in the rich folklore of that continent was ignored to give preference to that developed on the distant shores of the Mediterranean. Most missionary teachers of the freedmen, like most men of our time, had never read the interesting books of travel in Africa, and had never heard of the Tarikh Es-Soudan.

In the teaching of fine arts these instructors usually started with Greece by showing how that art was influenced from without, but they omitted the African influence which scientists now regard as significant and dominant in early Hellas. They failed to teach the student the Mediterranean Melting Pot with the Negroes from Africa bringing their wares, their ideas and their blood therein to influence the history of Greece, Carthage, and Rome. Making desire father to the thought, our teachers either ignored these influences or endeavored to belittle them by working out theories to the contrary.

The bias did not stop at this point, for it invaded the teaching of the professions. Negro law students were told that they belonged to the most criminal element in the country; and an effort was made to justify the procedure in the seats of injustice where law was interpreted as being one thing for the white man and a different thing for the Negro. In constitutional law the spinelessness of the United States Supreme Court in permitting the judicial nullification of the Fourteenth and Fifteenth Amendments was and still is boldly upheld in our few law schools.

In medical schools Negroes were likewise convinced of their inferiority in being reminded of their rôle as germ carriers. The prevalence of syphilis and tuberculosis among Negroes was especially emphasized without showing that these maladies are more deadly among the Negroes for the reason that they are Caucasian diseases; and since these plagues are new to Negroes, these sufferers have not had time to develop against them the immunity which time has permitted in the Caucasian. Other diseases to which Negroes easily fall prey were mentioned to point out the race as an undesirable element when this condition was due to the Negroes' economic and social status. Little emphasis was placed upon the immunity of the Negro from diseases like yellow fever and influenza which are so disastrous to whites. Yet, the whites were not considered inferior because of this differential resistance to these plagues.

In history, of course, the Negro had no place in this curriculum. He was pictured as a human being of the lower order, unable to subject passion to reason, and therefore useful only when made the hewer of wood and the drawer of water for others. No thought was given to the history of Africa except so far as it had been a field of exploitation for the Caucasian. You might study the history as it was offered in our system from the elementary school throughout the university, and you would never hear Africa mentioned except in the negative. You would never thereby learn that Africans first domesticated the sheep, goat, and cow, developed the idea of trial by jury, produced the first stringed instruments, and gave the world its greatest boon in the discovery of iron. You would never know that prior to the Mohammedan invasion about 1000 A.D. these natives in the heart of Africa had developed powerful kingdoms which were later organized as the Songhay Empire on the order of that of the Romans and boasting of similar grandeur.

Unlike other people, then, the Negro, according to this point of view, was an exception to the natural plan of things, and he had no such mission as that of an outstanding contribution to culture. The status of the Negro, then, was justly fixed as that of an inferior. Teachers of Negroes in their first schools after Emancipation did not proclaim any such doctrine, but the content of their curricula justified these inferences.

An observer from outside of the situation naturally inquires why the Negroes, many of whom serve their race as teachers, have not changed this program. These teachers, however, are powerless. Negroes have no control over their education and have little voice in their other affairs pertaining thereto. In a few cases Negroes have been chosen as members of public boards of education, and some have been appointed members of private boards, but these Negroes are always such a small minority that they do not figure in the final working out of the educational program. The education of the Negroes, then, the most important thing in the uplift of the Negroes, is almost entirely in the hands of those who have enslaved them and now segregate them.

With "mis-educated Negroes" in control themselves, however, it is doubtful that the system would be very much different from what it is or that it would rapidly undergo change. The Negroes thus placed in charge would be the products of the same system and would show no more conception of the task at hand than do the whites who have educated them and shaped their minds as they would have them function. Negro educators of today may have more sympathy and interest in the race than the whites now exploiting Negro institutions as educators, but the former have no more vision than their competitors. Taught from books of the same bias, trained by Caucasians of the same prejudices or by Negroes of enslaved minds, one generation of Negro teachers after another have served for no higher purpose than to do what they are told to do. In other words, a Negro teacher instructing Negro children is in many respects a white teacher thus engaged, for the program in each case is about the same.

There can be no reasonable objection to the Negro's doing what the white man tells him to do, if the white man tells him to do what is right; but right is purely relative. The present system under the control of the whites trains the Negro to be white and at the same time convinces him of the impropriety or the impossibility of his becoming white. It compels the Negro to become a good Negro for the performance of which his education is ill-suited. For the white man's exploitation of the Negro through economic restriction and segregation the present system is sound and will doubtless continue until this gives place to the saner policy of actual interracial cooperation—not the present farce of racial manipulation in which the Negro is a figurehead. History does not furnish a case of the elevation of a people by ignoring the thought and aspiration of the people thus served.

This is slightly dangerous ground here, however, for the Negro's mind has been all but perfectly enslaved in that he has been trained to think what is desired of him. The "highly educated" Negroes do not like to hear anything uttered against this procedure because they make their living in this way, and they feel that they must defend the system. Few mis-educated Negroes ever act otherwise; and, if they so express themselves, they are easily crushed by the large majority to the contrary so that the procession may move on without interruption.

The result, then, is that the Negroes thus mis-educated are of no service to themselves and none to the white man. The white man does not need the Negroes' professional, commercial or industrial assistance; and as a result of the multiplication of mechanical appliances he no longer needs them in drudgery or menial service. The "highly educated" Negroes, moreover, do not need the Negro professional or commercial classes because Negroes have been taught that whites can serve them more efficiently in these spheres. Reduced, then, to teaching and preaching, the Negroes will have no outlet but to go down a blind alley, if the sort of education which they are now receiving is to enable them to find the way out of their present difficulties.

CHAPTER IV

EDUCATION UNDER OUTSIDE CONTROL

"IN the new program of educating the Negro what would become of the white teachers of the race?" some one recently inquired. This is a simple question requiring only a brief answer. The remaining few Christian workers who went South not so long after the Civil War and established schools and churches to lay the foundation on which we should now be building more wisely than we do, we would honor as a martyred throng. Anathema be upon him who would utter a word derogatory to the record of these heroes and heroines! We would pay high tribute also to unselfish Southerners like Hay-good, Curry, Ruffner, Northern, and Vance, and to white men of our time, who believe that the only way to elevate people is to help them to help themselves.

The unfortunate successors of the Northern missionary teachers of Negroes, however, have thoroughly demonstrated that they have no useful function in the life of the Negro. They have not the spirit of their predecessors and do not measure up to the requirements of educators desired in accredited colleges. If Negro institutions are to be as efficient as those for the whites in the South the same high standard for the educators to direct them should be maintained. Negro schools cannot go forward with such a load of inefficiency and especially when the white presidents of these institutions are often less scholarly than Negroes who have to serve under them.

By law and custom the white presidents and teachers of Negro schools are prevented from participating freely in the life of the Negro. They occupy, therefore, a most uncomfortable dual position. When the author once taught in a school with a mixed faculty the white women connected with the institution would bow to him in patronizing fashion when on the campus, but elsewhere they did not see him. A white president of one Negro school never entertains a Negro in his home, preferring to shift such guests to the students' dining-room. Another white president of a Negro college maintains on the campus a guest cottage which Negroes can enter only as servants. Still another such functionary does not allow students to enter his home through the front door. Negroes trained under such conditions without protest become downright cowards, and in life will continue as slaves in spite of their nominal emancipation.

"What different method of approach or what sort of appeal would one make to the Negro child that cannot be made just as well by a white teacher?" some one asked not long ago. To be frank we must concede that there is no particular body of facts that Negro teachers can impart to children of their own race that may not be just as easily presented by persons of another race if they have the same attitude as Negro teachers; but in most cases tradition, race hate, segregation, and terrorism make such a thing impossible. The only thing to do in this case, then, is to deal with the situation as it is.

Yet we should not take the position that a qualified white person should not teach in a Negro school. For certain work which temporarily some whites may be able to do better than the Negroes there can be no objection to such service, but if the Negro is to be forced to live in the ghetto he can more easily develop out of it under his own leadership than under that which is super-imposed. The Negro will never be able to show all of his originality as long as his efforts are directed from without by those who socially proscribe him. Such "friends" will unconsciously keep him in the ghetto.

Herein, however, the emphasis is not upon the necessity for separate systems but upon the need for common sense schools and teachers who understand and continue in sympathy with those whom they instruct. Those who take the position to the contrary have the idea that education is merely a process of imparting information. One who can give out these things or devise an easy plan for so doing, then, is an educator. In a sense this is true, but it accounts for most of the troubles of the Negro. Real education means to inspire people to live more abundantly, to learn to begin with life as they find it and make it better, but the instruction so far given Negroes in colleges and universities has worked to the contrary. In most cases such graduates have merely increased the number of malcontents who offer no program for changing the undesirable conditions about which they complain. One should rely upon protest only when it is supported by a constructive program.

Unfortunately Negroes who think as the author does and dare express themselves are branded as opponents of interracial cooperation. As a matter of fact, however, such Negroes are the real workers in carrying out a program of interracial effort. Cooperation implies equality of the participants in the particular task at hand. On the contrary, however, the usual way now is for the whites to work out their plans behind closed doors, have them approved by a few Negroes serving nominally on a board, and then employ a white or mixed staff to carry out their program. This is not interracial cooperation. It is merely the ancient idea of calling upon the "inferior" to carry out the orders of the "superior." To express it in post-classic language, as did Jessie O. Thomas, "The Negroes do the 'coing' and the whites the 'operating.'"

This unsound attitude of the "friends" of the Negro is due to the persistence of the mediaeval idea of controlling underprivileged classes. Behind closed doors these "friends" say you need to be careful in advancing Negroes to commanding positions unless it can be determined beforehand that they will do what they are told to do. You can never tell when some Negroes will break out and embarrass their "friends." After being advanced to positions of influence some of them have been known to run amuck and advocate social equality or demand for their race the privileges of democracy when they should restrict themselves to education and religious development.

It is often said, too, that the time is not ripe for Negroes to take over the administration of their institutions, for they do not have the contacts for raising money; but what becomes of this argument when we remember what Booker T. Washington did for Tuskegee and observe what R. R. Moton and John Hope are doing today? As the first Negro president of Howard University Mordecai W. Johnson has raised more money for that institution among philanthropists than all of its former presidents combined. Furthermore, if, after three generations the Negro colleges have not produced men qualified to administer their affairs, such an admission is an eloquent argument that they have failed ingloriously and should be immediately closed.

Recently some one asked me how I connect my criticism of the higher education of the Negroes with new developments in this sphere and especially with the four universities in the South which are to be made possible by the millions obtained from governments, boards, and philanthropists. I believe that the establishment of these four centres of learning at Washington, Atlanta, Nashville, and New Orleans can be so carried out as to mark an epoch in the development of the Negro race. On the other hand, there is just as much possibility for a colossal failure of the whole scheme. If these institutions are to be the replica of universities like Harvard, Yale, Columbia and Chicago, if the men who are to administer them and teach in them are to be the products of roll-top desk theorists who have never touched the life of the Negro, the money thus invested will be just as profitably spent if it is used to buy peanuts to throw at the animals in a circus.

Some of the thought behind the new educational movement is to provide in the South for educating the Negroes who are now crowding Northern universities, especially the medical schools, many of which will not admit Negroes because of the racial friction in hospital practice. In the rush merely to make special provisions for these "undesirable students," however, the institutions which are to train them may be established on false ideas and make the same blunders of the smaller institutions which have preceded them. It will hardly help a poisoned patient to give him a large dose of poison.

In higher institutions for Negroes, organized along lines required for people differently circumstanced, some few may profit by being further grounded in the fundamentals, others may become more adept in the exploitation of their people, and a smaller number may cross the divide and join the whites in useful service; but the large majority of the products of such institutions will increase rather than diminish the load which the masses have had to carry ever since their emancipation. Such ill-prepared workers will have no foundation upon which to build. The education of any people should begin with the people themselves, but Negroes thus trained have been dreaming about the ancients of Europe and about those who have tried to imitate them.

In a course at Harvard, for example, students were required to find out whether Pericles was justly charged with trying to supplant the worship of Jupiter with that of Juno. Since that time Negroes thus engaged have learned that they would have been much better prepared for work among the Negroes in the Black Belt if they had spent that time learning why John Jasper of "sun-do-move" fame joined with Joshua in contending that the planet stood still "in the middle of the line while he fought the battle the second time."

Talking the other day with one of the men now giving the millions to build the four Negro universities in the South, however, I find that he is of the opinion that accredited institutions can be established in mushroom fashion with theorists out of touch with the people. In other words, you can go almost anywhere and build a three million dollar plant, place in charge a white man to do what you want accomplished, and in a short while he can secure or have trained to order the men necessary to make a university. "We want here," he will say, "a man who has his Master's degree in English. Send me another who has his Doctor's degree in sociology, and I can use one more in physics."

Now, experience has shown that men of this type may "fill in," but a university cannot be established with such raw recruits. The author once had some experience in trying to man a college in this fashion, and the result was a story that would make an interesting headline for the newspapers. When Dr. William Bainey Harper was establishing the University of Chicago he called to the headship of the various departments only men who had distinguished themselves in the creative world. Some had advanced degrees, and some had not. Several of them had never done any formal graduate work at all. All of them, however, were men whose thought was moving the world. It may be argued that the Negroes have no such men and must have them trained, but such a thing cannot be forced as we are now doing it. It would be much better to stimulate the development of the more progressive teachers of old than experiment with novices produced by the degradation of higher education.

The degradation of the doctorate especially dawned upon the author the other day more clearly than ever when a friend of his rushed into his office saying, "I have been trying to see you for several days. I have just failed to get a job for which I had been working, and I am told that I cannot expect a promotion until I get my 'darkter's 'gree.'" That is what he called it. He could not even pronounce the words, but he is determined to have his "darkter's 'gree" to get the job in sight.

This shameful status of higher education is due in a large measure to low standards of institutions with a tendency toward the diplomamill procedure. To get a job or to hold one you go in and stay until they "grind" you out a "darkter's 'gree." And you do not have to worry any further. The assumption is that almost any school will be glad to have you thereafter, and you will receive a large salary.

Investigation has shown, however, that men who have the doctorate not only lose touch with the common people, but they do not do as much creative work as those of less formal education. After having this honor conferred upon them, these so-called scholars often rest on their oars. Few persons have thought of the seriousness of such inertia among men who are put in the lead of things because of meeting statutory requirements of frontier universities which are not on the frontier.

The General Education Board and the Julius Rosenwald Fund have a policy which may be a partial solution of the undeveloped Negro college instructor's problem. These foundations are giving Negro teachers scholarships to improve themselves for work in the sphere in which they are now laboring in the South. These boards, as a rule, do not send one to school to work for the Doctor's degree. If they find a man of experience and good judgment, showing possibilities for growth, they will provide for him to study a year or more to refresh his mind with whatever there is new in his field. Experience has shown that teachers thus helped have later done much better work than Doctors of Philosophy made to order.

The Northern universities, moreover, cannot do graduate work for Negroes along certain lines when they are concentrating on the educational needs of people otherwise circumstanced. The graduate school for Negroes studying chemistry is with George W. Carver at Tuskegee. At least a hundred youths should wait daily upon the words of this scientist to be able to pass on to the generations unborn his great knowledge of agricultural chemistry. Negroes desiring to specialize in agriculture should do it with workers like T. M. Campbell and B. F. Hubert among the Negro farmers of the South.

In education itself the situation is the same. Neither Columbia nor Chicago can give an advanced course in Negro rural education, for their work in education is based primarily upon what they know of the educational needs of the whites. Such work for Negroes must be done under the direction of the trail blazers who are building school houses and reconstructing the educational program of those in the backwoods. Leaders of this type can supply the foundation upon which a university of realistic education may be established.

We offer no argument here against earning advanced degrees, but these should come as honors conferred for training crowned with scholastic distinction, not to enable a man to increase his salary or find a better paying position. The schools which are now directing attention exclusively to these external marks of learning will not contribute much to the uplift of the Negro.

In Cleveland not long ago the author found at the Western Reserve University something unusually encouraging.

A native of Mississippi, a white man trained in a Northern university and now serving as a professor in one, has under him in sociology a Negro student from Georgia. For his dissertation this Negro is collecting the sayings of his people in everyday life—their morning greetings, their remarks about the weather, their comments on things which happen around them, their reactions to things which strike them as unusual, and their efforts to interpret life as the panorama passes before them. This white Mississippian and black Georgian are on the right way to understand the Negro and, if they do not fall out about social equality, they will serve the Negro much better than those who are trying to find out whether Henry VIII lusted more after Anne Boleyn than after Catherine of Aragon or whether Elizabeth was justly styled as more untruthful than Philip II of Spain.

CHAPTER V

THE FAILURE TO LEARN TO MAKE A LIVING

THE greatest indictment of such education as Negroes have received, however, is that they have thereby learned little as to making a living, the first essential in civilization. Rural Negroes have always known something about agriculture, and in a country where land is abundant they have been able to make some sort of living on the soil even though they have not always employed scientific methods of farming. In industry where the competition is keener, however, what the Negro has learned in school has had little bearing on the situation, as pointed out above. In business the rôle of education as a factor in the uplift of the Negro has been still less significant. The Negroes of today are unable to employ one another, and the whites are inclined to call on Negroes only when workers of their own race have been taken care of. For the solution of this problem the "mis-educated" Negro has offered no remedy whatever.

What Negroes are now being taught does not bring their minds into harmony with life as they must face it. When a Negro student works his way through college by polishing shoes he does not think of making a special study of the science underlying the production and distribution of leather and its products that he may some day figure in this sphere. The Negro boy sent to college by a mechanic seldom dreams of learning mechanical engineering to build upon the foundation his father has laid, that in years to come he may figure as a contractor or a consulting engineer. The Negro girl who goes to college hardly wants to return to her mother if she is a washerwoman, but this girl should come back with sufficient knowledge of physics and chemistry and business administration to use her mother's work as a nucleus for a modern steam laundry. A white professor of a university recently resigned his position to become rich by running a laundry for Negroes in a Southern city. A Negro college instructor would have considered such a suggestion an insult. The so-called education of Negro college graduates leads them to throw away opportunities which they have and to go in quest of those which they do not find.

In the case of the white youth in this country, they can choose their courses more at random and still succeed because of numerous opportunities offered by their people, but even they show so much more wisdom than do Negroes. For example, a year or two after the author left Harvard he found out West a schoolmate who was studying wool. "How did you happen to go into this sort of thing?" the author inquired. His people, the former replied, had had some experience in wool, and in college he prepared for this work. On the contrary, the author studied Aristotle, Plato, Marsiglio of Padua, and Pascasius Rathbertus when he was in college. His friend who studied wool, however, is now independently rich and has sufficient leisure to enjoy the cultural side of life which his knowledge of the science underlying his business developed, but the author has to make his living by begging for a struggling cause.

An observer recently saw at the market near his office a striking example of this inefficiency of our system. He often goes over there at noon to buy a bit of fruit and to talk with a young woman who successfully conducts a fruit stand there in cooperation with her mother. Some years ago he tried to teach her in high school; but her memory was poor, and she could not understand what he was trying to do. She stayed a few weeks, smiling at the others who toiled, and finally left to assist her mother in business. She learned from her mother, however, how to make a living and be happy.

This observer was reminded of this young woman soon thereafter when there came to visit him a friend who succeeded in mastering everything taught in high school at that time and later distinguished himself in college. This highly educated man brought with him a complaint against life. Having had extreme difficulty in finding an opportunity to do what he is trained to do, he has thought several times of committing suicide. A friend encouraged this despondent man to go ahead and do it. The sooner the better. The food and air which he is now consuming may then go to keep alive some one who is in touch with life and able to grapple with its problems. This man has been educated away from the fruit stand.

This friend had been trying to convince this misfit of the unusual opportunities for the Negroes in business, but he reprimanded his adviser for urging him to take up such a task when most Negroes thus engaged have been failures.

"If we invest our money in some enterprise of our own," said he, "those in charge will misuse or misappropriate it. I have learned from my study of economics that we had just as well keep on throwing it away."

Upon investigation, however, it was discovered that this complainant and most others like him have never invested anything in any of the Negro enterprises, although they have tried to make a living by exploiting them. But they feel a bit guilty on this account, and when they have some apparent ground for fault-finding they try to satisfy their conscience which all but condemns them for their suicidal course of getting all they can out of the race while giving nothing back to it.

Gossiping and scandal-mongering Negroes, of course, come to their assistance. Mis-educated by the oppressors of the race, such Negroes expect the Negro business man to fail anyway. They seize, then, upon unfavorable reports, exaggerate the situation, and circulate falsehoods throughout the world to their own undoing. You read such headlines as GREATEST NEGRO BUSINESS FAILS, NEGRO BANK ROBBED BY ITS OFFICERS, and THE TWILIGHT OF NEGRO BUSINESS. The mis-educated Negroes, then, stand by saying:

"I told you so. Negroes cannot run business. My professors pointed that out to me years ago when I studied economics in college; and I never intend to put any of my money in any Negro enterprise."

Yet, investigation shows that in proportion to the amount of capital invested Negro enterprises manifest about as much strength as businesses of others similarly situated. Negro business men have made mistakes, and they are still making them; but the weak link in the chain is that they are not properly supported and do not always grow strong enough to pass through a crisis. The Negro business man, then, has not failed so much as he has failed to get support of Negroes who should be mentally developed sufficiently to see the wisdom of supporting such enterprises.

Now the "highly educated" Negroes who have studied economics at Harvard, Yale, Columbia, and Chicago, will say that the Negro cannot succeed in business because their professors who have never had a moment's experience in this sphere have written accordingly. The whites, they say, have the control of the natural resources and so monopolize the production of raw materials as to eliminate the competition of the Negro. Apparently this is true. All things being equal from the point of view of the oppressor, he sees that the Negro cannot meet the test.

The impatient, "highly educated" Negroes, therefore, say that since under the present system of capitalism the Negro has no chance to toil upward in the economic sphere, the only hope for bettering his condition in this respect is through socialism, the overthrow of the present economic régime, and the inauguration of popular control of resources and agencies which are now being operated for personal gain. This thought is gaining ground among Negroes in this country, and it is rapidly sweeping them into the ranks of what are commonly known as "Communists."

There can be no objection to this radical change, if it brings with it some unselfish genius to do the task better than it is now being done under the present régime of competition. Russia so far has failed to do well this particular thing under a proletarian dictatorship in an agricultural country. But whether this millennium comes or not, the capitalistic system is so strongly intrenched at present that the radicals must struggle many years to overthrow it; and if the Negro has to wait until that time to try to improve his condition he will be starved out so soon that he will not he here to tell the story. The Negro, therefore, like all other oppressed people, must learn to do the so-called "impossible."

The "uneducated" Negro business man, however, is actually at work doing the very thing which the "mis-educated" Negro has been taught to believe cannot be done. This much-handicapped Negro business man could do better if he had some assistance, but our schools are turning out men who do as much to impede the progress of the Negro in business as they do to help him. The trouble is that they do not think for themselves.

If the "highly educated" Negro would forget most of the untried theories taught him in school, if he could see through the propaganda which has been instilled into his mind under the pretext of education, if he would fall in love with his own people and begin to sacrifice for their uplift—if the "highly educated" Negro would do these things, he could solve some of the problems now confronting the race.

During recent years we have heard much of education in business administration departments in Negro colleges; but if they be judged by the products turned out by these departments they are not worth a "continental." The teachers in this field are not prepared to do the work, and the trustees of our institutions are spending their time with trifles instead of addressing themselves to the study of a situation which threatens the Negro with economic extermination.

Recently the author saw the need for a change of attitude when a young woman came almost directly to his office after her graduation from a business school to seek employment. After hearing her story he finally told her that he would give her a trial at fifteen dollars a week.

"Fifteen dollars a week!" she cried, "I cannot live on that, sir."

"I do not see why you cannot," he replied. "You have lived for some time already, and you say that you have never had permanent employment, and you have none at all now."

"But a woman has to dress and to pay board," said she;

"and how can she do it on such a pittance?"

The amount offered was small, but it was a great deal more than she is worth at present. In fact, during the first six or nine months of her connection with some enterprise it will be of more service to her than she will be to the firm. Coming out of school without experience, she will be a drag on a business until she learns to discharge some definite function in it. Instead of requiring the firm to pay her she should pay it for training her. Negro business today, then, finds the "mis-educated employees" its heaviest burden. Thousands of graduates of white business schools spend years in establishments in undergoing apprenticeship without pay and rejoice to have the opportunity thus to learn how to do things.

The schools in which Negroes are now being trained, however, do not give our young people this point of view. They may occasionally learn the elements of stenography and accounting, but they do not learn how to apply what they have studied. The training which they undergo gives a false conception of life when they believe that the business world owes them a position of leadership. They have the idea of business training that we used to have of teaching when it was thought that we could teach anything we had studied.

Graduates of our business schools lack the courage to throw themselves upon their resources and work for a commission. The large majority of them want to be sure of receiving a certain amount at the end of the week or month. They do not seem to realize that the great strides in business have been made by paying men according to what they do. Persons with such false impressions of life are not good representatives of schools of business administration.

Not long ago a firm of Washington, D. C., appealed to the graduates of several of our colleges and offered them an inviting proposition on the commission basis, but only five of the hundreds appealed to responded and only two of the five gave satisfaction. Another would have succeeded, but he was not honest in handling money because he had learned to purloin the treasury of the athletic organization while in college.

All of the others, however, were anxious to serve somewhere in an office for a small wage a week.

Recently one of the large insurance companies selected for special training in this line fifteen college graduates of our accredited institutions and financed their special training in insurance. Only one of the number, however, rendered efficient service in this field. They all abandoned the effort after a few days' trial and accepted work in hotels and with the Pullman Company, or they went into teaching or something else with a fixed stipend until they could enter upon the practice of professions. The thought of the immediate reward, shortsightedness, and the lack of vision and courage to struggle and win the fight made them failures to begin with. They are unwilling to throw aside their coats and collars and do the groundwork of Negro business and thus make opportunities for themselves instead of begging others for a chance.

The educated Negro from the point of view of commerce and industry, then, shows no mental power to understand the situation which he finds. He has apparently read his race out of that sphere, and with the exception of what the illiterate Negroes can do blindly the field is left wide open for foreign exploitation. Foreigners see this opportunity as soon as they reach our shores and begin to manufacture and sell to Negroes especially such things as caps, neckties, and housedresses which may be produced at a small cost and under ordinary circumstances. The main problem with the Negro in this field, however, is salesmanship; that is where he is weak.

It is unfortunate, too, that the educated Negro does not understand or is unwilling to start small enterprises which make the larger ones possible. If he cannot proceed according to the methods of the gigantic corporations about which he reads in books, he does not know how to take hold of things and organize the communities of the poor along lines of small businesses. Such training is necessary, for the large majority of Negroes conducting enterprises have not learned business methods and do not understand the possibilities of the field in which they operate. Most of them in the beginning had had no experience, and started out with such knowledge as they could acquire by observing some one's business from the outside. One of them, for example, had waited on a white business club in passing the members a box of cigars or bringing a pitcher of water. When they began to discuss business, however, he had to leave the room. About the only time he could see them in action was when they were at play, indulging in extravagances which the Negro learned to take up before he could afford them.

Negro businesses thus handicapped, therefore, have not developed stability and the capacity for growth. Practically all worth while Negro businesses which were flourishing in 1900 are not existing today. How did this happen? Well, Negro business men have too much to do. They have not time to read the business literature and study the market upon which they depend, and they may not be sufficiently trained to do these things. They are usually operating in the dark or by the hit-or-miss method. They cannot secure intelligent guidance because the schools are not turning out men properly trained to take up Negro business as it is to develop and make it what it ought to be rather than find fault with it. Too often when the founder dies, then, the business dies with him; or it goes to pieces soon after he passes away, for nobody has come into sufficiently close contact with him to learn the secret of his success in spite of his handicaps.

The business among Negroes, too, continues individualistic in spite of advice to the contrary. The founder does not take kindly to the cooperative plan, and such business education as we now give the youth does not make their suggestions to this effect convincing. If the founder happens to be unusually successful, too, the business may outgrow his knowledge, and becoming too unwieldy in his hands, may go to pieces by errors of judgment; or because of mismanagement it may go into the hands of whites who are usually called in at the last hour to do what they call refinancing but what really means the actual taking over of the business from the Negroes. The Negroes, then, finally withdraw their patronage because they realize that it is no longer an enterprise of the race, and the chapter is closed.

All of the failures of the Negro business, however, are not due to troubles from without. Often the Negro business man lacks common sense. The Negro in business, for example, too easily becomes a social "lion." He sometimes plunges into the leadership in local matters. He becomes popular in restricted circles, and men of less magnetism grow jealous of his inroads. He learns how richer men of other races waste money. He builds a finer home than anybody else in the community, and in his social program he does not provide for much contact with the very people upon whom he must depend for patronage. He has the finest car, the most expensive dress, the best summer home, and so far outdistances his competitors in society that they often set to work in child-like fashion to bring him down to their level.

CHAPTER VI

THE EDUCATED NEGRO LEAVES THE MASSES

ONE of the most striking evidences of the failure of higher education among Negroes is their estrangement from the masses, the very people upon whom they must eventually count for carrying out a program of progress. Of this the Negro churches supply the most striking illustration. The large majority of Negro communicants still belong to these churches, but the more education the Negroes undergo the less comfort they seem to find in these evangelical groups. These churches do not measure up to the standard set by the university preachers of the Northern centres of learning. Most Negroes returning as finished products from such institutions, then, are forever lost to the popular Negro churches. The unchurched of this class do not become members of such congregations, and those who have thus connected themselves remain chiefly for political or personal reasons and tend to become communicants in name only.

The Negro church, however, although not a shadow of what it ought to be, is the great asset of the race. It is a part of the capital that the race must invest to make its future. The Negro church, has taken the lead in education in the schools of the race, it has supplied a forum for the thought of the "highly educated" Negro, it has originated a large portion of the business controlled by Negroes, and in many cases it has made it possible for Negro professional men to exist. It is unfortunate, then, that these classes do not do more to develop the institution. In thus neglecting it they are throwing away what they have, to obtain something which they think they need. In many respects, then, the Negro church during recent generations has become corrupt. It could be improved, but those Negroes who can help the institution have deserted it to exploiters, grafters, and libertines. The "highly educated" Negroes have turned away from the people in the churches, and the gap between the masses and the "talented tenth" is rapidly widening.

Of this many examples may be cited. When the author recently attended in Washington, D. C., one of the popular Negro churches with a membership of several thousands he saw a striking case in evidence. While sitting there he thought of what a power this group could become under the honest leadership of intelligent men and women. Social uplift, business, public welfare—all have their possibilities there if a score or more of our "highly educated" Negroes would work with these people at that center. Looking carefully throughout the audience for such persons, however, he recognized only two college graduates, Kelly Miller and himself; but the former had come to receive from the church a donation to the Community Chest, and the author had come according to appointment to make an appeal in behalf of Miss Nannie H. Burroughs' school. Neither one had manifested any interest in that particular church. This is the way most of them receive attention from our "talented tenth."

Some "highly educated" Negroes say that they have not lost their interest in religion, that they have gone into churches with a more intellectual atmosphere in keeping with their new thoughts and aspirations. And then there is a sort of contagious fever which takes away from the churches of their youth others of less formal education. Talking with a friend from Alabama, the other day, the author found out that after her father had died and she had moved to Washington she forsook the Baptist church in which he had been a prominent worker and joined a ritualistic church which is more fashionable.

Such a change of faith is all right in a sense, for no sensible person today would dare to make an argument in favor of any particular religion. Religion is but religion, if the people live up to the faith they profess. What is said here with respect to the popular churches of Negroes, which happen to be chiefly Methodist and Baptist, would hold also if they were mainly Catholic and Episcopal, provided the large majority of Negroes belonged to those churches. The point here is that the ritualistic churches into which these Negroes have gone do not touch the masses, and they show no promising future for racial development. Such institutions are controlled by those who offer the Negroes only limited opportunity and then sometimes on the condition that they be segregated in the court of the gentiles outside of the temple of Jehovah.

How an "educated Negro" can thus leave the church of his people and accept such jimcrowism has always been a puzzle. He cannot be a thinking man. It may be a sort of slave psychology which causes this preference for the leadership of the oppressor. The excuse sometimes given for seeking such religious leadership is that the Negro evangelical churches are "fogy," but a thinking man would rather be behind the times and have his self-respect than compromise his manhood by accepting segregation. They say that in some of the Negro churches bishoprics are actually bought, but it is better for the Negro to belong to a church where one can secure a bishopric by purchase than be a member of one which would deny the promotion on account of color.

With respect to developing the masses, then, the Negro race has lost ground in recent years. In 1880 when the Negroes had begun to make themselves felt in teaching, the attitude of the leaders was different from what it is today. At that time men went off to school to prepare themselves for the uplift of a downtrodden people. In our time too many Negroes go to school to memorize certain facts to pass examinations for jobs. After they obtain these positions they pay little attention to humanity. This attitude of the "educated Negro" toward the masses results partly from the general trend of all persons toward selfishness, but it works more disastrously among the Negroes than among the whites because the lower classes of the latter have had so much more opportunity.

For some time the author has been making a special study of the Negroes in the City of Washington to compare their condition of today with that of the past. Now although the "highly educated" Negroes of the District of Columbia have multiplied and apparently are in better circumstances than ever, the masses show almost as much backwardness as they did in 1880. Sometimes you find as many as two or three store-front churches in a single block where Negroes indulge in heathen-like practices which could hardly be equaled in the jungle. The Negroes in Africa have not descended to such depths. Although born and brought up in the Black Belt of the South the author never saw there such idolatrous tendencies as he has seen under the dome of the Capitol.

Such conditions show that the undeveloped Negro has been abandoned by those who should help him. The educated white man, said an observer recently, differs from the "educated Negro" who so readily forsakes the belated element of his race. When a white man sees persons of his own race tending downward to a level of disgrace he does not rest until he works out some plan to lift such unfortunates to higher ground; but the Negro forgets the delinquents of his race and goes his way to feather his own nest, as he has done in leaving the masses in the popular churches.

This is sad indeed, for the Negro church is the only institution the race controls. With the exception of the feeble efforts of a few all but starved-out institutions, the education of the Negroes is controlled by the other element; and save the dramatization of practical education by Booker T. Washington, Negroes have not influenced the system at all in America. In business, the lack of capital, credit, and experience has prevented large undertakings to accumulate the wealth necessary for the ease and comfort essential to higher culture.

In the church, however, the Negro has had sufficient freedom to develop this institution in his own way; but he has failed to do so. His religion is merely a loan from the whites who have enslaved and segregated the Negroes; and the organization, though largely an independent Negro institution, is dominated by the thought of the oppressors of the race. The "educated" Negro minister is so trained as to drift away from the masses and the illiterate preachers into whose hands the people inevitably fall are unable to develop a doctrine and procedure of their own. The dominant thought is to make use of the dogma of the whites as means to an end. Whether the system is what it should be or not it serves the purpose.

In chameleon-like fashion the Negro has taken up almost everything religious which has come along instead of thinking for himself. The English split off from the Catholics because Henry VIII had difficulty in getting sanction from the Church to satisfy his lust for amorous women, and Negroes went with this ilk, singing "God save the King." Others later said the thing necessary is baptism by immersion; and the Negroes joined them as Baptists. Another circle of promoters next said we must have a new method of doing things and we shall call ourselves Methodists; and the Negroes, then, embraced that faith. The Methodists and Baptists split up further on account of the custom of holding slaves; and the Negroes arrayed themselves on the respective sides. The religious agitators divided still more on questions beyond human power to understand; and the Negroes started out in similar fashion to imitate them.

For example, thirty of the two hundred and thirteen religious bodies reported in 1926 were exclusively Negro, while thirty which were primarily white denominations had one or more Negro churches among their number. In other words, Negroes have gone into practically all sects established by the whites; and, in addition to these, they have established thirty of their own to give the system further complication and subdivision. The situation in these churches is aggravated, too, by having too many ministers and about five times as many supervisory officials as a church embracing all Negro communicants would actually need. All of the Negro Methodists in the world, if united, would not need more than twelve bishops, and these would have time to direct the affairs of both Methodists and Baptists in a united church. There is no need for three or four bishops, each teaching the same faith and practice while duplicating the work of the other in the same area merely because a long time ago somebody following the ignorant oppressors of the race in these churches committed the sin of dissension and strife. For all of this unnecessary expense impoverished Negroes have to pay.

The "theology" of "foreigners," too, is the important factor in this disunion of churches and the burden which they impose on an unenlightened people. Theologians have been the "bane of bliss and source of woe." While bringing the joy of conquest to their own camp they have confused the world with disputes which have divided the church and stimulated division and subdivision to the extent that it no longer functions as a Christian agency for the uplift of all men.

To begin with, theology is of pagan origin. Albert Magnus and Thomas Aquinas worked out the first system of it by applying to religious discussion the logic of Aristotle, a pagan philosopher, who believed neither in the creation of the world nor the immortality of the soul. At best it was degenerate learning, based upon the theory that knowledge is gained by the mind working upon itself rather than upon matter or through sense perception. The world was, therefore, confused with the discussion of absurdities as it is today by those of prominent churchmen. By their peculiar "reasoning," too, theologians have sanctioned most of the ills of the ages. They justified the Inquisition, serfdom, and slavery. Theologians of our time defend segregation and the annihilation of one race by the other. They have drifted away from righteousness into an effort to make wrong seem to be right.

While we must hold the Negroes responsible for following these ignorant theorists, we should not charge to their account the origination of this nonsense with which they have confused thoughtless people. As said above, the Negro has been so busy doing what he is told to do that he has not stopped long enough to think about the meaning of these things. He has borrowed the ideas of his traducers instead of delving into things and working out some thought of his own. Some Negro leaders of these religious factions know better, but they hold their following by keeping the people divided, in emphasizing nonessentials the insignificance of which the average man may not appreciate. The "highly educated" Negroes who know better than to follow these unprincipled men have abandoned these popular churches.

While serving as the avenue of the oppressor's propaganda, the Negro church, although doing some good, has prevented the union of diverse elements and has kept the race too weak to overcome foes who have purposely taught Negroes how to quarrel and fight about trifles until their enemies can overcome them. This is the keynote to the control of the so-called inferior races by the self-styled superior. The one thinks and plans while the other in excited fashion seizes upon and destroys his brother with whom he should cooperate.

CHAPTER VII

DISSENSION AND WEAKNESS

IN recent years the churches in enlightened centres have devoted less attention to dissension than formerly, but in the rural districts and small cities they have not changed much; and neither in urban communities nor in the country has any one succeeded in bringing these churches together to work for their general welfare. The militant sects are still fighting one another, and in addition to this the members of these sects are contending among themselves. The spirit of Christ cannot dwell in such an atmosphere.

Recent experiences show that these dissensions are about as rank as ever. For example, a rural community, in which an observer spent three weeks a year ago, has no church at all, although eight or ten families live there. No church can thrive among them because, with one or two exceptions, each family represents a different denomination, and the sectarian bias is so pronounced that one will not accept the procedure of the other. Each one loves his fellow man if he thinks as he does; but if his fellow man does not, he hates and shuns him.

In another rural community where the same observer recently spent two weeks he found a small and poorly attended Methodist church. Worshiping there one Sunday morning, he counted only four persons who lived in the community. Others might have come, for there was no other church for them in that place; but this particular church was not of their faith, and their number was too small to justify the establishment of one to their liking. The support given the unfortunate pastor there is so meager that he can hardly afford to come to them once a month, and consequently these peasants are practically without spiritual leadership. People who are so directed as to develop such an attitude are handicapped for life.

Some one recently inquired as to why the religious schools do not teach the people how to tolerate differences of opinion and to cooperate for the common good. This, however, is the thing which these institutions have refused to do. Religious schools have been established, but they are considered necessary to supply workers for denominational outposts and to keep alive the sectarian bias by which the Baptists hope to outstrip the Methodists or the latter the former. No teacher in one of these schools has advanced a single thought which has become a working principle in Christendom, and not one of these centres is worthy of the name of a school of theology. If one would bring together all of the teachers in such schools and carefully sift them he would not find in the whole group a sufficient number qualified to conduct one accredited school of religion. The large majority of them are engaged in imparting to the youth worn-out theories of the ignorant oppressor.

This lack of qualified teachers in Negro schools of theology, however, is not altogether the fault of the teachers themselves. It is due largely to the system to which they belong. Their schools of "theology" are impoverished by their unnecessary multiplication, and consequently the instructors are either poorly paid or not compensated at all. Many of them have to farm, conduct enterprises, or pastor churches to make a living while trying to teach. Often, then, only the inefficient can be retained under such circumstances. Yet those who see how they have failed because of these things nevertheless object to the unification of the churches as taught by Jesus of Nazareth, whom they have all but ceased to follow because of their sectarian bias obtained from thumb-worn books of misguided Americans and Europeans.

Recently an observer saw a result of this in the sermon of a Negro college graduate, trying to preach to a church of the masses. He referred to all the great men in the history of a certain country to show how religious they were, whether they were or not. When he undertook to establish the Christian character of Napoleon, however, several felt like leaving the place in disgust. The climax of the service was a prayer by another "mis-educated" Negro who devoted most of the time to thanking God for Cicero and Demosthenes. Here, then, was a case of the religion of the pagan handed down by the enslaver and segregationist to the Negro.

Returning from the table where he had placed his offering in a church on a Sunday morning not long thereafter, this observer saw another striking example of this failure to hit the mark. He stopped to inquire of his friend, Jim Minor, as to why he had not responded to the appeal for a collection.

"What!" said Jim, "I ain't givin' that man nothing. That man ain't fed me this morning, and I ain't feedin' him."

This was Jim's reaction to a "scholarly" sermon entitled "The Humiliation of the Incarnation." During the discourse, too, the minister had had much to say about John Knox Orthodox, and another of the communicants bowing at that shrine inquired of the observer later as to who this John Knox Orthodox was and where he lived. The observer could not answer all of the inquiries thus evoked, but he tried to explain the best he could that the speaker had "studied" history and theology.

This was the effect this sermon had on an earnest congregation. The minister had attended a school of theology but had merely memorized words and phrases, which meant little to him and nothing to those who heard his discourse. The school in which he had been trained followed the traditional course for ministers, devoting most of the time to dead languages and dead issues. He had given attention to polytheism, monotheism, and the doctrine of the Trinity. He had studied also the philosophical basis of the Caucasian dogma, the elements of that theology, and the schism by which fanatics made religion a football and multiplied wars only to moisten the soil of Europe with the blood of unoffending men.

This minister had given no attention to the religious background of the Negroes to whom he was trying to preach. He knew nothing of their spiritual endowment and their religious experience as influenced by their traditions and environment in which the religion of the Negro has developed and expressed itself. He did not seem to know anything about their present situation. These honest people, therefore, knew nothing additional when he had finished his discourse. As one communicant pointed out, their wants had not been supplied, and they wondered where they might go to hear a word which had some bearing upon the life which they had to live.

Not long ago when the author was in Virginia he inquired about a man who was once a popular preacher in that state. He is here, they said, but he is not preaching now. He went off to school, and when he came back the people could not understand what he was talking about. Then he began to find fault with the people because they would not come to church. He called them fogy, because they did not appreciate his new style of preaching and the things he talked about. The church went down to nothing, and he finally left it and took up farming.

In a rural community, then, a preacher of this type must fail unless he can organize separately members of the popular Methodist and Baptist churches who go into the ritualistic churches or establish certain "refined" Methodist or Baptist churches catering to the "talented tenth." For lack of adequate numbers, however, such churches often fail to develop sufficient force to do very much for themselves or for anybody else. On Sunday morning, then, their pastors have to talk to the benches. While these truncated churches go higher in their own atmosphere of self-satisfaction the mentally undeveloped are left to sink lower because of the lack of contact with the better trained. If the latter exercised a little more judgment, they would be able to influence these people for good by gradually introducing advanced ideas.

Because our "highly educated" people do not do this, large numbers of Negroes drift into churches led by the "uneducated" ministers who can scarcely read and write. These preachers do not know much of what is found in school books and can hardly make use of a library in working out a sermon; but they understand the people with whom they deal, and they make such use of the human laboratory that sometimes they become experts in solving vexing problems and meeting social needs. They would be much better preachers if they could have attended a school devoted to the development of the mind rather than to cramming it with extraneous matters which have no bearing on the task which lies before them. Unfortunately, however, very few of such schools of religion now exist.

For lack of intelligent guidance, then, the Negro church often fulfills a mission to the contrary of that for which it was established. Because the Negro church is such a free field and it is controlled largely by the Negroes themselves, it seems that practically all the incompetents and undesirables who have been barred from other walks of life by race prejudice and economic difficulties have rushed into the ministry for the exploitation of the people. Honest ministers who are trying to do their duty, then, find their task made difficult by these men who stoop to practically everything conceivable. Almost anybody of the lowest type may get into the Negro ministry. The Methodists claim that they have strict regulations to prevent this, but their net draws in proportionately as many undesirables as one finds among the Baptists.

As an evidence of the depths to which the institution has gone a resident of Cincinnati recently reported a case of its exploitation by a railroad man who lost his job and later all his earnings in a game in a den of vice in that city. To refinance himself he took an old black frock coat and a Bible and went into the heart of Tennessee, where he conducted at various points a series of distracted, protracted meetings which netted him two hundred and ninety-nine converts to the faith and four hundred dollars in cash. He was enabled thereby to return to the game in Cincinnati and he is still in the lead. Other such cases are frequently reported.

The large majority of Negro preachers of today, then, are doing nothing more than to keep up the mediaeval hell-fire scare which the whites have long since abandoned to emphasize the humanitarian trend in religion through systematized education. The young people of the Negro race could be held in the church by some such program, but the Negro's Christianity does not conceive of social uplift as a duty of the church; and consequently Negro children have not been adequately trained in religious matters to be equal to the social demands upon them. Turning their back on medievalism, then, these untrained youth think nothing of taking up moonshining, gambling, and racketeering as occupations; and they find great joy in smoking, drinking, and fornication as diversions. They cannot accept the old ideas, and they do not understand the new.

What the Negro church is, however, has been determined largely by what the white man has taught the race by precept and example. We must remember that the Negroes learned their religion from the early white Methodists and Baptists who evangelized the slaves and the poor whites when they were barred from proselytizing the aristocracy. The American white people themselves taught Negroes to specialize unduly in the "Praise the Lord," "Hallelujah" worship. In the West Indies among the Anglicans and among the Latin people Negroes do not show such emotionalism. They are cold and conservative.

Some of the American whites, moreover, are just as far behind in this respect as are the Negroes who have had less opportunity to learn better. While in Miami, Florida, not long ago the author found in two interracial "Holiness Churches" that the following was a third or fourth white. The whites joined whole-heartedly with the Negroes in their "holy rolling" and some of them seemed to be "rollers not holy."

A few months ago in Huntington, West Virginia, where the author was being entertained by friends, the party was disturbed throughout the evening by the most insane outbursts of white worshippers in a "Church of God" across the street. There they daily indulged in such whooping and screaming in "unknown tongues" that the Negroes have had to report them to the police as a nuisance. The author has made a careful study of the Negro church, but he has never known Negroes to do anything to surpass the performance of those heathen.

The American Negroes' ideas of morality, too, were borrowed from their owners. The Negroes could not be expected to raise a higher standard than their aristocratic governing class that teemed with sin and vice. This corrupt state of things did not easily pass away. The Negroes have never seen any striking examples among the whites to help them in matters of religion. Even during the colonial period the whites claimed that their ministers sent to the colonies by the Anglican Church, the progenitor of the Protestant Episcopal Church in America, were a degenerate class that exploited the people for money to waste it in racing horses and drinking liquor. Some of these ministers were known to have illicit relations with women and, therefore, winked at the sins of the officers of their churches, who sold their own offspring by slave women.

Although the author was born ten years after the Civil War the morals and religion of that régime continued even into his time. Many of the rich or well-to-do white men belonging to the churches in Buckingham County, Virginia, indulged in polygamy. They raised one family by a white woman and another by a colored or poor white woman. Both the owner of the largest slate quarry and the proprietor of the largest factory in that county lived in this fashion. One was an outstanding Episcopalian and the other a distinguished Catholic.

One day the foreman of the factory, a polygamous deacon of the local white Baptist Church, called the workmen together at noon for a short memorial service in honor of Parson Taylor, for almost half a century the pastor of the large white Baptist church in that section. The foreman made some remarks on the life of the distinguished minister, and then all sang "Shall We Meet Beyond the River?" But "to save his life" the author could not restrain himself from wondering all that time whether the foreman's white wife or colored paramour would greet him on the other side, and what a conflict there would be if they happened to get into an old-fashioned hair-pulling. In spite of his libertine connections, however, this foreman believed that he was a Christian, and when he died his eulogist commended his soul to God.

Some years later when the author was serving his six years' apprenticeship in the West Virginia coal mines he found at Nutallburg a very faithful vestryman of the white Episcopal Church at that point. He was one of the most devout from the point of view of his co-workers. Yet, privately, this man boasted of having participated in that most brutal lynching of the four Negroes who thus met their doom at the hands of an angry mob in Clifton Forge, Virginia, in 1892.

It is very clear, then, that if Negroes got their conception of religion from slaveholders, libertines, and murderers, there may be something wrong about it, and it would not hurt to investigate it. It has been said that the Negroes do not connect morals with religion. The historian would like to know what race or nation does such a thing. Certainly the whites with whom the Negroes have come into contact have not done so.

CHAPTER VIII

PROFESSIONAL EDUCATION DISCOURAGED

IN the training for professions other than the ministry and teaching the Negro has not had full sway. Any extensive comment on professional education by the Negro, then, must be mainly negative. We have not had sufficient professional schools upon which we can base an estimate of what the Negro educator can do in this sphere. If mistakes have been made in mis-educating the Negro professionally it must be charged not so much to the account of the Negroes themselves as to that of their friends who have performed this task. We are dealing here, then, mainly with information obtained from the study of Negroes who have been professionally trained by whites in their own schools and in mixed institutions.

The largest numbers of Negroes in professions other than the ministry or education are physicians, dentists, pharmacists, lawyers and actors. The numbers in these and other lines have not adequately increased because of the economic status of the Negroes and probably because of a false conception of the rôle of the professional man in the community and its relation to him. The people whom the Negro professional men have volunteered to serve have not always given them sufficient support to develop that standing and solidarity which will make their position professional and influential. Most whites in contact with Negroes, always the teachers of their brethren in black, both by precept and practice, have treated the professions as aristocratic spheres to which Negroes should not aspire. We have had, then, a much smaller number than those who under different circumstances would have dared to cross the line; and those that did so were starved out by the whites who would not treat them as a professional class. This made it impracticable for Negroes to employ them in spheres in which they could not function efficiently. For example, because of a law that a man could not be admitted to the bar in Delaware without practicing a year under some lawyer in the state (and no white lawyer would grant a Negro such an opportunity until a few years ago) it was only recently that a Negro was admitted there.

Negroes, then, learned from their oppressors to say to their children that there were certain spheres into which they should not go because they would have no chance therein for development. In a number of places young men were discouraged and frightened away from certain professions by the poor showing made by those trying to function in them. Few had the courage to face this ordeal; and some professional schools in institutions for Negroes were closed about thirty or forty years ago, partly on this account.

This was especially true of the law schools, closed during the wave of legislation against the Negro, at the very time the largest possible number of Negroes needed to know the law for the protection of their civil and political rights. In other words, the thing which the patient needed most to pass the crisis was taken from him that he might more easily die. This one act among many others is an outstanding monument to the stupidity or malevolence of those in charge of Negro schools, and it serves as a striking demonstration of the mis-education of the race.

Almost any observer remembers distinctly the hard trials of the Negro lawyers. A striking example of their difficulties was supplied by the case of the first to be permanently established in Huntington, West Virginia. The author had entrusted to him the matter of correcting an error in the transfer of some property purchased from one of the most popular white attorneys in the state. For six months this simple transaction was delayed, and the Negro lawyer could not induce the white attorney to act. The author finally went to the office himself to complain of the delay. The white attorney frankly declared that he had not taken up the matter because he did not care to treat with a Negro attorney; but he would deal with the author, who happened to be at that time the teacher of a Negro school, and was, therefore, in his place.

At one time the Negroes in medicine and correlated fields were regarded in the same light They had difficulty in making their own people believe that they could cure a complaint, fill a tooth, or compound a prescription. The whites said that they could not do it; and, of course, if the whites said so, it was true, so far as most Negroes were concerned. In those fields, however, actual demonstrations to the contrary have convinced a sufficient number of both Negroes and whites that such an attitude toward these classes is false, but there are many Negroes who still follow those early teachings, especially the "highly educated" who in school have been given the "scientific" reasons for it. It is a most remarkable process that while in one department of a university a Negro may be studying for a profession, in another department of the same university he is being shown how the Negro professional man cannot succeed. Some of the "highly educated," then, give their practice to those who are often inferior to the Negroes whom they thus pass by. Although there has been an increase in these particular spheres, however, the professions among Negroes, with the exception of teaching and preaching, are still undermanned.

In the same way the Negro was once discouraged and dissuaded from taking up designing, drafting, architecture, engineering and chemistry. The whites, they were told, will not employ you and your people cannot provide such opportunities. The thought of pioneering or of developing the Negro to the extent that he might figure in this sphere did not dawn on those monitors of the Negroes preparing for their life's work. This tradition is still a heavy load in Negro education, and it forces many Negroes out of spheres in which they might function into those for which they may not have any aptitude.

In music, dramatics and correlated arts, too, the Negro has been unfortunately misled. Because the Negro is gifted as a singer and can render more successfully than others the music of his own people, he has been told that he does not need training. Scores of those who have undertaken to function in this sphere without adequate education, then, have developed only to a certain point beyond which they have not had ability to go. We cannot easily estimate how popular Negro musicians and their music might have become had they been taught to the contrary.

Of these, several instances may be cited. A distinguished man, talking recently as a member of a large Episcopal church, which maintains a Negro mission, mentioned his objection to the budget of fifteen hundred dollars a year for music for these segregated communicants. Inasmuch as the Negroes were naturally gifted in music he did not believe that any expensive training or direction was required. The small number of Negro colleges and universities which undertake the training of the Negro in music is further evidence of the belief that the Negro is all but perfect in this field and should direct his attention to the traditional curricula.

The same misunderstanding with respect to the Negro in dramatics is also evident. We have long had the belief that the Negro is a natural actor who does not require any stimulus for further development. In this assertion is the idea that because the Negro is good at dancing, joking, minstrelsy and the like he is "in his place" when "cutting a shine" and does not need to be trained to function in the higher sphere of dramatics. Thus misled, large numbers of Negroes ambitious for the stage have not bloomed forth into great possibilities. Too many of them have finally ended with rôles in questionable cafés, cabarets, and night clubs of America and Europe; and instead of increasing the prestige of the Negro they have brought the race into disgrace.

We scarcely realize what a poor showing we make in dramatics in spite of our natural aptitude in this sphere. Only about a half dozen Negro actors have achieved greatness, but we have more actors and showmen than any other professionals except teachers and ministers. Where are these thousands of men and women in the histrionic sphere? What do we hear of them? What have they achieved? Their record shows that only a few measure up to the standard of the modern stage. Most of these would-be artists have no preparation for the tasks undertaken.

A careful study of the Negro in dramatics shows that only

those who have actually taken the time to train themselves as they should be have finally endured. Their salvation has been to realize that adequate training is the surest way to attain artistic maturity. And those few who have thus understood the situation clearly demonstrate our ineptitude in the failure to educate the Negroes along the lines in which they could have admirably succeeded. Some of our schools have for some time undertaken this work as imitators of institutions dealing with persons otherwise circumstanced. Desirable results, therefore, have not followed, and the Negro on the stage is still mainly the product of the trial and error method.

Several other reasons may be given for the failure of a larger number of Negro actors to reach a higher level. In the first place, they have been recognized by the white man only in purely plantation comedy and minstrelsy, and because of the large number entering the field it has failed to offer a bright future for many of such aspirants. Repeatedly told by the white man that he could not function as an actor in a different sphere, the American Negro has all but ceased to attempt anything else. The successful career of Ira Aldridge in Shakespeare was forgotten until recently recalled by the dramatic success of Paul Robeson in Othello. The large majority of Negroes have settled down, then, to contentment as ordinary clowns and comedians. They have not had the courage or they have not learned how to break over the unnatural barriers and occupy higher ground.

The Negro author is no exception to the traditional rule. He writes, but the white man is supposed to know more about everything than the Negro. So who wants a book written by a Negro about one? As a rule, not even a Negro himself, for if he is really "educated," he must show that he has the appreciation for the best in literature. The Negro author, then, can neither find a publisher nor a reader; and his story remains untold. The Negro editors and reporters were once treated the same way, but thanks to the uneducated printers who founded most of our newspapers which have succeeded, these men of vision have made it possible for the "educated"

Negroes to make a living in this sphere in proportion as they recover from their education and learn to deal with the Negro as he is and where he is.

The Mis-Education of The Negro

CHAPTER IX

POLITICAL EDUCATION NEGLECTED

SOME time ago when Congressman Oscar De Priest was distributing by thousands copies of the Constitution of the United States certain wiseacres were disposed to make fun of it. What purpose would such an act serve? These critics, however, probably did not know that thousands and thousands of Negro children in this country are not permitted to use school books in which are printed the Declaration of Independence or the Constitution of the United States. Thomas Jefferson and James Madison are mentioned in their history as figures in politics rather than as expounders of liberty and freedom. These youths are not permitted to learn that Jefferson believed that government should derive its power from the consent of the governed.

Not long ago a measure was introduced in a certain State Legislature to have the Constitution of the United States thus printed in school histories, but when the bill was about to pass it was killed by some one who made the point that it would never do to have Negroes study the Constitution of the United States. If the Negroes were granted the opportunity to peruse this document, they might learn to contend for the rights therein guaranteed; and no Negro teacher who gives attention to such matters of the government is tolerated in those backward districts. The teaching of government or the lack of such instruction, then, must be made to conform to the policy of "keeping the Negro in his place."

In like manner, the teaching of history in the Negro area has had its political significance. Starting out after the Civil War, the opponents of freedom and social justice decided to work out a program which would enslave the Negroes' mind inasmuch as the freedom of body had to be conceded. It was well understood that if by the teaching of history the white man could be further assured of his superiority and the Negro could be made to feel that he had always been a failure and that the subjection of his will to some other race is necessary the freedman, then, would still be a slave. If you can control a man's thinking you do not have to worry about his action. "When you determine what a man shall think you do not have to concern yourself about what he will do. If you make a man feel that he is inferior, you do not have to compel him to accept an inferior status, for he will seek it himself. If you make a man think that he is justly an outcast, you do not have to order him to the back door. He will go without being told; and if there is no back door, his very nature will demand one.

This program, so popular immediately after the Civil War, was not new, but after this upheaval, its execution received a new stimulus. Histories written elsewhere for the former slave area were discarded, and new treatments of local and national history in conformity with the recrudescent propaganda were produced to give whites and blacks the biased point of view of the development of the nation and the relations of the races. Special treatments of the Reconstruction period were produced in apparently scientific form by propagandists who went into the first graduate schools of the East to learn modern historiography about half a century ago. Having the stamp of science, the thought of these polemics was accepted in all seats of learning. These rewriters of history fearlessly contended that slavery was a benevolent institution; the masters loved their slaves and treated them humanely; the abolitionists meddled with the institution which the masters eventually would have modified; the Civil War brought about by "fanatics" like William Lloyd Garrison and John Brown was unnecessary; it was a mistake to make the Negro a citizen, for he merely became worse off by incurring the displeasure of the master class that will never tolerate him as an equal; and the Negro must live in this country in a state of recognized inferiority.

Some of these theories may seem foolish, but historians even in the North have been won to this point of view. They ignore the recent works of Miss Elizabeth Donnan, Mrs. H. T. Catterall, and Dr. Frederic Bancroft, who have spent years investigating slavery and slavetrading. These are scientific productions with the stamp of the best scholarship in

America, treatises produced from such genuine documents as the court records of the slaveholding section itself, and these authors have rendered the public a valuable service in removing the whitewash which pseudo-historians have been giving to slavery and slaveholders for more than a century.

In the preparation of Negroes, many of whom teach in the South, these biased Northern historians even convert them to such a faith. A few years ago the author happened to listen to a conversation of Negro lawyers in one of our Southern cities, in which they unanimously conceded practically every contention set forth in this program of propaganda. They denounced, therefore, all reconstructionists who advocated equality and justice for all. These Negroes had the biased point of view of the rewriters like Claude Bowers and had never been directed to the real history of that drama as set forth by A. A. Taylor, Francis B. Simkins and Robert H. Woodly of the new Southern school of thought. These Negro critics were especially hard on Negroes of our day who engage in agitation for actual democracy. Negroes themselves in certain parts join with the whites, then, in keeping out of the schools teachers who may be bold enough to teach the truth as it is. They usually say the races here are getting along amicably now, and we do not want these peaceful relations disturbed by the teaching of new political thought.

What they mean to say with respect to the peaceful relation of the races, then, is that the Negroes have been terrorized to the extent that they are afraid even to discuss political matters publicly. There must be no exposition of the principles of government in the schools, and this must not be done in public among Negroes with a view to stimulating political activity. Negroes engaged in other spheres in such communities finally come to the point of accepting silence on these matters as a fixed policy. Knowing that action to the contrary means mob rule which may destroy the peace and property of the community, they constitute themselves a sort of a vigilant committee to direct their fellows accordingly.

A few years ago a rather youthful looking high school principal in one of the large cities was unceremoniously dismissed because he said jocosely to the president of the board of education, in reply to his remark about his youthful bearing, "I am old enough to vote." "Horrors!" said the infuriated official. "Put him out. We brought him here to teach these Negroes how to work, and here he is thinking about voting," A few prominent Negroes of the place muttered a little, but they did nothing effective to correct this injustice.

In certain parts, therefore, the Negroes under such terrorism have ceased to think of political matters as their sphere. Where such things come into the teaching in more advanced work they are presented as matters of concern to a particular element rather than as functions in which all citizens may participate. The result is that Negroes grow up without knowledge of political matters which should concern all elements. To prevent the Negroes from learning too much about these things the whites in the schools are sometimes neglected also, but the latter have the opportunity to learn by contact, close observation, and actual participation in the affairs of government.

Negroes in certain parts, then, have all but abandoned voting even at points where it might be allowed. In some cases not as many as two thousand Negroes vote in a whole state. By special legislation providing for literacy tests and the payment of taxes their number of voters has been reduced to a negligible quantity, and the few who can thus function do not do so because they are often counted out when they have the deciding vote.

The tests established for the restriction of suffrage were not intended to stimulate political education but to eliminate the Negro vote by subterfuge. Negroes presenting themselves for registration are asked to do the all but impossible thing of expounding parts of the Constitution which have baffled high courts; but whites are asked simple questions which almost any illiterate man can answer. In this way the Negroes, however intelligent, are turned down; and all ignorant whites are permitted to vote. These laws, then, have retarded rather than stimulated the political education of both races. Such knowledge is apparently useless for Negroes and unnecessary for the whites, for the Negroes do not immediately profit by having it and the whites may function as citizens without it.

The effect of such a one-sided system is decidedly bad. One does not realize it until he talks with men and women of these districts, who because of the denial of these privileges have lost interest in political matters. A book agent working in the plantation area of Mississippi tested the knowledge of Negroes of these matters by asking them questions about the local and State government. He discovered that they knew practically nothing in this sphere. It was difficult to find any who knew who was president of the United States. One meets teachers, physicians, and ministers who do not know the ordinary operations of courts, the functions of the counsel, jury or judge, unless such knowledge has come by the bitter experience of having been imposed upon by some tribunal of injustice. Some of the "educated" Negroes do not pay attention to such important matters as "the assessment of property and the collection of taxes, and they do not inform themselves as to how these things are worked out. An influential Negro in the South, then, is one who has nothing to do or say about politics and advises others to follow the same course.

The elimination of the Negro from politics, then, has been most unfortunate. The whites may have profited thereby temporarily, but they showed very little foresight. How the whites can expect to make of the Negroes better citizens by leading them to think that they should have no part in the government of this country is a mystery. To keep a man above vagabondage and crime he needs among other things the stimulus of patriotism, but how can a man be patriotic when the effect of his education is to the contrary?

What little chance the Negro has to learn by participation in politics in most parts of the South is unfortunately restricted now to corruption. The usual stir about electing delegates to the National Republican Convention from the Southern States and the customary combat the Negroes have with Lily-white corruptionists are about all the political matters which claim their attention in the Lower South. Neither the white nor the black faction, as a rule, makes any effort to restore suffrage to Negroes. The objective is merely the control of delegates and Federal patronage for the financial considerations involved. To do this they resort to numerous contests culminating in closing hotels and bolting doors for secret meetings. Since this is the only activity in which Negroes can participate they have learned to look upon it as honorable. Large numbers of Negroes become excited over the contest and give much publicity to it on the rostrum and in the press as a matter of great importance. The methods of these corruptionists of both races, however, should be condemned as a disgrace to the state and nation.

Instead of doing something to get rid of this ilk, however, we find the "highly educated" Negroes trying to plunge also into the mire. One of the most discouraging aspects in Negro life recently observed was that of a presidential campaign. Prominent Negroes connected with three of our leading institutions of learning temporarily abandoned their work to round up Negro votes for one of the candidates. The objective, of course, was to control the few ordinary jobs which are allotted to Negro politicians for their campaign services. When the successful candidate had been inaugurated, however, he carefully ignored them in the make-up of the personnel of his administration and treated Negroes in general with contempt. When you think of the fact that the Negroes who are being thus used are supposedly the most reputable Negro leaders and our most highly educated men you have to wonder whether the Negro has made any progress since Emancipation. The only consolation one can get out of it is that they may not represent the whole race.

In the North the Negroes have a better chance to acquire knowledge of political matters of the simple kind, but the bosses do not think it is advisable to enlighten them thoroughly. Negroes in parts are employed in campaigns, but they are not supposed to discuss such issues of the day as free trade, tariff for protection, the World Court, and the League of Nations. These Negro workers are supposed to tell their people how one politician seeking office has appointed more Negro messengers or charwomen in the service than the other or how the grandfather of the candidate stood with Lincoln and Grant through their ordeal and thus brought the race into its own. Another important task of these Negroes thus employed is also to abuse the opposing party, showing how hostile it has been to the Negro while the highly favorable party was doing so much for the race.

The course of these bosses has been interesting. At first the white man used the Negro leader by giving him a drink occasionally. The next step was to give him sufficient money to set up drinks in the name of the white candidate. When drinking at the expense of the candidate became too common the politicians fell back on the distribution of funds in small amounts. When this finally proved to be insufficient, however, the politicians had to go a bit further and provide Jim Crow jobs in certain backrooms with the understanding that the functions of the so-called office would be merely nominal and the incumbents would have no close contact with white people. In this stage the Negroes find themselves today.

The undesirable aspect of the affair is that the Negro in spite of the changes from one method of approach to that of another is never brought into the inner circle of the party with which he is affiliated. He is always kept on the outside and is used as a means to an end. To obtain the meager consideration which he receives the Negro must work clandestinely through the back door. It has been unnecessary for the white man to change this procedure, for until recent years he has generally found it possible to satisfy the majority of Negroes with the few political positions earmarked as "Negro jobs" and to crush those who clamor for more recognition.

It is unfortunate, too, that such a large number of Negroes do not know any better than to stake their whole fortune on politics. History does not show that any race, especially a minority group, has ever solved an important problem by relying altogether on one thing, certainly not by parking its political strength on one side of the fence because of empty promises. There are Negroes who know better, but such thinkers are kept in the background by the traducers of the race to prevent the enlightenment of the masses. The misleading politicians are the only persons through whom the traducers act with respect to the Negro, and there are always a sufficient number of mentally undeveloped voters who will supply them a large following.

Even the few Negroes who are elected to office are often similarly uninformed and show a lack of vision. They have given little attention to the weighty problems of the nation; and in the legislative bodies to which they are elected, they restrict themselves as a rule to matters of special concern to the Negroes themselves, such as lynching, segregation and disfranchisement, which they have well learned by experience. This indicates a step backwards, for the Negroes who sat in Congress and in the State Legislatures during the Reconstruction worked for the enactment of measures of concern to all elements of the population regardless of color. Historians have not yet forgot what those Negro statesmen did in advocating public education, internal improvements, labor arbitration, the tariff, and the merchant marine.

CHAPTER X

THE LOSS OF VISION

HISTORY shows, then, that as a result of these unusual forces in the education of the Negro he easily learns to follow the line of least resistance rather than battle against odds for what real history has shown to be the right course. A mind that remains in the present atmosphere never undergoes sufficient development to experience what is commonly known as thinking. No Negro thus submerged in the ghetto, then, will have a clear conception of the present status of the race or sufficient foresight to plan for the future; and he drifts so far toward compromise that he loses moral courage. The education of the Negro, then, becomes a perfect device for control from without. Those who purposely promote it have every reason to rejoice, and Negroes themselves exultingly champion the cause of the oppressor.

A comparison of the record of the spokesmen of the race today with that of those of the eighteenth century shows a moral surrender. During the prolonged struggle between the French and English in America the Negroes held the balance of power at several strategic points and used it accordingly; today the Negro finds himself inconsequential because he can be parked on one side of the fence. The same balance of power was evident also during the American Revolution when Negro soldiers insisted on serving side by side with others; today many Negroes are content as menials in the army. At that time Negroes preached to mixed congregations; today we find Negroes busy separating them. The eighteenth-century Negro resented any such thing as social distinctions; today Negroes are saying that they do not want social equality. Negroes of that epoch said with the ancient poet, "I am a man and deem nothing that relates to man a matter of indifference to me"; today, however, the average Negro says, "Now, I am a colored man, and you white folks must settle that matter among yourselves."

At a still later date the American Negro showed more courage than he does today with all of his so-called enlightenment. When the free Negroes were advised a hundred years ago to go to Africa they replied that they would never separate themselves from the slave population of this country as they were brethren by the "ties of consanguinity, of suffering, and of wrong." Today, however, the Negro in the North turns up his nose at the crude migrant from the South who brings to the North the race problem but along with it more thrift and actual progress than the Northern Negro ever dreamed of.

When, again in 1816, free Negroes like Richard Allen, James Forten, and Robert Purvis, were referred to as a foreign element whose social status might not be secure in this country, instead of permitting the colonizationists to shove them aside as criminals to be deported to a distant shore, they replied in no uncertain terms that this soil in America which gave them birth is their only true home. "Here their fathers fought, bled, and died for this country and here they intended to stay." Today when such things come up you find Negroes appearing upon the scene to see how much pay they can obtain to assist in the proposed undoing of the race.

Further emphasizing this thought of resistance a few years later, Nathaniel Paul, a Baptist preacher of Albany, informed the colonizationists that the free Negroes would not permit their traducers to formulate a program for the race. You may go ahead with your plan to deport this element in order to make slavery secure, he warned; but the free Negroes will never emigrate to Africa. "We shall stay here and fight until the foul monster is crushed. Slavery must go."

"Did I believe it would always continue," said he, "and that man to the end of time would be permitted with impunity to usurp the same undue authority over his fellow, I would disavow any allegiance or obligation I was under to my fellow creatures, or any submission that I owed to the laws of my country! I would deny the superintending power of divine Providence in the affairs of this life; I would ridicule the religion of the Savior of the world, and treat as the worst of men the ministers of the everlasting gospel; I would consider my Bible as a book of false and delusive fables, and commit it to the flames; nay, I would still go farther; I would at once confess myself an atheist, and deny the existence of a holy God."

And these Negroes of a century ago stood their ground and fought the pro-slavery deportationists to a standstill, for with the exception of a few pioneers the emigrants to Liberia were largely slaves manumitted on the condition that they would settle in Africa. These freedmen, then, could have no ideals but those of the slave-holding section from which they were sent. They established, therefore, a slavocracy in Liberia. If Liberia has failed, then, it is no evidence of the failure of the Negro in government. It is merely evidence of the failure of slavery.

The Negroes attacking Jim-Crowism almost a century ago fearlessly questioned the constitutionality of such a provision. Speaking through Charles Lenox Remond of that day, they said, "There is a distinction between social and civil rights. We all claim the privilege of selecting our society and associations, but, in civil rights, one man has not the prerogative to define rights for another. These [race] distinctions react in all their wickedness—to say nothing of their concocted and systematized odiousness and absurdity—upon those who are illiberal and mean enough to practice them."

In our day, however, we find some "highly educated" Negroes approving such Jim-Crowism. For example, not many years ago an outstanding Baptist preacher, dabbling in politics in West Virginia, suggested to the whites that they enact a Jim Crow car law in that State, and we had difficulty in crushing that sentiment. A few years thereafter the author heard one of our bishops say that we should not object to such separation, for we want to be by ourselves. When this distinguished churchman died the traducers of the Negro lauded him to the skies; and thoughtless members of the race, thinking that he deserved it, joined in the loud acclaim.

In this way the large majority of "educated" Negroes in the United States have accepted segregation and have become its fearless champions. Their filled but undeveloped minds do not enable them to understand that, although an opiate furnishes temporary relief, it does not remove the cause of the pain. In this case we have yielded on principle to satisfy the mob, but have not yet found an ultimate solution of the problem at hand. In our so-called democracy we are accustomed to give the majority what they want rather than educate them to understand what is best for them. We do not show the Negro how to overcome segregation, but we teach him how to accept it as final and just.

Numerous results from this policy may be cited. The white laboring man refuses to work with Negroes because of the false tradition that the Negro is an inferior, and at the same time the Negro for the same reason becomes content with menial service and drudgery. The politician excludes the Negro from the councils of his party and from the government because he has been taught that such is necessary to maintain the supremacy of his race; the Negro, trained in the same school of thought, accepts this as final and contends for such meager consideration as the bosses may begrudgingly grant him. An irate resident in an exclusive district protests against an invasion by Negroes because he has learned that these poverty-stricken people are carriers of disease and agents of crime; the Negroes, believing that such is the truth, remain content in the ghetto. The irrational parent forces the separation of the races in some schools because his child must occupy a seat next to a pupil of "tainted" African blood; the educated Negro accepts this as inevitable and welcomes the makeshift for his people. Children of Negroes are excluded from the playgrounds because of the assertion that they will contaminate those of the whites; the Negroes yielding, settle down to a policy of having their children grow up in neglected fashion in the most undesirable part of the city. The Negro is forced to ride in a Jim Crow car to stamp upon him more easily the badge of his "inferiority"; the "educated Negro" accepts it as settled and abandons the fight against this social proscription.

And thus goes segregation which is the most far-reaching development in the history of the Negro since the enslavement of the race. In fact, it is a sequel of slavery. It has been made possible by our system of mis-educating innocent people who did not know what was happening. It is so subtle that men have participated in promoting it without knowing what they were doing.

There are a few defenders of segregation who are doubtless sincere. Although nominally free they have never been sufficiently enlightened to see the matter other than as slaves. One can cite cases of Negroes who opposed emancipation and denounced the abolitionists. A few who became free reenslaved themselves. A still larger number made no effort to become free because they did not want to disconnect themselves from their masters, and their kind still object to full freedom.

Ever since the Civil War when Negroes were first given a chance to participate in the management of their affairs they have been inconsistent and compromising. They have tried to gain one thing on one day by insisting on equality for all, while at the same time endeavoring to gain another point the next day by segregation. At one moment Negroes fight for the principle of democracy, and at the very next moment they barter it away for some temporary advantage. You cannot have a thing and dispose of it at the same time.

For example, the Negro political leaders of the Reconstruction period clamored for suffrage and the right of holding office, serving in the militia, and sitting on the jury; but few of them wanted white and colored children to attend the same school. When expressing themselves on education most of them took the position of segregationists; and Charles Sumner in his fight for the civil rights of the Negro had to eliminate mixed schools from his program not only because many whites objected but also because the Negroes themselves did not seem to want them. All of these leaders might not have been looking for jobs in those days; but as nominal freemen, who were still slaves, they did not feel comfortable in the presence of their former masters.

These timorous men were very much like some Negroes

who were employed near the author's home in Virginia by a Northern farmer, who had moved into the State after the Civil War. When breakfast time came the first morning he called them in to eat at the table with his family. These actual slaves, however, immediately lost their appetite. One finally called the employer aside and settled the matter in another way. He said:

"Now boss, you ain't used to de rules ob dis country. We just can't sit at de table wid wite folks. We been use ter eating a cake er bread out yonder 'tween de plow handles. Les us go out dar."

The system, therefore, has extended from one thing to another until the Negroes today find themselves hedged in by the color bar almost every way they turn; and, set off by themselves, the Negroes cannot learn from the example of others with whom they might come into contact. In the ghetto, too, they are not permitted to construct and carry out a program of their own. These segregating institutions interfere with the development of self-help among Negroes, for often Negroes fail to raise money to establish institutions which they might control, but they readily contribute large sums for institutions which segregate persons of African blood.

Denied participation in the higher things of life, the "educated" Negro himself joins, too, with ill-designing persons to handicap his people by systematized exploitation. Feeling that the case of the Negro is hopeless, the "educated" Negro decides upon the course of personally profiting by whatever he can do in using these people as a means to an end. He grins in their faces while "extracting money" from them, hut his heart shows no fond attachment to their despised cause. With a little larger income than they receive he can make himself somewhat comfortable in the ghetto; and he forgets those who have no way of escape.

Some of this "educated" class join with unprincipled real estate men in keeping Negroes out of desirable parts of the city and confining them to unsanitary sections. Such persons help the profiteer to collect from Negroes thus cornered a larger rental than that exacted from whites for the same property. In similar fashion a Negro minister sometimes goes into a community where the races are moving along amicably together in their churches and rents a shack or an old empty store to start a separate church for "our people," not to supply any practical need but to exploit those who have never learned to think. Professional men, too, walking in their footsteps, impose also upon the poor innocent Negroes who do not know when they are being treated properly and when they are not, but high fees may be obtained from them inasmuch as they cannot always go to others for service.

Settling in a community with mixed schools, the educated Negro often advocates their separation that his daughter may secure a position in the system. The Negro politician is accustomed to corner the Negro vote, by opening a separate office from which he may bargain with the chieftains of the machine for the highest price available. When paid off by some position, which is not very lofty, this office-holder accepts such employment with the understanding that he will be set off by himself as if he were destructive of the rest of mankind.

In the present crisis, however, the "highly educated" Negroes find very little to exploit, and in their untoward condition they have no program of finding a way out. They see numerous instances of Negroes losing their jobs in white establishments. In fact, these things occur daily. Janitors who have been giving satisfaction are abruptly told that they will no longer be needed. Negro waiters in hotels are being informed that their places will go to white workers. Negro truck drivers are ordered to step down and let the needy of the other race go up. We hear so much of this that we wonder what the outcome will be.

In this readjustment, of course, when there are fewer opportunities left for those who cannot or do not have the opportunity to operate machines the Negroes will naturally be turned out of their positions by their employers who think first of their own race. In the ultimate passing of the depression, however, Negroes will not be much better off when some of the whites now displacing them will rise to higher levels. In the economic order of tomorrow there will be little use for the factotum or scullion. Man will not need such personal attention when he can buy a machine to serve him more efficiently. The menial Negroes, the aggregate of parasites whom the "highly educated" Negro has exploited, will not be needed on tomorrow. What, then, will become of "our highly educated" Negroes who have no initiative?

We have appealed to the talented tenth for a remedy, but they have nothing to offer. Their minds have never functioned in this all-important sphere. The "educated" Negro shows no evidence of vision. He should see a new picture. The Negroes are facing the alternative of rising in the sphere of production to supply their proportion of the manufacturers and merchants or of going down to the graves of paupers. The Negro must now do for himself or die out as the world undergoes readjustment. If the whites are to continue for some time in doing drudgery to the exclusion of Negroes, the latter must find another way out. Nothing forces this upon one more dramatically than when he learns that white women in Montgomery, Alabama, are coming to the back door of Negro homes asking for their washing. If the whites have reached this extremity, and they must be taken care of first, what will be left for the Negroes?

At this moment, then, the Negroes must begin to do the very thing which they have been taught that they cannot do. They still have some money, and they have needs to supply. They must begin immediately to pool their earnings and organize industries to participate in supplying social and economic demands. If the Negroes are to remain forever removed from the producing atmosphere, and the present discrimination continues, there will be nothing left for them to do.

There is no reason for lack of confidence because of the recent failure of Negro enterprises, although the "highly educated" Negroes assert the contrary. This lack of confidence is the cause of the failure of these enterprises. If the Negroes had manifested enough confidence in them and had properly supported them, they would have been strong enough to stand the test in the crisis. Negro banks, as a rule, have failed because the people, taught that their own pioneers in business cannot function in this sphere, withdrew their deposits. An individual cannot live after you extract the blood from his veins. The strongest bank in the United States will last only so long as the people will have sufficient confidence in it to keep their money there. In fact, the confidence of the people is worth more than money.

The lack of confidence of the Negro in himself and in his possibilities is what has kept him down. His mis-education has been a perfect success in this respect. Yet it is not necessary for the Negro to have more confidence in his own workers than in others. If the Negro would be as fair to his own as he has been to others, this would be all that is necessary to give him a new lease on life and start the trend upward.

Here we find that the Negro has failed to recover from his slavish habit of berating his own and worshipping others as perfect beings. No progress has been made in this respect because the more "education" the Negro gets the worse off he is. He has just had so much longer to learn to decry and despise himself. The race looking to this educated class for a solution of its problems does not find any remedy; and, on the contrary, sees itself further and further away from those things to which it has aspired. By forgetting the schoolroom for the time being and relying upon an awakening of the masses through adult education we can do much to give the Negro a new point of view with respect to economic enterprise and group cooperation. The average Negro has not been sufficiently mis-educated to become hopeless.

Our minds must become sufficiently developed to use segregation to kill segregation, and thus bring to pass that ancient and yet modern prophecy, "The wrath of man shall praise thee." If the Negro in the ghetto must eternally be fed by the hand that pushes him into the ghetto, he will never become strong enough to get out of the ghetto. This assumption of Negro leadership in the ghetto, then, must not be confined to matters of religion, education, and social uplift; it must deal with such fundamental forces in life as make these things possible. If the Negro area, however, is to continue as a district supported wholly from without, the inept dwellers therein will merit and will receive only the contempt of those who may occasionally catch glimpses of them in their plight.

As Frederick Douglass said in 1852, "It is vain that we talk of being men, if we do not the work of men. We must become valuable to society in other departments of industry than those servile ones from which we are rapidly being excluded. We must show that we can do as well as they. When we can build as well as live in houses; when we can make as well as wear shoes; when we can produce as well as consume wheat, corn and rye—then we shall become valuable to society.

"Society," continued Douglass, "is a hard-hearted affair. With it the helpless may expect no higher dignity than that of paupers. The individual must lay society under obligation to him or society will honor him only as a stranger and sojourner."

CHAPTER XI

THE NEED FOR SERVICE RATHER THAN LEADERSHIP

IN this untoward situation the Negro finds himself at the close of the third generation from Emancipation. He has been educated in the sense that persons directed a certain way are more easily controlled, or as Ovid remarked, "In time the bull is brought to bear the yoke." The Negro in this state continues as a child. He is restricted in his sphere to small things, and with these he becomes satisfied. His ambition, does not rise any higher than to plunge into the competition with his fellows for these trifles. At the same time those who have given the race such false ideals are busy in the higher spheres from which Negroes by their mis-education and racial guidance have been disbarred.

Examples of this failure of the mis-educated Negro to have high ideals may be cited. The author has known numerous cases of Negro lawyers, physicians and business men who, while attending local Sunday schools, churches, and lodges, have fallen out about trifles like a resolution or the chairmanship of a committee, which so embittered them as to make themselves enemies for life and stumbling blocks preventing any such thing as organization or community cooperation.

It is a common on occurrence to see a Negro well situated as a minister or teacher aspiring to a political appointment which temporarily pays little more than what he is receiving and offers no distinction except that of being earmarked as a Jim Crow job set aside for some Negro who has served well the purposes of the bosses as a wardheeler in a campaign. Negroes who have begun promising business enterprises sometimes abandon them temporarily for the same sort of empty honor. In this way they have been known to hamper their business by incurring the displeasure of ambitious politicians who might otherwise patronize them.

Negroes of this point of view have developed in that

part of the country where it is thought that the most distinguished persons in the community are those who hold and exploit the local offices or those who are further honored with positions in the state and nation. While this may apply in the case of their oppressors the few positions allotted the Negroes are magnified beyond all reasonable bounds. This comes as a natural result, however, for the "education" of the Negro requires it. The ambitious mis-educated Negro in the struggle for the little things allotted by others prevents any achievement of the people in matters more constructive. Potentially the colored people are strong although they are actually weak.

This much-ado-about-nothing renders impossible cooperation, the most essential thing in the development of a people. The ambitious of this class do more to keep the race in a state of turmoil and to prevent it from serious community effort than all the other elements combined. The one has a job that the other wants; or the one is a leader of a successful faction, and the other is struggling to supplant him. Everything in the community, then, must yield ground to this puerile contest.

In one city of a few thousand Negroes there is no chance for community cooperation because of the antagonism of the Methodist and Baptist preachers in charge of the two largest churches. The one is determined to dictate the appointment of the teaching corps and the social welfare workers; the other is persistently struggling to undo everything accomplished by his opponent. The one is up today, and the other in ascendency tomorrow. Several efforts have been made to start business enterprises there, but none has succeeded because one faction tears down what the other builds up.

In another city the cleavage is along political lines. Preachers are there, but a lawyer and a dentist plunging into politics have dispossessed the clergy of the stage. The leader of one faction is so bitterly opposed to the other that he even warns strangers against going to the home of his adversary. To present a sane proposition to the community through one of these leaders means local warfare rather than an effort to work together for the common good. Consequently, although there are thousands of Negroes living together in one quarter they have no business enterprises of worth. The selfish struggle for personal aggrandizement, which has not yet brought either faction more than an appointment on the police force or a clerkship in one of the city offices, thus blocks the social and economic progress of thousands of unoffending people.

In another state the ambition of the highly educated Negro is restricted to becoming principals of the high schools. The neglected state school has not developed sufficiently to become attractive. The warring area, then, is in the cities. In one of them, where several Negroes own considerable wealth which, if pooled and properly used, would produce all but wonderful results, the petty strife has been most disastrous. Little thought is given to social uplift, and economic effort is crushed by factional wrangling. Before the author had been in one of the towns an hour a stalwart of one faction sounded him on becoming a candidate for the position held by the principal of the high school. A few minutes thereafter another approached him for advice as to how "to get him out."

The high cost of this childishness to the community can be estimated only by taking into consideration the fact that this strife is all but endless. If it were a matter that developed now and then only to be forgotten by people directing their attention thereafter to more important things, it would not do much harm; but this confusion continues for years. Sometimes it grips a community for a whole generation, vitiating the entire life of the people.

In spite of the meager rewards, however, the idea of leadership looms high in the Negro mind. It always develops thus among oppressed people. The oppressor must have some dealing with the despised group, and rather than have contact with individuals he approaches the masses through his own spokesman. The term itself connotes a backward condition. In its strides upward a race shuffles off its leaders because they originate outside of the group. They constitute a load that sinks the oppressed in the mire of trials and tribulations.

Leadership is usually superimposed for the purpose of "directing the course of the ostracized group along sane lines." This was accomplished during the days of slavery by restricting the assembly of Negroes to certain times and places and compelling them to meet in the presence of a stipulated number of the "wisest and discreetest men of the community." These supervisors of the conduct of Negroes would prevent them from learning the truth which might make them "unruly" or ambitious to become free.

After the Negroes became free the same end was reached by employing a Negro or some white man to spy upon and report behind closed doors on a plan to enslave the Negroes' minds. In case that actual employment as a spy seemed too bold, the person to be used as such an instrument took up some sort of enterprise which the oppressors of the race warmly supported to give him the desired influence in the community. This "racial racketeer" might be a politician, minister, teacher, director of a community center, or head of a "social uplift agency." As long as he did certain things and expressed the popular opinion on questions he lacked nothing, and those who followed him found their way apparently better paid as the years went by. His leadership, then, was recognized and the ultimate undoing of the Negroes in the community was assured.

Such leadership, too, has continued into our day and it goes from bad to worse. The very service which this racial toady renders hardens him to the extent that he loses his soul. He becomes equal to any task the oppressor may impose upon him, and at the same time he becomes artful enough to press his case convincingly before the thoughtless multitude. What is right is sacrificed because everything that is right is not expedient; and what is expedient soon becomes unnecessary.

Recently a citizen, observing how we have been thus betrayed, suggested that there be called a national meeting to take steps for a program of development of the race from within under "a new leadership." Such a movement can be made to mean something, and then it can degenerate into an assembly of abuse and vituperation followed by the usual whereas-therefore-be-it-resolved effort which has never meant anything in the awakening and the development of an oppressed people.

The Negroes, however, will not advance far if they continue to waste their energy abusing those who misdirect and exploit them. The exploiters of the race are not so much at fault as the race itself. If Negroes persist in permitting themselves to be handled in this fashion they will always find some one at hand to impose upon them. The matter is one which rests largely with the Negroes themselves. The race will free itself from exploiters just as soon as it decides to do so. No one else can accomplish this task for the race. It must plan and do for itself.

Checking up on what they do, Negroes often find themselves giving money and moral support to various persons and institutions which influence the course of the race in the wrong way. They do not often ask themselves whether the support thus given will redound in the long run to the good of the people with whom they are identified. They do not inquire whether the assistance thus given offers temporary relief but eventually results in irreparable loss. So many Negroes often do themselves harm when they actually believe that they are doing good. Under their present teachers they cannot easily learn to do any better, for such training as we undergo does not open our eyes sufficiently for us to see far ahead of us.

If the Negro could abandon the idea of leadership and instead stimulate a larger number of the race to take up definite tasks and sacrifice their time and energy in doing these things efficiently the race might accomplish something. The race needs workers, not leaders. Such workers will solve the problems which race leaders talk about and raise money to enable them to talk more and more about. When you hear a man talking, then, always inquire as to what he is doing or what he has done for humanity. Oratory and resolutions do not avail much. If they did, the Negro race would be in a paradise on earth. It may be well to repeat here the saying that old men talk of what they have done, young men of what they are doing, and fools of what they expect to do. The Negro race has a rather large share of the last mentioned class.

If we can finally succeed in translating the idea of leadership into that of service, we may soon find it possible to lift the Negro to a higher level. Under leadership we have come into the ghetto; by service within the ranks we may work our way out of it. Under leadership we have been constrained to do the biddings of others; by service we may work out a program in the light of our own circumstances. Under leadership we have become poverty-stricken; by service we may teach the masses how to earn a living honestly. Under leadership we have been made to despise our own possibilities and to develop into parasites; by service we may prove sufficient unto the task of self-development and contribute our part to modern culture.

CHAPTER XII

HIRELINGS IN THE PLACES OF PUBLIC SERVANTS

IF the highly educated Negroes have not learned better the simple lessons of life one cannot expect the laboring classes to conduct themselves differently. In the large number of cases the employers of Negroes in common labor, in which most of them are now engaged, assert that there is no hope for advancement of Negroes in their employ because Negroes will not work under foremen of their own color. In other words, the average Negro has not yet developed to the point that one is willing to take orders from another of his own race.

While it is true that such an answer is often given as a mere excuse for not placing Negroes in responsible positions when it can be done without any particular trouble, the investigation among Negroes themselves reveals numerous facts to prove that there is more truth than falsehood in this statement. Hundreds of employes of African blood frankly say that they will not work under a Negro. One is afraid that the other may prosper more than he does and be recognized accordingly.

Some of these instances are interesting. A head of one of the Government departments, in which Negro women are employed to do unskilled labor, reports that he placed in charge of the group of these workers an intelligent colored woman who seemed to have all of the necessary qualifications which he had found in other women thus employed. Those working under her, however, refused to obey instructions, kept the place in turmoil and soon destroyed the morale of the whole force. As soon as he placed a white woman in charge, however, order was reestablished on the premises, and everything moved along smoothly.

Another employer conducting a wholesale business placed a Negro foreman in charge of others of his race to function as one of the important departments of the establishment.

The Negroes working under him, who had formerly taken orders without question from the white foreman, soon undertook to take liberties with the promoted Negro and to ignore his orders. Knowing that the Negro foreman was well qualified, however, and being personally interested in him, the employer instead of doing what so many others under such circumstances had done, dismissed those who refused to cooperate and supplied the vacancies with others until an efficient working force could thus be obtained. Only a few employers, however, have had such patience and have manifested such interest in the advancement of the Negro. As a rule they merely dispose of Negro foremen with the excuse that one Negro will not take orders from another.

This refusal of Negroes to take orders from one another is due largely to the fact that slaveholders taught their bondmen that they were as good as or better than any others and, therefore, should not be subjected to any member of their race. If they were to be subordinated to some one it should be to the white man of superior culture and social position. This keeps the whole race on a lower level, restricted to the atmosphere of trifles which do not concern their traducers. The greater things of life which can be attained only by wise leadership, then, they have no way to accomplish.

The strong have always used this as a means of dealing with the so-called weaker races of the world. The Caucasian arrays the one against the other so that they may never combine their forces and thus deprive their so-called superiors of control over them, which they could easily do if organized. One white man was thus able to maintain himself on a plantation where there were thirty or forty slaves because the Negroes were mis-educated in such a way as to keep them divided into distinct factions. In petty strife their power would be lost in the process of attrition. Today we find the same thing in Africa where this end is reached by embittering one tribe against another; and it worked the same way in India until recently when it began to break down under the masterful leadership of Mahatma Gandhi.

The Negroes of the United States have followed leadership slavishly but sometimes unfortunately that of those leaders who are selected for them by the traducers of the race. The enemies of the race, for example, will find a Negro willing to do certain things they desire to have accomplished and will finance him and give him sufficient publicity to get before the world, for the few favors which he may dispense among his followers as a result of his influence and economic position will bring to him the adequate number of Negroes for the constituency which he desires.

Negroes, however, sometimes choose their own leaders but unfortunately they are too often of the wrong kind. Negroes do not readily follow persons with constructive programs. Almost any sort of exciting appeal or trivial matter presented to them may receive immediate attention and temporarily at least liberal support. When the bubble collapses, of course, these same followers will begin to decry Negro leadership and call these misrepresentatives of the group rascals and scoundrels. Inasmuch as they have failed to exercise foresight, however, those who have deceived them should not be blamed so much as those who have liberally supported these impostors. Yet the fault here is not inherently in the Negro but in what he has been taught.

The Negroes' point of view, therefore, must be changed before they can construct a program which will bring them out of the wilderness. For example, no good can be expected from one of our teachers who said that she had to give up her class in Sunday school to accept an extra job of waiting on table at that hour because she had bought a twenty-four-hundred-dollar coat and her husband had purchased an expensive car. Such a teacher has no message for the Negro child. Her example would tend to drag the youth downward, and the very thought of having such a person in the schoolroom is most depressing.

We must feel equally discouraged when we see a minister driving up to his church on Sunday morning in a Cadillac. He does not come to feed the multitude spiritually. He comes to fleece the flock. The appeal he makes is usually emotional. While the people are feeling happy the expensive machine is granted, and the prolonged vacation to use it is easily financed. Thus the thoughtless drift backward toward slavery.

When you see a physician drive to one's door in his Pierce Arrow, you cannot get the impression he has come to treat the patient for a complaint. He has come to treat him for a dollar. Such physicians, as a rule, know less and less medicine as the years go by, although they make much money by learning human psychology and using it for personal gain. With leeches of this type feeding upon an all but impoverished people and giving them nothing back there can be no hope for advancement.

No people can go forward when the majority of those who should know better have chosen to go backward, but this is exactly what most of our misleaders do. Not being learned in the history and background of the race, they figure out that there is no hope for the masses; and they decide, then, that the best thing they can do is to exploit these people for all they can and use the accumulations selfishly. Such persons have no vision and therefore perish at their own hands.

It is an injustice to the Negro, however, to mis-educate him and suffer his manners to be corrupted from infancy unto old age and then blame him for making the mistakes which such guidance necessitates. People who have been restricted and held down naturally condescend to the lower levels of delinquency. When education has been entirely neglected or improperly managed we see the worst passions ruling with uncontrolled and incessant sway. Good sense degenerates into craft, anger wrangles into malignity, restraint which is thought most solitary comes too late, and the most judicial admonitions are urged in vain."

Philosophers have long conceded, however, that every man has two educations: that which is given to him, and the other that which he gives himself. Of the two kinds the latter is by far the more desirable. Indeed all that is most worthy in man he must work out and conquer for himself. It is that which constitutes our real and best nourishment.

What we are merely taught seldom nourishes the mind like that which we teach ourselves."

The same eternal principle applies to a race forced to live apart from others as a separate and distinct group. Inasmuch as the education of the Negro has come from without we can clearly see that he has received only a part of the development which he should have undergone or he has developed negatively. The Negro lacks mental power, which cannot be expected from ill-fed brains.

This naturally brings up a serious question. The people on the outside, who are directing the race from afar, will take this condition of affairs as evidence that the Negro is not prepared for leadership. What they ought to say is that they have not prepared the Negro to assume the responsibility of his own uplift. Instead of doing this, however, they play up this result of their own failure as an argument for imposing upon the Negro race the guidance of others from without.

As to whether or not a white man should be a leader of the Negroes may be dismissed as a silly question. What has the color to do with it? Such a worker may be white, brown, yellow, or red, if he is heart and soul with the people whom he would serve. It just happens, however, that most white men now in control of Negro institutions are not of this required type. Practically all of those with whom I have talked and communicated believe in imposing some sort of disability upon Negroes. Some object to the freedom of intermarriage as a substitute for concubinage, scoff at the idea of the enfranchisement of the Negroes, approve their segregation, and justify the economic exploitation of the race. Now if these are the persons to elevate the Negroes, to what point do they expect to lift them, and what will the Negroes be when they get there?

With this same thought in mind a white director of Negroes recently said to the author:

"I realize that I have no useful function in my present position as a president of a Negro institution. I do not approve of their aspirations to many things. I cannot accept the students in my house as I would white students because it might lead to an interracial romance. Marrying is such a difficult problem at the best that I should not like to see one of my children make a failure in life by marrying a Negro."

"In other words," continued he, "we live in two different worlds. While I am among them I cannot become a part of them. How then can I help them under these circumstances?"

I am acquainted with another white educator at the head of a Negro institution, who will not address a colored girl as Miss, and to avoid the use of a title in speaking to women of the race he addresses them as his kin. One of them was sharp enough to reply to him thus when he accosted her as auntie:

"Oh, I am so glad that I have found my lost relatives at last. My mother often told me that I had some distinguished kin, and just to think that you are my nephew makes me feel glad."

Another such exploiter in charge of a Negro college never wears his hat on the campus. His confidential explanation is that he might have to lift it when he meets a Negro woman. Of course, that would never do. "White supremacy" would be lost in the Negro school.

As we realize more and more that education is not merely imparting information which is expected to produce certain results, we see very clearly the inconsistency of the position of white persons as executives of Negro institutions. These misfits belong to the very group working out the segregation of the Negro, and they come into these institutions mainly to earn a living. They make no particular contribution to the development of education, for they are not scholarly enough to influence educational theory; and they are so far out of sympathy with the Negro that they cannot make any contribution to educational practice. These "foreigners" are not bringing to such institutions large sums of money which the

Negroes cannot obtain, for the institutions now directed by Negroes are receiving larger appropriations than those under the management of whites.

Our so-called thinkers, however, seldom see the inevitable results of this unsound policy. Not long ago when the author wrote the textbook entitled NEGRO MAKERS OF HISTORY it was adversely criticised by a Negro who said that the book should have had as an illustration the cut of the white man who established a certain Negro college. The author had to explain that the book was to give an account of what the Negro has done, not of what has been done for him.

The school referred to, moreover, was in no sense a Negro school. It had very few Negro teachers and only one Negro trustee. The policy of the school was determined altogether by others without giving the Negro credit for having a thought on education. In other words, it was merely a school which Negroes were permitted to attend. If they picked up here and there something to help them, well and good; if not, may God help them!

It is all right to have a white man as the head of a Negro college or to have a red man at the head of a yellow one, if in each case the incumbent has taken out his naturalization papers and has identified himself as one of the group which he is trying to serve. It seems that the white educators of this day are unwilling to do this, and for that reason they can never contribute to the actual development of the Negro from within. You cannot serve people by giving them orders as to what to do. The real servant of the people must live among them, think with them, feel for them, and die for them.

The white worker in Negro institutions, too, can never be successful without manifesting some faith in the people with whom he has cast his lot. His efforts must not be merely an attempt to stimulate their imitation of things in a foreign sphere. He must study his community sufficiently to discover the things which have a trend in the proper direction that he may stimulate such forces and thus help the community to do better the good things which it may be capable of doing and at the same time may be interested in doing. If these people are to be brought the ideas of "foreigners," and must be miraculously transformed into something else before anything can be made of them, such effort will be a fruitless task like most of the so-called education and uplift of the Negroes in America.

The Negro, in spite of his confinement to the ghetto, has some opportunities to develop his special capacities if they are properly studied and understood. The real servant of the people, then, will give more attention to those to be served than to the use that somebody may want to make of them. He will be more concerned with what he can do to increase the ease, comfort, and happiness of the Negro than with how the Negro may be used to contribute to the ease, comfort, and happiness of others.

The servant of the people, unlike the leader, is not on a high horse elevated above the people and trying to carry them to some designated point to which he would like to go for his own advantage. The servant of the people is down among them, living as they live, doing what they do and enjoying what they enjoy. He may be a little better informed than some other members of the group; it may be that he has had some experience that they have not had, but in spite of this advantage he should have more humility than those whom he serves, for we are told that "Whosoever is greatest among you, let him be your servant."

CHAPTER XIII

UNDERSTAND THE NEGRO

"WE do not offer here any course in Negro history, Negro literature, or race relations," recently said a professor of a Negro college. "We study the Negro along with other people."

"An excellent idea," the interviewer replied. "No one should expect you to do any more than this, but how do you do it when the Negro is not mentioned in your textbooks except to be condemned? Do you, a teacher in a Negro school, also condemn the race in the same fashion as the writers of your textbooks of history and literature?"

"No," said he, "we bring the Negro in here and there."

"How often does 'here and there' connote?"

"Well, you know," said he, "Negroes have not done much; and what they have accomplished may be briefly covered by referring to the achievements of a few men and women.

"Why do you emphasize the special study of the Negro?" said he further. "Why is it necessary to give the race special attention in the press, on the rostrum, or in the schoolroom? This idea of projecting the Negro into the foreground does the race much harm by singing continually of his woes and problems and thus alienating the public which desires to give its attention to other things."

It is true that many Negroes do not desire to hear anything about their race, and few whites of today will listen to the story of woe. With most of them the race question has been settled. The Negro has been assigned to the lowest drudgery as the sphere in which the masses must toil to make a living; and socially and politically the race has been generally proscribed. Inasmuch as the traducers of the race have "settled" the matter in this fashion, they naturally oppose any effort to change this status.

Many Negro professional men who are making a living

attending to the affairs of these laborers and servants in their mentally undeveloped state and many teachers who in conservative fashion are instructing their children to maintain the status quo ante bellum, also oppose any movement to upset this arrangement. They are getting paid for their efforts Why should they try innovations? The gods have so decreed it. Human beings cannot change it. Why be foolish?

A Negro with sufficient thought to construct a program of his own is undesirable, and the educational systems of this country generally refuse to work through such Negroes in promoting their cause. The program for the uplift of the Negroes in this country must be handed over to an executive force like orders from the throne, and they must carry it out without question or get out of line and let the procession go on. Although the Negro is being daily forced more and more by segregation into a world peculiarly his own, his unusually perplexing status is given little or no thought, and he is not considered capable of thinking for himself.

The chief difficulty with the education of the Negro is that it has been largely imitation resulting in the enslavement of his mind. Somebody outside of the race has desired to try out on Negroes some experiment which interested him and his coworkers; and Negroes, being objects of charity, have received them cordially and have done what they required. In fact, the keynote in the education of the Negro has been to do what he is told to do. Any Negro who has learned to do this is well prepared to function in the American social order as others would have him.

Looking over the courses of study of the public schools, one finds little to show that the Negro figures in these curricula. In supplementary matter a good deed of some Negro is occasionally referred to, but oftener the race is mentioned only to be held up to ridicule. With the exception of a few places like Atlantic City, Atlanta, Tulsa, St. Louis, Birmingham, Knoxville, and the states of Louisiana and North Carolina no effort is made to study the Negro in the public schools as they do the Latin, the Teuton, or the Mongolian. Several mis-educated Negroes themselves contend that the study of the Negro by children would bring before them the race problem prematurely and, therefore, urge that the study of the race be deferred until they reach advanced work in the college or university. These misguided teachers ignore the fact that the race question is being brought before black and white children daily in their homes, in the streets, through the press and on the rostrum. How, then, can the school ignore the duty of teaching the truth while these other agencies are playing up falsehood?

The experience of college instructors shows that racial attitudes of the youth are not easily changed after they reach adolescence. Although students of this advanced stage are shown the fallacy of race superiority and the folly of social distinctions, they nevertheless continue to do the illogical thing of still looking upon these despised groups as less worthy than themselves and persist in treating them accordingly. Teachers of elementary and secondary schools giving attention to this interracial problem have succeeded in softening and changing the attitude of children whose judgment has not been so hopelessly warped by the general attitude of the communities in which they have been brought up.

In approaching this problem in this fashion to counteract the one-sided education of youth the thinking people of this country have no desire to upset the curricula of the schools or to force the Negro as such into public discussion; but, if the Negro is to be elevated he must be educated in the sense of being developed from what he is, and the public must be so enlightened as to think of the Negro as a man. Furthermore, no one can be thoroughly educated until he learns as much about the Negro as he knows about other people.

Upon examining the recent catalogues of the leading Negro colleges, one finds that invariably they give courses in ancient, mediaeval, and modern Europe, but they do not give such courses in ancient, mediaeval, and modern Africa. Yet Africa, according to recent discoveries, has contributed about as much to the progress of mankind as Europe has, and the early civilization of the Mediterranean world was decidedly influenced by Africa.

Negro colleges offer courses bearing on the European colonists prior to their coming to America, their settlement on these shores, and their development here toward independence. Why are they not equally generous with the Negroes in treating their status in Africa prior to enslavement, their first transplantation to the West Indies, the Latinization of certain Negroes in contradistinction to the development of others under the influence of the Teuton, and the effort of the race toward self-expression?

A further examination of their curricula shows, too, that invariably these Negro colleges offer courses in Greek philosophy and in that of modern European thought, but they direct no attention to the philosophy of the African. Negroes of Africa have and always have had their own ideas about the nature of the universe, time, and space, about appearance and reality, and about freedom and necessity. The effort of the Negro to interpret man's relation to the universe shows just as much intelligence as we find in the philosophy of the Greeks. There were many Africans who were just as wise as Socrates.

Again, one observes in some of these catalogues numerous courses in art but no well defined course in Negro or African art which early influenced that of the Greeks. Thinkers are now saying that the early culture of the Mediterranean was chiefly African. Most of these colleges do not even direct special attention to Negro music in which the Negro has made his outstanding contribution in America. The unreasonable attitude is that because the whites do not have these things in their schools the Negroes must not have them in theirs. The Catholics and Jews, therefore, are wrong in establishing special schools to teach their principles of religion, and the Germans in America are unwise in having their children taught their mother tongue.

Such has been the education of Negroes. They have been taught facts of history, but have never learned to think. Their conception is that you go to school to find out what other people have done, and then you go out in life to imitate them. What they have done can be done by others, they contend;

and they are right. They are wrong, however, in failing to realize that what others have done, we may not need to do. If we are to do identically the same thing from generation to generation, we would not make any progress. If we are to duplicate from century to century the same feats, the world will grow tired of such a monotonous performance.

In this particular respect "Negro education" is a failure, and disastrously so, because in its present predicament the race is especially in need of vision and invention to give humanity something new. The world does not want and will never have the heroes and heroines of the past. What this age needs is an enlightened youth not to undertake the tasks like theirs but to imbibe the spirit of these great men and answer the present call of duty with equal nobleness of soul.

Not only do the needs of generations vary, but the individuals themselves are not duplicates the one of the other; and being different in this respect, their only hope to function efficiently in society is to know themselves and the generation which they are to serve. The chief value in studying the records of others is to become better acquainted with oneself and with one's possibilities to live and to do in the present age. As long as Negroes continue to restrict themselves to doing what was necessary a hundred or a thousand years ago, they must naturally expect to be left out of the great scheme of things as they concern men of today.

The most inviting field for discovery and invention, then, is the Negro himself, but he does not realize it. Frederika Bremer, when reflecting upon her visit to America about 1850, gave this country a new thought in saying to Americans, "The romance of your history is the fate of the Negro." In this very thought lies unusual possibilities for the historian, the economist, the artist, and the philosopher. Why should the Negro writer seek a theme abroad when he has the greatest of all at home?

The bondage of the Negro brought captive from Africa is one of the greatest dramas in history, and the writer who merely sees in that ordeal something to approve or condemn fails to understand the evolution of the human race. Negroes now studying dramatics go into our schools to reproduce Shakespeare, but mentally developed members of this race would see the possibilities of a greater drama in the tragedy of the man of color. Negroes graduating from conservatories of music dislike the singing of our folk songs. For some reason such misguided persons think that they can improve on the productions of the foreign drama or render the music of other people better than they can themselves.

A knowledge of real history would lead one to think that slavery was one of the significant developments which, although evil in themselves, may redound sometimes to the advantage of the oppressed rather than to that of the oppressor. Some one has said that the music of Poland was inspired by incidents of a struggle against the despots invading and partitioning their prostrate land. The Greeks never had an art until the country was overrun by hostile Orientals. Some one then began to immortalize in song the sons who went forth to fight for the native land. Another carved in marble the thought evoked by the example of the Greek youth who blocked the mountain pass with his body or who bared his breast to the javelin to defend the liberty of his country. These things we call art.

In our own country the other elements of the population, being secure in their position, have never faced such a crisis; and the Europeans, after whose pattern American life is fashioned, have not recently had such experience. White Americans, then, have produced no art at all, and that of Europe has reached the point of stagnation. Negroes who are imitating whites, then, are engaged in a most unprofitable performance. Why not interpret themselves anew to the world?

If we had a few thinkers we could expect great achievements on tomorrow. Some Negro with unusual insight would write an epic of bondage and freedom which would take its place with those of Homer and Virgil. Some Negro with esthetic appreciation would construct from collected fragments of Negro music a grand opera that would move humanity to repentance. Some Negro of philosophic penetration would find a solace for the modern world in the soul of the Negro, and then men would be men because they are men.

The Negro in his present plight, however, does not see possibilities until it is too late He exercises much "hindsight," and for that reason he loses ground in the hotly contested battles of life. The Negro as a rule waits until a thing happens before he tries to avert it. He is too much like a man whom the author once saw knocked down in a physical combat. Instead of dodging the blow when it was being dealt he arose from his prostration dodging it.

For example, the author has just received a letter from a lady in Pittsburgh complaining that the librarian in one of its schools insists upon reading to the children "a great deal of literature containing such words as 'nigger,' 'Blackie,' 'Little Black Sambo,' etc." This lady, therefore, would like to place in that school some books by Negro authors. This is a commendable effort, but it comes a little late; we hope not too late.

For centuries such literature has been circulated among the children of the modern world; and they have, therefore, come to regard the Negro as inferior. Now that some of our similarly mis-educated Negroes are seeing how they have been deceived they are awakening to address themselves to a long neglected work. They should have been thinking about this generations ago, for they have a tremendous task before them today in dispelling this error and counteracting the results of such bias in our literature.

There has just come, too, from a friend of humanity in Edinburgh, Scotland, a direful account of the increase in race prejudice in those parts. Sailors who had frequented the stronghold of race prejudice in South Africa undertook recently to prevent Negro men from socializing with Scotch women at a dance; and certain professors of the University of Edinburgh with the same attitude show so much of it in their teaching that this friend entreats us to send them informing books on the Negro. We are doing it.

Here again, however, the effort to uproot error and popularize the truth comes rather late. The Negro since freedom has gone along grinning, whooping, and "cutting capers" while the white man has applied himself to the task of defining the status of the Negro and compelling him to accept it as thus settled forever. While the Negro has been idle, propaganda has gone far ahead of history. Unfortunately, too, Negro "scholars" have assisted in the production of literature which gives this point of view.

CHAPTER XIV

THE NEW PROGRAM

IT seems only a reasonable proposition, then, that, if under the present system which produced our leadership in religion, politics, and business we have gone backward toward serfdom or have at least been kept from advancing to real freedom, it is high time to develop another sort of leadership with a different educational system. In the first place, we must bear in mind that the Negro has never been educated. He has merely been informed about other things which he has not been permitted to do. The Negroes have been shoved out of the regular schools through the rear door into the obscurity of the backyard and told to imitate others whom they see from afar, or they have been permitted in some places to come into the public schools to see how others educate themselves. The program for the uplift of the Negro in this country must be based upon a scientific study of the Negro from within to develop in him the power to do for himself what his oppressors will never do to elevate him to the level of others.

Being without actual education, we have very few persons prepared to help the Negroes whom they have set out to lead. These persons are not all dishonest men and women. Many of them are sincere, and believe that they are doing the race some great good in thus holding it backward. They must be awakened and shown the error of their ways.

We have very few teachers because most of those with whom we are afflicted know nothing about the children whom they teach or about their parents who influence the pupils more than the teachers themselves. When a boy comes to school without knowing his lesson he should be studied instead of being punished. The boy who does well in the beginning of the year and lags behind near the end of the term should not always be censured or ridiculed. As a rule, such children are not responsible for their failures. Their parents and their social status account mainly for these shortcomings. The Negro teacher, then, must treat the disease rather than its symptoms.

But can you expect teachers to revolutionize the social order for the good of the community? Indeed we must expect this very thing. The educational system of a country is worthless unless it accomplishes this task. Men of scholarship and consequently of prophetic insight must show us the right way and lead us into the light which shines brighter and brighter.

In the church where we have much freedom and independence we must get rid of preachers who are not prepared to help the people whom they exploit. The public must refuse to support men of this type. Ministers who are the creations of the old educational system must be awakened, and if this is impossible they must be dethroned. Those who keep the people in ignorance and play upon their emotions must be exiled. The people have never been taught what religion is, for most of the preachers find it easier to stimulate the superstition which develops in the unenlightened mind. Religion in such hands, then, becomes something with which you take advantage of weak people. Why try to enlighten the people in such matters when superstition serves just as well for exploitation?

The ministers with the confidence of the people must above all things understand the people themselves. They must find out the past of their parishioners, whether they were brought up in Georgia, Alabama or Texas, whether they are housed under desirable circumstances, what they do to make a living, what they do with their earnings, how they react to the world about them, how they spend their leisure, or how they function along with other elements of the social order.

In our schools, and especially in schools of religion, attention should be given to the study of the Negro as he developed during the antebellum period by showing to what extent that remote culture was determined by ideas which the Negro brought with him from Africa. To take it for granted that the ante-bellum Negro was an ignoramus or that the native brought from Africa had not a valuable culture merely because some prejudiced writers have said so does not show the attitude of scholarship, and Negro students who direct their courses accordingly will never be able to grapple with the social problems presented today by the Negro church.

The preachers of today must learn to do as well as those of old. Richard Allen so interpreted Christianity anew to his master that he was converted, and so did Henry Evans and George Bentley for other whites in North Carolina and Tennessee. Instead of accepting and trying to carry out the theories which the exploiters of humanity have brought them for a religious program the Negroes should forget their differences and in the strength of a united church bring out a new interpretation of Christ to this unwilling world. Following the religious teachings of their traducers, the Negroes do not show any more common sense than a people would in permitting criminals to enact the laws and establish the procedure of the courts by which they are to be tried.

Negro preachers, too, must be educated to their people rather than away from them. This, of course, requires a new type of religious school. To provide for such training the Negro church must get rid of its burdensome supervisory force. If the number of bishops of the various Negro Methodist churches were reduced to about twelve or fifteen, as they should be, the amount of a hundred thousand dollars or more now being paid to support the unnecessary number could be used to maintain properly at least one accredited college; and what is now being raised here and there to support various struggling but starving institutions kept alive by ambitious bishops and preachers could be saved to the people. With this money diverted to a more practical use the race would be able to establish some other things which would serve as assets rather than as liabilities.

We say liabilities, for practically all of our denominational schools which are bleeding the people for the inadequate support which they receive are still unable to do accredited work. There are so many of them that the one impoverishes the other. Outstanding men of the church, therefore, have to acquire their advanced education by attending other schools in the beginning or by taking additional training elsewhere after learning all our denominational schools can offer. This is a loss of ground which should be regained if the church is to go forward.

By proper unification and organization the Negro churches might support one or two much needed universities of their own. With the present arrangement of two or three in the same area and sometimes as many in one city there is no chance for emerging from the trying poverty-stricken state. And even if these institutions could do well what they undertake they do not supply all educational needs. To qualify for certification in the professions Negroes must go to other schools, where, although they acquire the fundamentals, they learn much about their "inferiority" to discourage them in their struggle upward.

We should not close any accredited Negro colleges or universities, but we should reconstruct the whole system. We should not eliminate many of the courses now being offered, but we should secure men of vision to give them from the point of view of the people to be served. We should not spend less money for the higher education of the Negro, but should redefine higher education as preparation to think and work out a program to serve the lowly rather than to live as an aristocrat.

Such subjects of certitude as mathematics, of course, would continue and so would most of the work in practical languages and science. In theology, literature, social science, and education, however, radical reconstruction is necessary. The old worn-out theories as to man's relation to God and his fellowman, the system of thought which has permitted one man to exploit, oppress, and exterminate another and still be regarded as righteous must be discarded for the new thought of men as brethren and the idea of God as the lover of all mankind.

After Negro students have mastered the fundamentals of English, the principles of composition, and the leading facts in the development of its literature, they should not spend all of their time in advanced work on Shakespeare, Chaucer and Anglo-Saxon. They should direct their attention also to the folklore of the African, to the philosophy in his proverbs, to the development of the Negro in the use of modern language, and to the works of Negro writers.

The leading facts of the history of the world should be studied by all, but of what advantage is it to the Negro student of history to devote all of his time to courses bearing on such despots as Alexander the Great, Caesar, and Napoleon, or to the record of those nations whose outstanding achievement has been rapine, plunder, and murder for world power? Why not study the African background from the point of view of anthropology and history, and then take up sociology as it concerns the Negro peasant or proletarian who is suffering from sufficient ills to supply laboratory work for the most advanced students of the social order? Why not take up economics as reflected by the Negroes of today and work out some remedy for their lack of capital, the absence of cooperative enterprise, and the short life of their establishments. Institutions like Harvard, Yale and Columbia are not going to do these things, and educators influenced by them to the extent that they become blind to the Negro will never serve the race efficiently.

To educate the Negro we must find out exactly what his background is, what he is today, what his possibilities are, and how to begin with him as he is and make him a better individual of the kind that he is. Instead of cramming the Negro's mind with what others have shown that they can do, we should develop his latent powers that he may perform in society a part of which others are not capable.

During his life the author has seen striking examples of how people should and should not be taught. Some of these are worth relating. Probably the most interesting was that of missionary work in China. In 1903 the author crossed the Pacific Ocean with twenty-six missionaries who were going to take the Orient by storm. One Todd, from North Carolina, was orating and preaching almost every day to stimulate his coworkers to go boldly to the task before them. Dr. De Forest, long a missionary to Japan, informed them that the work required more than enthusiasm: that they could not rush into the homes of the natives saying, "Peace be to this house." for it might turn out the other way and give somebody the opportunity to say, "Peace be to his ashes."

Dr. De Forest explained to them how he chose a decidedly different course, preferring first to study the history, the language, the manners and the customs of the people to approach them intelligently; and not until he had been in the country four years did he undertake to exhort, but after that time he had had great success and had been invited to preach before the Mikado himself. Now Todd did not take this advice, and he had not been in China five months before he and his wife had been poisoned by their native cook who had become incensed at the way they interfered with the institutions of his people.

Another striking illustration was the education of the Filipinos. Not long after the close of the Spanish-American War the United States Government started out to educate the Filipinos over night. Numbers of "highly trained" Americans were carried there to do the work They entered upon their task by teaching the Filipinos just as they had taught American children who were otherwise circumstanced. The result was failure. Men trained at institutions like Harvard, Yale, Columbia, and Chicago could not reach these people and had to be dismissed from the service. Some of these "scholarly" Americans had to be maintained by the subscription of friends until they could be returned to this country on Government transportation.

In the meantime, however, there came along an insurance man, who went to the Philippines to engage in business. He had never taught at all, and he had never studied authorities like Bagley, Judd, and Thorndike; but he understood people Seeing that others had failed, he went into the work himself. He filled the schoolroom with thousands of objects from the pupil's environment. In the beginning he did not use books very much, because those supplied were not adapted to the needs of the children. He talked about the objects around them. Everything was presented objectively. When he took up the habits of the snake he brought the reptile to the school for demonstration. When he taught the crocodile he had one there. In teaching the Filipinos music he did not sing "Come shake the Apple-Tree." They had never seen such an object. He taught them to sing "Come shake the Lomboy Tree," something which they had actually done. In reading he did not concentrate on the story of how George Washington always told the truth. They had never heard of him and could not have appreciated that myth if some one had told them about it. This real educator taught them about their own hero, José Rizal, who gave his life as a martyr for the freedom of his country. By and by they got rid of most books based on the life of American people and worked out an entirely new series dealing with the life of Filipinos. The result, then, was that this man and others who saw the situation as he did succeeded, and the work of the public schools in the Philippines is today the outstanding achievement of the Americans in that country.

We do not mean to suggest here, however, that any people should ignore the record of the progress of other races. We would not advocate any such unwise course. We say, hold on to the real facts of history as they are, but complete such knowledge by studying also the history of races and nations which have been purposely ignored. We should not underrate the achievements of Mesopotamia, Greece, and Rome; but we should give equally as much attention to the internal African kingdoms, the Songhay empire, and Ethiopia, which through Egypt decidedly influenced the civilization of the Mediterranean world. We would not ignore the rise of Christianity and the development of the Church; but we would at the same time give honorable mention to the persons of African blood who figured in these achievements, and who today are endeavoring to carry out the principles of Jesus long since repudiated by most so-called Christians. We would not underestimate the achievements of the captains of industry who in the commercial expansion of the modern world have produced the wealth necessary to ease and comfort; but we would give credit to the Negro who so largely supplied the demand for labor by which these things have been accomplished.

In our own particular history we would not dim one bit the luster of any star in our firmament. We would not learn less of George Washington, "First in War, First in Peace and First in the Hearts of his Countrymen"; but we would learn something also of the three thousand Negro soldiers of the American Revolution who helped to make this "Father of our Country" possible. We would not neglect to appreciate the unusual contribution of Thomas Jefferson to freedom and democracy; but we would invite attention also to two of his outstanding contemporaries, Phillis Wheatley, the writer of interesting verse, and Benjamin Banneker, the mathematician, astronomer, and advocate of a world peace plan set forth in 1793 with the vital principles of Woodrow Wilson's League of Nations. We would in no way detract from the fame of Perry on Lake Erie or Jackson at New Orleans in the second struggle with England; but we would remember the gallant black men who assisted in winning these memorable victories on land and sea. We would not cease to pay tribute to Abraham Lincoln as the "Savior of the Country"; but we would ascribe praise also to the one hundred and seventy-eight thousand Negroes who had to be mustered into the service of the Union before it could be preserved, and who by their heroism demonstrated that they were entitled to freedom and citizenship.

CHAPTER XV

VOCATIONAL GUIDANCE

BUT how can the Negro in this new system learn to make a living, the most important task to which all people must give attention? In view of the Negro's economic plight most of the schools are now worked up over what is called "vocational guidance" in an effort to answer this very question. To what, however, are they to guide their Negro students? Most Negroes now employed are going down blind alleys, and unfortunately some schools seem to do no more than to stimulate their going in that direction.

This may seem to be a rash statement, but a study of our educational system shows that our schools are daily teaching Negroes what they can never apply in life or what is no longer profitable because of the revolution of industry by the multiplication of mechanical appliances. For example, some of our schools are still teaching individual garment making which offers no future today except in catering to the privileged and rich classes. Some of these institutions still offer instruction in shoemaking when the technique developed under their handicaps makes impossible competition with that of the modern factory based upon the invention of a Negro, Jan Matzeliger.

These facts have been known for generations, but some of these institutions apparently change not. Education, like religion, is conservative. It makes haste slowly only, and sometimes not at all. Do not change the present order of thinking and doing, many say, for you disturb too many things long since regarded as ideal. The dead past, according to this view, must be the main factor in determining the future. We should learn from the living past, but let the dead past remain dead.

A survey of employment of the Negroes in this country shows a most undesirable situation The education of the masses has not enabled them to advance very far in making a living and has not developed in the Negro the power to change this condition. It is revealed that in many establishments the Negro when a young man starts as a janitor or porter and dies in old age in the same position. Tradition fixes his status as such, and both races feel satisfied.

When this janitor or porter dies the dailies headline the passing of this Negro who knew his place and rendered satisfactory service in it. "Distinguished" white men, for whom he ran errands and cleaned cuspidors, volunteer as honorary pall-bearers and follow his remains to the final resting place. Thoughtless Negro editors, instead of expressing their regret that such a life of usefulness was not rewarded by promotion, take up the refrain as some great honor bestowed upon the race.

Among people thus satisfied in the lower pursuits of life and sending their children to school to memorize theories which they never see applied, there can be no such thing as vocational guidance. Such an effort implies an objective; and in the present plight of economic dependence there is no occupation for which the Negro may prepare himself with the assurance that he will find employment. Opportunities which he has today may be taken from him tomorrow; and schools changing their curricula in hit-and-miss fashion may soon find themselves on the wrong track just as they have been for generations.

Negroes do not need some one to guide them to what persons of another race have developed. They must be taught to think and develop something for themselves. It is most pathetic to see Negroes begging others for a chance as we have been doing recently. "Do not force us into starvation." we said. "Let us come into your stores and factories and do a part of what you are doing to profit by our trade." The Negro as a slave developed this fatal sort of dependency; and, restricted mainly to menial service and drudgery during nominal freedom, he has not grown out of it. Now the Negro is facing the ordeal of either learning to do for himself or to die out gradually in the bread line in the ghetto.

If the schools really mean to take a part in necessary uplift they must first supply themselves with teachers. Unfortunately we have very few such workers. The large majority of persons supposedly teaching Negroes never carry to the schoolroom any thought as to improving their condition. From the point of view of these so-called teachers they have done their duty when in automaton fashion they impart in the schoolroom the particular facts which they wrote out in the examination when they "qualified" for their respective positions. Most of them are satisfied with receiving their pay and spending it for the toys and gewgaws of life.

For example, the author is well acquainted with a Negro of this type, who is now serving as the head of one of the largest schools in the United States. From the point of view of our present system he is well educated. He holds advanced degrees from one of the leading institutions of the world; and he is known to be well informed on all the educational theories developed from the time of Socrates down to the day of Dewey. Yet this "educator" says repeatedly that in his daily operations he never has anything to do with Negroes because they are impossible. He says that he never buys anything from a Negro store, and he would not dare to put a penny in a Negro bank.

From such teachers large numbers of Negroes learn this fateful lesson. For example, not long ago a committee of Negroes in a large city went to the owner of a chain store in their neighborhood and requested that he put a Negro manager in charge. This man replied that he doubted that the Negroes themselves wanted such a thing. The Negroes urging him to make the change assured him that they were unanimously in favor of it. The manager, however, asked them to be fair enough with his firm and themselves to investigate before pressing the matter any further. They did so and discovered that one hundred thirty-seven Negro families in that neighborhood seriously objected to buying from Negroes and using articles handled by them. These Negroes, then, had to do the groundwork of uprooting the inferiority idea which had resulted from their mis-education.

To what, then, can a Negro while despising the enterprise of his fellows guide the youth of his race; and where do you figure out that the youth thus guided will be by 1950? The whites are daily informing Negroes that they need not come to them for opportunities. Can the Negro youth, miseducated by persons who depreciate their efforts, learn to make, opportunities for themselves? This is the real problem which the Negroes must solve; and he who is not interested in it and makes no effort to solve it is worthless in the present struggle.

Our advanced teachers, like "most highly educated" Negroes, pay little attention to the things about them except when the shoe begins to pinch on one or the other side. Unless they happen to become naked they never think of the production of cotton or wool; unless they get hungry they never give any thought to the output of wheat or corn; unless their friends lose their jobs they never inquire about the outlook for coal or steel, or how these things affect the children whom they are trying to teach. In other words, they live in a world, but they are not of it. How can such persons guide the youth without knowing how these things affect the Negro community?

The Negro community, in a sense, is composed of those around you, but it functions in a different way. You cannot see it by merely looking out of the windows of the schoolroom. This community requires scientific investigation. While persons of African blood are compelled to sustain closer relation to their own people than to other elements in society, they are otherwise influenced socially and economically. The Negro community suffers for lack of delimitation because of the various ramifications of life in the United States. For example, there may be a Negro grocer in the neighborhood, but the Negro chauffeur for a rich man down town and the washerwoman for an aristocratic family in "quality row" will be more than apt to buy their food and clothing at the larger establishment with which their employers have connections, although they may be insulted there. Negroes of the District of Columbia have millions of dollars deposited in banks down town, where Negro women are not allowed in the ladies' rest rooms.

Right in the heart of the highly educated Negro section of Washington, too, is a restaurant catering through the front door exclusively to the white business men, who must live in the Negroes' section to supply them with the necessities of life, and catering at the same time through the back door to numbers of Negroes who pile into that dingy room to purchase whatever may be thrown at them. Yet less than two blocks away are several Negroes running cafés where they can be served for the same amount and under desirable circumstances. Negroes who do this, we say, do not have the proper attitude toward life and its problems, and for that reason we do not take up time with them. They do not belong to our community. The traducers of the race, however, are guiding these people the wrong way. Why do not the "educated" Negroes change their course by identifying themselves with the masses?

For similar reasons the Negro professional man may not always have a beautiful home and a fine car. His plight to the contrary may result from action like that of a poor man who recently knocked on the author's door about midnight to use his telephone to call the ambulance of the Casualty Hospital to take immediate charge of his sick wife. Although living nearer to the Freedmen's Hospital, where more sympathetic consideration would have been given this patient, he preferred to take her to the other hospital where she would have to be carried through the back yard and placed in a room over a stable. He worked there, however; and because of long association with his traducers and the sort of treatment that they have meted out to him he was willing to entrust to their hands the very delicate matter of the health of his wife. This was a part of his community.

Large numbers of Negroes live in such a community. You say that such an atmosphere is not congenial and you will not lose time with these people who are thus satisfied, but the exploiting preacher, the unprincipled politician, the notorious gambler, and the agent of vice are all there purposely misleading these people who have not as yet shaken from their minds the shackles of slavery. What is going to become of them? What is going to become of you?

We avoid them because we find enjoyment among others; but they are developing their own community. Their teacher lives in another community which may or may not be growing. Will his community so expand as to include theirs? If not, their community may encroach upon his. It is a sort of social dualism. What will the end be? The teacher will help to answer this question.

Such guidance, however, must not be restricted to the so-called common people. So many Negroes now engaged in business have no knowledge of its possibilities and limitations. Most of them are as unwise as a Negro business man who came to Washington recently in a ten-thousand-dollar car representing a firm with only one hundred thousand dollars invested. It is only a matter of time before his firm will be no more. He started out destroying his business at the very source. While Negroes are thus spending their means and themselves in riotous living the foreigners come to dwell among them in modest circumstances long enough to get rich and to join those who close in on these unfortunates economically until all the hopes for their redemption are lost.

If the Negroes of this country are to escape starvation and rise out of poverty unto comfort and ease, they must change their way of thinking and living. Never did the author see a more striking demonstration of such a necessity than recently when a young man came to him looking for a job. He was well bedecked with jewelry and fine clothes, and while he was in the office he smoked almost enough cigars to pay one's board for that day. A man of this type in a poverty-stricken group must suffer and die.

A young woman recently displaced in a position from which she received considerable income for a number of years approached the author not long ago to help her solve the problem of making a living. He could not feel very sympathetic toward her, however, for she had on a coat which cost enough to maintain one comfortably for at least two years.

While talking with him, moreover, she was so busy telling him about what she wanted that she had little time to inform him as to what she can do to supply her needs.

A man whom the author knows is decidedly handicapped by having lost a lucrative position. He must now work for a little more than half of what he has been accustomed to earn. With his former stipend he was able to maintain two or three girls in addition to his wife, and he drank the best of bootleg stuff available. In now trying to do all of these things on a small wage he finds himself following a most tortuous course to make his ends meet, and he suffers within as well as without.

This undesirable attitude toward life results from the fact that the Negro has learned from others how to spend money much more rapidly than he has learned how to earn it. During these days, therefore, it will be very wise for Negroes to concentrate on the wise use of money and the evil results from the misuse of it. In large cities like Washington, Baltimore, Philadelphia, New York, and Chicago they earn millions and millions every year and throw these vast sums immediately away for trifles which undermine their health, vitiate their morals, and contribute to the undoing of generations of Negroes unborn.

This enlightenment as to economic possibilities in the Negro community must not only include instruction as to how enterprises can be made possible but how they should be apportioned among the various parts of the Negro community. Such knowledge is especially necessary in the case of Negroes because of the fatal tendency toward imitation not only of the white man but the imitation of others in his own group. For example, a Negro starts a restaurant on a corner and does well. Another Negro, observing this prosperity, thinks that he can do just as well by opening a similar establishment next door. The inevitable result is that by dividing the trade between himself and his forerunner he makes it impossible for either one to secure sufficient patronage to continue in business.

In undertakings of great importance this same undesirable tendency toward duplication of effort is also apparent. It has been a common thing to find two or three banks in a Negro community, each one struggling for an existence in competing for the patronage of the small group of people, all of whom would hardly be able to support one such financial institution. These banks continue their unprofitable competition and never think of merging until some crisis forces them to the point that they have to do so or go into bankruptcy. The Negro community, then, never has a strong financial institution with sufficient resources to stimulate the efforts of the business men who otherwise might succeed.

The same shortsightedness has been evident in, the case of the insurance companies organized by Negroes. One was established here and then another followed there in imitation of the first. We have been accustomed to boast that the Negroes have about fifty insurance companies in this country, marking the corners of the streets of the cities with large signs displaying what they are doing for the race. Instead of boasting of such unwise expansion we should have received such information with sorrow, for what the race actually needs is to merge all of the insurance companies now supported by Negroes and make one good one. Such a step away from duplication would be a long stride toward our much needed awakening, and it would certainly give us prestige in the business world.

This imitation and duplication are decidedly disastrous to economic enterprise as we can daily observe. A few days ago a young man in the East lamented the fact that after investing his life's earnings in the drug business and making every effort to stimulate the enterprise, he has failed. Some one took occasion, thereupon, to remind him that men have grown rich, as a rule, not by doing what thousands of others are doing but by undertaking something new. If instead of going into the retail dispensing of drugs, he had conceived and carried out the idea of the chain-drug store, he would have become an independently rich man.

There is always a chance to do this because the large majority of people do not think and, therefore, leave the field wide open for those who have something new with which to please the public. Negroes even found this possible during the days of slavery when the race supposedly had no chance at all.

About a hundred years ago Thomas Day, a North Carolina Negro, realized that the rough furniture of the people in his community did not meet the requirements of those of modern taste. He, therefore, worked out a style of ornate and beautiful furniture which attracted the attention of the most aristocratic people of the state and built up for himself a most successful business. Persons in that state are still talking about the Day furniture, and not long ago it became the subject of a magazine article. If North Carolina would turn out more Negroes of this type today, instead of the rather large number who are going to teach and preach, some of its present economic problems might thereby be solved.

During these same years another Negro was showing himself to be equally ingenious. This was Henry Boyd. After buying himself in Kentucky, he went to Cincinnati to start life as a free man. There he encountered so much prejudice against Negro labor that he could not find employment at his trade of cabinetmaking. A new thought came to him, however; and in this way he solved his own problem.

Boyd became convinced that people had been sleeping long enough on straw ticks and wooden slats, and he invented the corded bed, the most comfortable bed prior to the use of springs which brought still more ease. Boyd's corded bed became popular throughout the Ohio and Mississippi Valleys, and he built up a profitable trade which required the employment of twenty-five white and black artisans. Other enterprising Negro business men like Boyd gave the Negro element of Cincinnati more of an aspect of progress before the Civil War than it has today. Has the Negro less chance today than he had a century ago?

For about thirty years the author knew an old Negro lady at Gordonsville, Virginia, who gave the world something new in frying chicken. She discovered the art of doing this thing in the way that others could not, and she made a good living selling her exceptionally prepared chicken and fried puffs at the windows of the cars when the trains stopped at the station. Well-to-do men and women of both races would leave the Pullman train with its modern diner attached and go out and supply themselves and their friends with this old lady's tastefully made up lunches.

Another woman of color living in Columbia, Missouri, recently gave the world another new idea. She had learned cooking, especially baking, but saw no exceptional opportunity in the usual application of the trade. After studying her situation and the environment in which she had to live, she hit upon the scheme of popularizing her savorous sweet potato biscuits, beaten whiter than all others by an invention of her own; and the people of both races made a well-beaten path to her home to enjoy these delicious biscuits. In this way she has made herself and her relatives independent.

This is the way fortunes are made, but Negroes, who are conscientiously doing their best to rise in the economic sphere, do not follow the noble examples of those who had less opportunity than we have today. We spend much time in slavish imitation, but our white friends strike out along new lines. Almost all of the large fortunes in America have been made in this way.

John D. Rockefeller did not set out in life to imitate Vanderbilt. Rockefeller saw his opportunity in developing the oil industry. Carnegie had better sense than to imitate Rockefeller, for that task was already well done, and he consolidated the steel interests. Henry Ford knew better than to take up what Carnegie had exploited, for there appeared a still larger possibility for industrial achievement in giving the world the facility of cheap transportation in the low-priced car.

While such guidance as the Negro needs will concern itself first with material things, however, it must not stop with these as ends in themselves. In the acquisition of these we lay the foundation for the greater things of the spirit. A poor man properly directed can write a more beautiful poem than one who is surfeited. The man in the hovel composes a more charming song than the one in the palace. The painter in the ghetto gets an inspiration for a more striking portrait than his landlord can appreciate. The ill-fed sculptor lives more abundantly than the millionaire who purchases the expression of his thought in marble and bronze. For the Negro, then, the door of opportunity is wide open. Let him prepare himself to enter this field where competition is no handicap. In such a sphere he may learn to lead the world, while keeping pace with it in the development of the material things of life.

CHAPTER XVI

THE NEW TYPE OF PROFESSIONAL MAN REQUIRED

NEGROES should study for the professions for all sane reasons that members of another race should go into these lines of endeavor and also on account of the particular call to serve the lowly of their race. In the case of the law we should cease to make exceptions because of the possibilities for failure resulting from prejudice against the Negro lawyer and thE lack of Negro business enterprises to require his services Negroes must become like English gentlemen who study the law of the land, not because they intend to practice the profession, but because every gentleman should know the law. In the interpretation of the law by the courts, too, all the rights of the Negroes in this country are involved, and a larger number of us must qualify for this important service. We may have too many lawyers of the wrong kind, but we have not our share of the right kind.

The Negro lawyer has tended to follow in the footsteps of the average white practitioner and has not developed the power which he could acquire if he knew more about the people whom he should serve and the problems they have to confront. These things are not law in themselves, but they determine largely whether or not the Negro will practice law and the success he will have in the profession. The failure to give attention to these things has often meant the downfall of many a Negro lawyer.

There are, moreover, certain aspects of law to which the white man would hardly address himself but to which the Negro should direct special attention. Of unusual importance to the Negro is the necessity for understanding the misrepresentations in criminal records of Negroes, and race distinctions in the laws of modern nations. These matters require a systematic study of the principles of law and legal procedure. and, in addition thereto, further study of legal problems as they meet the Negro lawyer in the life which he must live.

This offers the Negro law school an unusual opportunity.

Because our lawyers do not give attention to these problems they often fail in a crisis. They are interested in the race and want to defend its cause. The case, however, requires not only the unselfish spirit they sometimes manifest but much more understanding of the legal principles, involved. Nothing illustrates this better than the failure of one of our attorneys to measure up in the case brought up to the United States Supreme Court from Oklahoma to test the validity of the exclusion of Negroes from Pullman cars. The same criticism may be made of the segregation case of the District of Columbia brought before this highest tribunal by another Negro attorney. In both of these cases the lawyers started wrong and therefore ended wrong. They lacked the knowledge to present their cases properly to the court.

Our lawyers must learn that the judges are not attorneys themselves, for they have to decide on the merits of what is presented to them. It is not the business of the judges to amend their pleadings or decide their cases according to their good intentions. Certainly such generosity cannot be expected from prejudiced courts which are looking for every loophole possible to escape from a frank decision on the rights of Negroes guaranteed by the constitution. These matters require advanced study and painstaking research; but our lawyers, as a rule, are not interested in this sort of mental exercise.

The Negro medical schools have had a much better opportunity than the few Negro law schools which have functioned in the professional preparation of Negroes. On account of the racial contact required of white physicians who are sometimes unwilling to sustain this relation to Negroes the Negro physicians and dentists have a better chance among their people than the Negro lawyers; and the demand for the services of the former assures a larger income than Negro lawyers are accustomed to earn. But in spite of this better opportunity Negro medical institutions and their graduates have done little more than others to solve the peculiar problems confronting the Negro race

Too many Negroes go into medicine and dentistry merely for selfish purposes, hoping thereby to increase their income and spend it in joyous living. They have the ambition to own fine automobiles, to dress handsomely, and to figure conspicuously in society. The practice of these professions among poor Negroes yields these results. Why not be a physician or dentist then?

Too many of our physicians are like the one whom the author recently visited in New York City. "When I heard you coming up the stairs," said he, "I began to feel glad, for I was sure that you were another patient from whom I might extract at least two dollars for a prescription."

Yet one would wonder how that physician could prosper in his profession, for he had no special equipment for the practice of any kind of advanced phases of medicine. About all he could do was to look at the patient's tongue, feel his pulse, ask him a few questions, write a prescription and collect the fee. The apparatus required for the modern treatment of serious maladies he did not have and seemed to have no ambition to possess.

The Negroes of today are very much in need of physicians who in their professional work will live up to what they are taught in school, and will build upon their foundation by both experience and further training. In his segregated position in the ghetto the Negro health problem presents more difficulties than that of the whites who are otherwise circumstanced. The longevity of the Negro depends in part upon the supply of Negro physicians and nurses who will address themselves unselfishly to the solution of this particular problem. Since the Negroes are forced into undesirable situations and compelled to inhabit germ-infested districts, they cannot escape ultimate extermination if our physicians do not help them to work out a community health program which will provide for the Negroes some way to survive.

Negro medical schools and their graduates must do more preaching of the necessity for improving conditions which determine health and eradicate disease. A large number of physicians and nurses must be trained, and new opportunities for them to practice must be found This can be done by turning out better products from these schools and the extension of hospitals among Negroes who have been so long neglected In this campaign, however, the Negro physicians must supply the leadership, and others must join with them in these efforts.

From medical schools, too, we must have Negroes with a program of medical research. Today the world is inclined to give attention to the health of the Negro since unsanitary conditions of the race will mean the lose of health among the whites. Philanthropists, however, hardly know how to proceed or which way to go because they have so long neglected the Negroes that they do not know how to provide wisely for them; and the Negro physicians themselves have failed to give adequate attention to these conditions. Negro medical students have not directed sufficient attention to the antebellum background of the Negro who, still under that influence, indulges in superstitious and religious practices which impede the progress of medicine among them. One would be surprised to know the extent to which primitive medicine is practiced Among American Negroes today. Often in the rural districts they seldom see a physician. The midwife and the herb doctor there control the situation.

The greatest problem now awaiting solution is the investigation of the differential resistance of races to disease. What are the diseases of which Negroes are more susceptible than whites? What are the diseases of which the whites are more susceptible than Negroes? The Negro escapes yellow fever and influenza, but the white man dies. The white man withstands syphilis and tuberculosis fairly well, but the Negro afflicted with these maladies easily succumbs. These questions offer an inviting field of research for Negro medical students.

While we hear much about medicine, law and the like their importance must not be unduly emphasized. Certainly men should not crowd into these spheres to make money, but all professions among Negroes except those of teaching and preaching are undermanned. All Negroes in professions constitute less than two and a half per cent of those over ten years of age who are gainfully employed. At the same time the whites find certain of their professions overcrowded, and some of their practitioners could not exist without the patronage of Negroes.

Negroes, too, should undergo systematic training for those professions in which they have shown special aptitude as in the arts. They must not wait for the Americans to approve their plunging into unknown spheres. The world is not circumscribed by the United States, and the Negro must become a pioneer in making use of a larger portion of the universe. If the people here do recognize the Negro in these spheres let him seek a hearing in the liberal circles of Europe. If he has any art Europeans will appreciate it and assure him success in forbidden fields

In Europe, it should be noted, the Negro artist is not wanted as a mere imitator Europeans will recognize him in the role of an enlightened artist portraying the life of his people. As an English abolitionist said more than a century ago, "The portrait of the Negro has seldom been drawn but by the pencil of his oppressor and the Negro has sat for it in the distorted attitude of slavery." A new method of approach, however, is now possible. There has been an awakening in Europe to the realization of the significance of African culture, and circles there want to see that life depicted by the Negro who can view it from within. There is a philosophy in it that the world must understand. From its contemplation may come a new social program Herein lies the opportunity of the Negro artist as a world reformer. Will he see it and live or continue the mere imitation of others and die?

CHAPTER XVII

HIGHER STRIVINGS IN THE SERVICE OF THE COUNTRY

ANOTHER factor the Negro needs is a new figure in politics, one who will not concern himself so much with what others can do for him as with what he can do for himself. He will know sufficient about the system of government not to carry his trouble to the federal functionaries and thus confess himself a failure in the community in which he lives. He will know that his freedom from peonage and lynching will be determined by the extent that he can develop into a worthy citizen and impress himself upon his community.

The New Negro in politics will not be so unwise as to join the ignorant delegations from conferences and convention which stage annual pilgrimages to the White House to complain to the President because they have socially and economically failed to measure up to demands of self-preservation. The New Negro in politics will understand clearly that in the final analysis federal functionaries cannot do anything about these matters within the police powers of the states, and he will not put himself in the position of being received with coldness and treated with contempt as these ignorant misleaders of the Negro race have been from time immemorial. The New Negro in politics, then, will appeal to his own and to such friends of other races in his locality as believe in social justice. If he does something for himself others will do more for him.

The increasing vigor of the race, then, will not be frittered away in partisan strife in the interest of the oppressors of the race. It ought not to be possible for the political bosses to induce almost any Negro in the community to abandon his permanent employment to assist them and their ilk in carrying out some program for the selfish purposes of the ones engineering the scheme. It ought not to be possible for the politicians to distribute funds at the rate of fifty or a hundred dollars a head among the outstanding ministers and use them and their congregations in vicious partisan strife.

It is most shameful that some ministers resort to religion as a camouflage to gain influence in the churches only to use such power for selfish political purpose.

The Negro should endeavor to be a figure in politics, not a tool for the politicians. This higher rôle can be played not by parking all of the votes of a race on one side of the fence as both blacks and whites have done in the South, but by independent action. The Negro should not censure the Republican party for forgetting him and he should not blame the Democratic party for opposing him. Neither can the South blame any one but itself for its isolation in national politics. Any people who will vote the same way for three generations without thereby obtaining results ought to be ignored and disfranchised.

As a minority element the Negro should not knock at the door of any particular political party. He should appeal to the Negroes themselves and from them should come harmony and concerted action for a new advance to that larger freedom of men. The Negro should use his vote rather than give it away to reward the dead for some favors done in the distant past. He should clamor not for the few offices earmarked as Negro jobs but for the recognition of these despised persons as men according to the provision of the Constitution of the United States.

The few state and national offices formerly set aside for Negroes have paled into insignificance when compared with the many highly lucrative positions now occupied by Negroes as a result of their development in other spheres. Sometimes a Negro prominent in education, business or professional life can earn more in a few months than the most successful politicians can earn in years. These political jobs, moreover, have diminished in recent years because the increase of race prejudice, which this policy has doubtless aided, supplies the political leaders with an excuse for not granting their Negro coworkers anything additional.

The New Negro in politics must learn something that the old "ward-heelers" have never been able to realize, namely, not only that the few offices allotted Negroes are insignificant but that even if the Negro received a proportionate share of the spoils, the race cannot hope to solve any serious problem by the changing fortunes of politics. Real politics, the science of government, is deeply rooted in the economic foundation of the social order. To figure greatly in politics the Negro must be a great figure in politics. A class of people slightly lifted above poverty, therefore, can never have much influence in political circles. The Negro must develop character and worth to make him a desirable everywhere so that he will not have to knock at the doors of political parties but will have them thrown open to him.

The New Negro in politics must not ask the party for money, he must not hire himself for a pittance to swing voters in line. He must contribute to the campaign of the party pleasing him, rather than draw upon it for an allowance to drive the wolf from the door during the three months of the political canvass. It will be considered a stroke of good fortune that a Negro of such influence and character has aligned himself with a party, and this fact will speak eloquently for the element to which he belongs.

The New Negro in politics, moreover, must not be a politician. He must be a man. He must try to give the world something rather than extract something from it. The world, as he should see it, does not owe him anything, certainly not a political office; and he should not try solely to secure one, and thus waste valuable years which might be devoted to the development of something of an enduring value. If he goes into office, it should be as a sacrifice, because his valuable time is required elsewhere. If he is needed by his country in a civil position, he may respond to the call as a matter of duty, for his usefulness is otherwise assured. From such a Negro, then, we may expect sound advice, intelligent guidance, and constructive effort fort the good of all elements of our population.

When such Negroes go into office you will not find them specializing in things which peculiarly concern the Negroes, offering merely antilynching bills and measures for pensioning the freedmen. The New Negro in politics will see his opportunity not in thus restricting himself but in visioning the whole social and economic order with his race as a part of it. In thus working for the benefit of all as prompted by his liberal mindedness the New Negro will do much more to bring the elements together for common good than he will be able to do in prating only of the ills of his particular corner and extending his hand for a douceur.

In suggesting herein the rise of the New Negro in politics the author does not have in mind the so-called radical Negroes who have read and misunderstood Karl Marx and his disciples and would solve the political as well as the economic problems of the race by an immediate application of these principles. History shows that although large numbers of people have actually tried to realize such pleasant dreams, they have in the final analysis come back to a social program based on competition. If no one is to enjoy the fruits of his exceptional labor any more than the individual who is not prepared to render such extraordinary service, not one of a thousand will be sufficiently humanitarian to bestir himself to achieve much of importance, and force applied in this case to stimulate such action has always broken down. If the excited whites who are bringing to the Negroes such strange doctrines are insane enough to believe them, the Negroes themselves should learn to think before it is too late

History shows that it does not matter who is in power or what revolutionary forces take over the government, those who have not learned to do for themselves and have to depend solely on others never obtain any more rights or privileges in the end than they had in the beginning. Even if the expected social upheaval comes, the Negro will be better prepared to take care of himself in the subsequent reconstruction if he develops the power to ascend to a position higher up after the radically democratic people will have recovered from their revelry in an impossible Utopia.

To say that the Negro cannot develop sufficiently in the business world to measure arms with present-day capitalists is to deny actual facts, refute history, and discredit the

Negro as a capable competitor in the economic battle of life. No man knows what he can do until he tries. The Negro race has never tried to do very much for itself. The race has great possibilities. Properly awakened, the Negro can do the so-called impossible in the business world and thus help to govern rather than merely be governed.

In the failure to see this and the advocacy of the destruction of the whole economic order to right social wrong we see again the tendency of the Negro to look to some force from without to do for him what he must learn to do for himself. The Negro needs to become radical, and the race will never amount to anything until it does become so, but this radicalism should come from within. The Negro will be very foolish to resort to extreme measures in behalf of foreign movements before he learns to suffer and die to right his own wrongs. There is no movement in the world-working especially for the Negro. He must learn to do this for himself or be exterminated just as the American Indian has faced his doom in the setting sun.

Why should the Negro wait for some one from without to urge him to self-assertion when he sees himself robbed by his employer, defrauded by his merchant, and hushed up by government agents of injustice? Why wait for a spur to action when he finds his manhood insulted, his women outraged, and his fellowmen lynched for amusement? The Negroes have always had sufficient reason for being radical, and it looks silly to see them taking up the cause of others who pretend that they are interested in the Negro when they merely mean to use the race as a means to an end. When the desired purpose of these so-called friendly groups will have been served, they will have no further use for the Negro and will drop him just as the Republican machine has done

The radicals bring forward, too, the argument that the Negro, being of a minority group, will always be overpowered by others From the point of view of the selfish elements this may be true, and certainly it has worked thus for some time; but things do not always turn out according to mathematical calculations. In fact, the significant developments in history have never been thus determined. Only the temporary and the trivial can be thus forecast. The human factor is always difficult for the materialist to evaluate and the prophecies of the alarmist are often upset Why should we expect less in the case of the Negro?

CHAPTER XVIII

THE STUDY OF THE NEGRO

The facts drawn from an experience of more than twenty years enable us to make certain deductions with respect to the study of the Negro. Only one Negro out of every ten thousand is interested in the effort to set forth what his race has thought and felt and attempted and accomplished that it may not become a negligible factor in the thought of the world. By traditions and education, however, the large majority of Negroes have become interested in the history and status of other races, and they spend millions annually to promote such knowledge. (Along with this sum, of course, should be considered the large amount paid for devices in trying not to be Negroes.)

The chief reason why so many give such a little attention to the background of the Negro is the belief that this study is unimportant. They consider as history only such deeds as those of Mussolini who after building up an efficient war machine with the aid of other Europeans would now use it to murder unarmed and defenseless Africans who have restricted themselves exclusively to attending to their own business. If Mussolini succeeds in crushing Abyssinia he will be recorded in "history" among the Caesars, and volumes written in praise of the conqueror will find their way to the homes and libraries of thousands of miseducated Negroes. The oppressor has always indoctrinated the weak with this interpretation of the crimes of the strong.

The war lords have done good only accidentally or incidentally while seeking to do evil. The movements which have ameliorated the condition of humanity and stimulated progress have been inaugurated by men of thought in lifting their fellows out of drudgery unto ease and comfort, out of selfishness unto altruism. The Negro may well rejoice that his hands, unlike those of his oppressors, are not stained with so much blood extracted by brute force. Real history is not the record of the successes and disappointments, the vices, the follies, and the quarrels of those who engage in contention for power.

The Association for the Study of Negro Life and History is projected on the fact that there is nothing in the past of the Negro more shameful than what is found in the past of other races The Negro is as human as the other members of the family of mankind. The Negro, like others, has been up at times; and at times he has been down. With the domestication of animals, the discovery of iron, the development of stringed instruments, an advancement in fine art, and the inauguration of trial by jury to his credit, the Negro stands just as high as others in contributing to the progress of the world.

The oppressor, however, raises his voice to the contrary. He teaches the Negro that he has no worth-while past, that his race has done nothing significant since the beginning of time, and that there is no evidence that he will ever achieve anything great. The education of the Negro then must be carefully directed lest the race may waste time trying to do the impossible. Lead the Negro to believe this and thus control his thinking. If you can thereby determine what he will think, you will not need to worry about what he will do. You will not have to tell him to go to the back door. He will go without being told; and if there is no back door he will have one cut for his special benefit.

If you teach the Negro that he has accomplished as much good as any other race he will aspire to equality and justice without regard to race. Such an effort would upset the program of the oppressor in Africa and America. Play up before the Negro, then, his crimes and shortcomings. Let him learn to admire the Hebrew, the Greek, the Latin and the Teuton. Lead the Negro to detest the man of African blood—to hate himself. The oppressor then may conquer exploit, oppress and even annihilate the Negro by segregation without fear or trembling. With the truth hidden there will be little expression of thought to the contrary.

The American Negro has taken over an abundance of information which others have made accessible to the oppressed, but he has not yet learned to think and plan for himself as others do for themselves. Well might this race be referred to as the most docile and tractable people on earth. This merely means that when the oppressors once start the large majority of the race in the direction of serving the purposes of their traducers, the task becomes so easy in the years following that they have little trouble with the masses thus controlled. It is a most satisfactory system, and it has become so popular that European nations of foresight are sending some of their brightest minds to the United States to observe the Negro in "inaction" in order to learn how to deal likewise with Negroes in their colonies. What the Negro in America has become satisfied with will be accepted as the measure of what should be allotted him elsewhere. Certain Europeans consider the "solution of the race problem in the United States" one of our great achievements.

The mis-educated Negro joins the opposition with the objection that the study of the Negro keeps alive questions which should be forgotten. The Negro should cease to remember that he was once held a slave, that he has been oppressed, and even that he is a Negro. The traducer, however, keeps before the public such aspects of this history as will justify the present oppression of the race. It would seem, then, that the Negro should emphasize at the same time the favorable aspects to justify action in his behalf. One cannot blame the Negro for not desiring to be reminded of being the sort of creature that the oppressor has represented the Negro to be; but this very attitude shows ignorance of the past and a slavish dependence upon the enemy to serve those whom he would destroy. The Negro can be made proud of his past only by approaching it scientifically himself and giving his own story to the world. What others have written about the Negro during the last three centuries has been mainly for the purpose of bringing him where he is today and holding him there.

The method employed by the Association for the Study of Negro Life and History, however, is not spectacular propaganda or fire-eating agitation. Nothing can be accomplished in such fashion. "Whom the gods would destroy they first make mad." The Negro, whether in Africa or America, must be directed toward a serious examination of the fundamentals of education, religion, literature, and philosophy as they have been expounded to him. He must be sufficiently enlightened to determine for himself whether these forces have come into his life to bless him or to bless his oppressor. After learning the facts in the case the Negro must develop the power of execution to deal with these matters as do people of vision. Problems of great importance cannot be worked out in a day. Questions of great moment must be met with far-reaching plans.

The Association for the Study of Negro Life and History is teaching the Negro to exercise foresight rather than "hindsight." Liberia must not wait until she is offered to Germany before realizing that she has few friends in Europe. Abyssinia must not wait until she is invaded by Italy before she prepares for selfdefense. A scientific study of the past of modern nations would show these selfish tendencies as inevitable results from their policies in dealing with those whom they have professed to elevate. For example, much of Africa has been conquered and subjugated to save souls How expensive has been the Negro's salvation! One of the strong arguments for slavery was that it brought the Negro into the light of salvation. And yet the Negro today is all but lost.

The Association for the Study of Negro Life and History, however, has no special brand for the solution of the race problem except to learn to think. No general program of uplift for the Negroes in all parts of the world will be any more successful than such a procedure would be in the case of members of other races under different circumstances. What will help a Negro in Alabama may prove harmful to one in Maine. The African Negro may find his progress retarded by applying "methods used for the elevation of the Negro in America." A thinking man, however, learns to deal wisely with conditions as he finds them rather than to take orders from some one who knows nothing about his status and cares less. At present the Negro, both in Africa and America, is being turned first here and there experimentally by so-called friends who in the final analysis assist the Negro merely in remaining in the dark.

In the furtherance of the program of taking up these matters dispassionately the Association had made available an outline for the systematic study of the Negro as he has touched the life of others and as others have functioned in their relation to him, The African Background Outlined: A Handbook. This book is written from the point of view of history, literature, art, education, religion and economic imperialism. In seventeen chapters as Part I of the work a brief summary of the past in Africa is presented; and courses on "The Negro in Africa," "The Negro in the European Mind," "The Negro in America," "The Negro in Literature," "The Negro in Art," "The Education of the Negro," "The Religious Development of the Negro," and "Economic Imperialism," follow as Part II with ample bibliographical comment for every heading and subhead of these outlines. This facilitates the task of clubs, young peoples' societies, and special classes organized where the oppressors of the race and the Negroes cooperating with them are determined that the history and status of the Negro shall not be made a part of the curricula.

In this outline there is no animus, nothing to engender race hate. The Association does not bring out such publications. The aim of this organization is to set forth facts in scientific form, for facts properly set forth will tell their own story. No advantage can be gained by merely inflaming the Negro's mind against his traducers. In a manner they deserve to be congratulated for taking care of their own interests so well. The Negro needs to become angry with himself because he has not handled his own affairs wisely. In other words, the Negro must learn from others how to take care of himself in this trying ordeal. He must not remain content with taking over what others set aside for him and then come in the guise of friends to subject even that limited information to further misinterpretation.

APPENDIX

A PARTICIPANT who recently attended an historical meeting desired to take up the question as to what the race should be called. Africans, Negroes, colored people, or what? This is a matter of much concern to him because he hopes thereby to solve the race problem. If others will agree to call Negroes Nordics, he thinks, he will reach the desired end by taking a short cut.

This may sound all but insane, but there are a good many "highly educated" Negroes who believe that such can be accomplished by this shift in terminology; and they have spent time and energy in trying to effect a change. Many of this class suffer mentally because of the frequent use of "offensive expressions" in addressing Negroes. When dealing with them, then, one has to be very careful. For this reason our friends in other races have to seek guidance in approaching us. For example, Lady Simon, the wife of Sir John Simon of the British Cabinet, has recently asked an American Negro what his people prefer to be called, and later in England she took up the same matter with another member of this race. Being an advocate of freedom, she has written considerably to advance its cause. She would not like to use in her works, then, an expression which may hurt some one's feelings.

Although a student of social problems, this learned woman cannot fathom this peculiar psychology. Americans, too, must confess the difficulty of understanding it, unless it is that the "highly educated Negro mind" tends to concern itself with trifles rather than with the great problems of life. We have known Negroes to ask for a separate Y. M. C. A. or Y. W. C. A., a separate church or a separate school, and then object to calling the institution colored or Negro. These segregationists have compromised on principle, but they are unwilling to acknowledge their crime against justice. The name, they believe, will save them from the disgrace.

It does not matter so much what the thing is called as

what the thing is. The Negro would not cease to be what he is by calling him something else; but, if he will struggle and make something of himself and contribute to modern culture, the world will learn to look upon him as an American rather than as one of an undeveloped element of the population.

The word Negro or black is used in referring to this particular element because most persons of native African descent approach this color. The term does not imply that every Negro is black; and the word white does not mean that every white man is actually white. Negroes may be colored, but many Caucasians are scientifically classified as colored. We are not all Africans, moreover, because many of us were not born in Africa; and we are not all Afro-Americans, because few of us are natives of Africa transplanted to America.

There is nothing to be gained by running away from the name. The names of practically all races and nations at times have connoted insignificance and low social status. Angles and Saxons, once the slaves of Romans, experienced this; and even the name of the Greek for a while meant no more than this to these conquerors of the world. The people who bore these names, however, have made them grand and illustrious. The Negro must learn to do the same.

It is strange, too, that while the Negro feels ashamed of his name, persons abroad do not usually think of it in this sense. One does find in Europe a number of West Indian and American Negroes of some Caucasian blood, who do not want to be known as Negroes. As a rule, however, a European of African Negro blood feels proud of this racial heritage and delights to be referred to as such. The writer saw a striking case of this in London in the granddaughter of a Zulu chief. She is so far removed from the African type that one could easily mistake her for a Spaniard; and yet she thinks only for her African connection and gets her inspiration mainly from the story of her people beyond the Pillars of Hercules.

The writer was agreeably surprised a few days later, too, when he met a prominent Parisian with the same attitude. He has produced several volumes in which he champions the cause of the Negro because he has in his veins the same blood. A well-to-do European woman, the daughter of a Dutchman and an African mother, is similarly enthusiastic over her Negro blood. The first thing she mentioned in conversing with the writer was that black mother. This young woman expressed the regret that she did not have more of that color that she, too, might say, as do members of certain tribes of Africa: "I am black and comely. I am black and beautiful. I am beautifully black."

These people surprise you when you think of the attitude of many American Negroes on this question. These race-conscious people can think, but it is seldom that the American Negro indulges in such an exercise. He has permitted other people to determine for him the attitude that he has toward his own people. This means the enslavement of his mind and eventually the enslavement of his body.

Some Europeans rather regard the word Negro as romantic. Going now along the streets of Paris, one will see advertised such places as "l'Elan Noir," and the "Café au Nègre de Toulouse." In one of these cases the writer was especially attracted by the "Choppe-du Nègre" end took dinner there one day. The cuisine was excellent, the music rendered by the orchestra was charming, and a jolly crowd came to enjoy themselves. However, he was the only "Nègre" there.

Walking along a street in Geneva not long ago, the writer's attention was attracted to something of the sort, which is still more significant. It was a wholesale coffee house called "A La Case de l'Oncle Tom." He entered and asked: "Why did you give this store such a name?" The proprietress laughed and explained that her grandfather, François Prudhom, who had read "Uncle Tom's Cabin" and had been deeply impressed thereby, selected this name for the store when he established it in 1866. THE VALUE OF COLOR

NOT long ago the writer saw on a street ear one of the prettiest women in the world. She was a perfectly black woman becomingly dressed in suitable gray and modest adornments which harmonized with her color. She was naturally a commanding figure without any effort to please others, for her bearing was such that she would not fail to attract attention. He could not restrain myself from gazing at her; and, looking around to see whether others were similarly concerned, he found the whites in the car admiring her also, even to the point of commenting among themselves.

This woman's common sense, manifested in knowing how to dress, had made her color an asset rather than a liability. The writer easily recalled, then, that tribe in Africa that feels unusually proud of being black. We are told that they are so anxious to be black that if they find one of the group with a tendency to depart the least from this color they go to the heart of nature and extract from it its darkest dye and paint therewith that native's face that he may continue perfectly black.

Here in America, however, we are ashamed of being black. So many of us who are actually black powder our faces and make ourselves blue. In so doing we become all but hideous by the slavish aping of those around us in keeping with our custom of imitation. We fail to take ourselves for what we are actually worth, and do not make the most of ourselves.

We show lack of taste in the selection of our dress. We long for what others wear whether it harmonizes with our color or not They have given particular attention to design with respect to their race and have written books to this effect. Thinking, however, that the Negro is not supposed to wear anything but what the poor may pick up, the artists have not thought seriously of him. Both teachers and students of nearby schools thus concerned, then, repeatedly appeal to us for help in the study of design with respect to the Negro, but we have nothing scientific to offer them. We have no staff of artists who can function in this sphere.

To be able to supply this need requires the most painstaking effort to understand colors and color schemes. It is a very difficult task because of the variation of color within the race. Sometimes in one family of ten you will hardly find two of the same shade. To dress them all alike may be economical, but the world thereby misses that much of beauty. The Negro mother, then, needs to be the real artist, and the schools now training the youth to be the parents of tomorrow should give as much attention to these things esthetic as they do to language, literature or mathematics.

In neglecting to know himself better from this point of view, then, the Negro is making a costly mistake. He should be deeply concerned with the esthetic possibilities of his situation. In this so-called Negro race we have the prettiest people in the world, when they dress in harmony with the many shades and colors with which we are so richly endowed. Why do we so away from home to find what we already have on hand?

Recently one saw in Washington a demonstration of the value of color when the Masonic conclave staged a tremendous parade in this national city. The whites were attracted to the upstanding, outstanding Negroes so becomingly bedecked in costumes of the Orient. This, however, was accidental. The color of the Negroes happened to be Oriental, and the colors of this order were originally worked out to suit the people of those parts. The dead white of the Caucasian does not harmonize with such garb. Why, then should the Negro worry about what others wear?

Carrying the imitation of others to an extreme today, we do not find ourselves far in advance of the oppressed antebellum Negroes, who, unable to dress themselves, had to take whatever others threw at them. We make a most hideous spectacle, then, when we are on dress parade in our social atmosphere. So many of us clad in unbecoming colors often look like decorated pet horses turned loose for an hour or so of freedom.

Appreciating the value of color, the artists in European cities are trying to change their hue to that of the colored people. They can understand how inexpressive the dead white is, and they are trying to make use of what we are seeking to conceal. The models in their shops are purposely colored to display to good effect the beautiful costumes which require color. Some of these Europeans frankly tell Negroes how they envy them for their color.

One is not surprised, then, to find European cafés and hotels employing American or African Negroes to supply this color which the Europeans lack. Pictures of such black men are sometimes displayed to great effect. That of Josephine Baker adorns the windows of large stores in Paris. Here in America, too, we observe that art centres are likewise getting away from the dead white to enjoy the richness of color.

The writer felt somewhat encouraged recently when he talked with a Washington lady who runs "The Pandora," a unique establishment devoted to design. Upon inquiring about her progress in the effort to teach colored people how to wear what becomes them, she reported considerable success. Sometimes customers insist on purchasing unbecoming attire, but usually she has shown them the unwisdom of so doing, and most of them now take her advice.

In this way this enterprising woman is not only conducting a pioneer business, but she is rendering a social service. She has not had any special training in this work, but on her initiative she is building upon what she has learned by studying the Negroes in her community. Others of us may do likewise, if we try to help the Negro rather than exploit him.

Book II:

Stolen Legacy

Book II: TABLE OF CONTENTS

INTRODUCTION

THE AIMS OF THE BOOK

PART I

CHAPTER I: GREEK PHILOSOPHY IS STOLEN EGYPTIAN PHILOSOPHY

CHAPTER II: SO-CALLED GREEK PHILOSOPHY WAS ALIEN TO THE GREEKS AND THEIR CONDITIONS OF LIFE

CHAPTER III: GREEK PHILOSOPHY WAS THE OFFSPRING OF THE EGYPTIAN MYSTERY SYSTEM

CHAPTER IV: THE EGYPTIANS EDUCATED THE GREEKS

CHAPTER V: THE PRE-SOCRATIC PHILOSOPHERS AND THE TEACHINGS ASCRIBED TO THEM

CHAPTER VI: THE ATHENIAN PHILOSOPHERS

CHAPTER VII: THE CURRICULUM OF THE EGYPTIAN MYSTERY SYSTEM

CHAPTER VIII: THE MEMPHITE THEOLOGY IS THE BASIS OF ALL IMPORTANT DOCTRINES OF GREEK PHILOSOPHY

PART II

CHAPTER IX: SOCIAL REFORMATION THROUGH THE NEW PHILOSOPHY OF AFRICAN REDEMPTION

APPENDIX

George G. M. James

INTRODUCTION

Characteristics of Greek Philosophy

The term Greek philosophy, to begin with is a misnomer, for there is no such philosophy in existence. The ancient Egyptians had developed a very complex religious system, called the Mysteries, which was also the first system of salvation.

As such, it regarded the human body as a prison house of the soul, which could be liberated from its bodily impediments, through the disciplines of the Arts and Sciences, and advanced from the level of a mortal to that of a God. This was the notion of the summum bonum or greatest good, to which all men must aspire, and it also became the basis of all ethical concepts. The Egyptian Mystery System was also a Secret Order, and membership was gained by initiation and a pledge to secrecy. The teaching was graded and delivered orally to the Neophyte; and under these circumstances of secrecy, the Egyptians developed secret systems of writing and teaching, and forbade their Initiates from writing what they had learnt.

After nearly five thousand years of prohibition against the Greeks, they were permitted to enter Egypt for the purpose of their education. First through the Persian invasion and secondly through the invasion of Alexander the Great. From the sixth century B.C. therefore to the death of Aristotle (322 B.C.) the Greeks made the best of their chance to learn all they could about Egyptian culture; most students received instructions directly from the Egyptian Priests, but after the invasion by Alexander the Great, the Royal temples and libraries were plundered and pillaged, and Aristotle's school converted the library at Alexandria into a research centre. There is no wonder then, that the production of the unusually large number of books ascribed to Aristotle has proved a physical impossibility, for any single man within a life time.

The history of Aristotle's life, has done him far more harm than good, since it carefully avoids any statement relating to his visit to Egypt, either on his own account or in company with Alexander the Great, when he invaded Egypt. This silence of history at once throws doubt upon the life and achievements of Aristotle. He is said to have spent twenty years under the tutorship of Plato, who is regarded as a Philosopher, yet he graduated as the greatest of Scientists of Antiquity. Two questions might be asked (a) How could Plato teach Aristotle what he himself did not know? (b) Why should

Stolen Legacy 143

Aristotle spend twenty years under a teacher from whom he could learn nothing? This bit of history sounds incredible. Again, in order to avoid suspicion over the extraordinary number of books ascribed to Aristotle. history tells us that Alexander the Great, gave him a large sum of money to get the books. Here again the history sounds incredible, and three statements must here be made.

(a) In order to purchase books on science, they must have been in circulation so as to enable Aristotle to secure them. (b) If the books were in circulation before Aristotle purchased them, and since he is not supposed to have visited Egypt at all, then the books in question must have been circulated among Greek philosophers. (c) If circulated among Greek philosophers, then we would expect the subject matter of such books to have been known before Aristotle's time, and consequently he could not be credited either with producing them or introducing new ideas of science.

Another point of considerable interest to be accounted for was the attitude of the Athenian government towards this so-called Greek philosophy, which it regarded as foreign in origin and treated it accordingly. Only a brief study of history is necessary to show that Greek philosophers were undesirable citizens, who throughout the period of their investigations were victims of relentless persecution, at the hands of the Athenian government. Anaxagoras was imprisoned and exiled; Socrates was executed; Plato was sold into slavery and Aristotle was indicted and exiled; while the earliest of them all, Pythagoras, was expelled from Croton in Italy. Can we imagine the Greeks making such an about turn, as to claim the very teachings which they had at first persecuted and openly rejected? Certainly, they knew they were usurping what they had never produced, and as we enter step by step into our study the greater do we discover evidence which leads us to the conclusion that Greek philosophers were not the authors of Greek philosophy, but the Egyptian Priests and Hierophants.

Aristotle died in 322 B.C. not many years after he had been aided by Alexander the Great to secure the largest quantity of scientific books from the Royal Libraries and Temples of Egypt. In spite however of such great intellectual treasure, the death of Aristotle marked the death of philosophy among the Greeks, who did not seem to possess the natural ability to advance these sciences. Consequently history informs us that the Greeks were forced to make a study of Ethics, which they also borrowed from the Egyptian "Summum Bonum" or greatest good. The two other

Athenian Philosophers must be mentioned here, I mean Socrates and Plato; who also became famous in history as philosophers and great thinkers. Every school boy believes that when he hears or reads the command "know thyself", he is hearing or reading words which were uttered by Socrates. But the truth is that the Egyptian temples carried inscriptions on the outside addressed to Neophytes and among them was the injunction "know thyself". Socrates copied these words from the Egyptian Temples, and was not the author. All mystery temples, inside and outside of Egypt carried such inscriptions, just like the weekly bulletins of our modern Churches.

Similarly, every school boy believes that when he hears or reads the names of the four cardinal virtues, he is hearing or reading names of virtues determined by Plato. Nothing has been more misleading, for the Egyptian Mystery System contained ten virtues, and from this source Plato copied what have been called the four cardinal virtues, justice, wisdom, temperance, and courage. It is indeed surprising how, for centuries, the Greeks have been praised by the Western World for intellectual accomplishments which belong without a doubt to the Egyptians or the peoples of North Africa.

Another noticeable characteristic of Greek philosophy is the fact that most of the Greek philosophers used the teachings of Pythagoras as their model; and consequently they have introduced nothing new in the field of philosophy. Included in the Pythagorean system we find the doctrines of (a) opposites (b) Harmony (c) Fire (d) Mind, since it is composed of fire atoms. (e) Immortality, expressed as transmigration of Souls, (f) The Summum Bonum or the purpose of philosophy. And these of course are reflected in the systems of Heraclitus, Parmenides, Democritus, Socrates, Plato and Aristotle.

The next thing that is peculiar about Greek philosophy is its use in literature. The Egyptian Mystery System was the first secret Order of History and the publication of its teachings was strictly prohibited. This explains why Initiates like Socrates did not commit to writing their philosophy, and why the Babylonians and Chaldaeans who were very closely associated with them also refrained from publishing those teachings.

We can at once see how easy it was for an ambitious and even envious nation to claim a body of unwritten knowledge which would make them great in the eyes of the primitive world. The absurdity however, is easily recognized when we remember that the Greek

Stolen Legacy 145

language was used to translate several systems of teachings which the Greeks could not succeed in claiming. Such were the translation of Hebrew Scriptures into Greek, called the Septuagint; and the translation of the Christian Gospels, Acts and the Epistles in Greek, still called the Greek New Testament. It is only the unwritten philosophy of the Egyptians translated into Greek that has met with such an unhappy fate: a legacy stolen by the Greeks.

On account of reasons already given, I have been compelled to handle the subject matter of this book, in the way it has been handled: namely (a) with a frequency of repetition, because it is the method of Greek philosophy, to use a common principle to explain several different doctrines, and (b) the quotation and analysis of doctrines, because it is the object of this book to establish the Egyptian Origin and this cannot be so satisfactorily done if the doctrines are not presented. Greek philosophy is somewhat of a drama, whose chief actors were Alexander the Great, Aristotle and his successors in the peripatetic school, and the Roman Emperor Justinian. Alexander invaded Egypt and captured the Royal Library at Alexandria and plundered it. Aristotle made a library of his own with plundered books, while his school occupied the building and used it as a research centre. Finally, Justinian the Roman Emperor abolished the Temples and schools of philosophy i.e. another name for the Egyptian Mysteries which the Greeks claimed as their product, and on account of which, they have been falsely praised and honoured for centuries by the world, as its greatest philosophers and thinkers. This contribution to civilization was really and truly made by the Egyptians and the African Continent, but not by the Greeks or the European Continent. We sometimes wonder why the people of African descent find themselves in such a social plight as they do, but the answer is plain enough. Had it not been for this drama of Greek philosophy and its actors, the African Continent would have had a different reputation, and would have enjoyed a status of respect among the nations of the world. This unfortunate position of the African Continent and its peoples appears to be the result of misrepresentation upon which the structure of race prejudice has been built, i.e. the historical world opinion that the African Continent is backward, that its people are backward, and that their civilization is also backward.

Finally, the dishonesty in the movement of the publication of a Greek philosophy, becomes very glaring, when we refer to the fact, purposely that by calling the theorem of the Square on the Hypotenuse, the Pythagorean theorem, it has concealed the truth for centuries from the world, who ought to know that the Egyptians taught Pythagoras and the Greeks, what mathematics they knew.

I want to mention here that among the many books which I found helpful in my present work are "The Intellectual Adventure of Man" and "The Egyptian Religion" by Professor Henri Frankfort and "The Mediterranean World in Ancient Times" by Professor Eva Sandford.

George G. M. James

The Aims of the Book

The aim of the book is to establish better race relations in the world, by revealing a fundamental truth concerning the contribution of the African Continent to civilization. It must be borne in mind that the first lesson in the Humanities is to make a people aware of their contribution to civilization; and the second lesson is to teach them about other civilizations. By this dissemination of the truth about the civilization of individual peoples, a better understanding among them, and a proper appraisal of each other should follow. This notion is based upon the notion of the Great Master Mind: Ye shall know the truth, and the truth shall make you free. Consequently, the book is an attempt to show that the true authors of Greek philosophy were not the Greeks; but the people of North Africa, commonly called the Egyptians; and the praise and honour falsely given to the Greeks for centuries belong to the people of North Africa, and therefore to the African Continent. Consequently this theft of the African legacy by the Greeks led to the erroneous world opinion that the African Continent has made no contribution to civilization, and that its people are naturally backward. This is the misrepresentation that has become the basis of race prejudice, which has affected all people of color.

For centuries the world has been misled about the original source of the Arts and Sciences: for centuries Socrates, Plato and Aristotle have been falsely idolized as models of intellectual greatness; and for centuries the African continent has been called the Dark Continent, because Europe coveted the honor of transmitting to the world, the Arts and Sciences.

I am happy to be able to bring this information to the attention of the world, so that on the one hand, all races and creeds might know the truth and free themselves from those prejudices which have corrupted human relations: and on the other hand, that the people of African origin might be emancipated from their serfdom of inferiority complex, and enter upon a new era of freedom, in which they would feel like free men, with full human rights and privileges.

George G. M. James

PART I

CHAPTER I

Greek Philosophy is Stolen Egyptian Philosophy

1. The Teachings of the Egyptian Mysteries Reached Other Lands Many Centuries Before It Reached Athens. According to history, Pythagoras after receiving his training in Egypt, returned to his native island, Samos, where he established his order for a short time, after which he migrated to Croton (540 B.C.) in Southern Italy, where his order grew to enormous proportions, until his final expulsion from that country. We are also told that Thales (640 B.C.) who had also received his education in Egypt, and his associates: Anaximander, and Anaximenes, were natives of Ionia in Asia Minor, which was a stronghold of the Egyptian Mystery schools, which they carried on. (Sandford's The Mediterranean World, p. 195–205). Similarly, we are told that Xenophanes (576 B.C.), Parmenides, Zeno and Melissus were also natives of Ionia and that they migrated to Elea in Italy and established themselves and spread the teachings of the Mysteries.

In like manner we are informed that Heraclitus (530 B.C.), Empedocles, Anaxagoras and Democritus were also natives of Ionia who were interested in physics. Hence in tracing the course of the so-called Greek philosophy, we find that Ionian students after obtaining their education from the Egyptian priests returned to their native land, while some of them migrated to different parts of Italy, where they established themselves.

Consequently, history makes it clear that the surrounding neighbours of Egypt had all become familiar with the teachings of Egyptian Mysteries many centuries before the Athenians, who in 399 B.C. sentenced Socrates to death (Zeller's Hist. of Phil., p. 112; 127; 170–172) and subsequently caused Plato and Aristotle to flee for their lives from Athens, because philosophy was something foreign and unknown to them. For this same reason, we would expect either the Ionians or the Italians to exert their prior claim to philosophy, since it made contact with them long before it did with the Athenians, who were always its greatest enemies, until Alexander's conquest of Egypt, which provided for Aristotle free access to the Library of Alexandria.

The Ionians and Italians made no attempt to claim the authorship of philosophy, because they were well aware that the Egyptians were the true authors. On the other hand, after the death of Aristotle, his Athenian pupils, without the authority of the state, undertook to compile a history of philosophy, recognized at that time as the Sophia or Wisdom of the Egyptians, which had become current and traditional in the ancient world, which compilation, because it was produced by pupils who had belonged to Aristotle's school, later history has erroneously called Greek philosophy, in spite of the fact that the Greeks were its greatest enemies and persecutors, and had persistently treated it as a foreign innovation. For this reason, the so-called Greek philosophy is stolen Egyptian philosophy, which first spread to Ionia, thence to Italy and thence to Athens. And it must be remembered that at this remote period of Greek history, i.e., Thales to Aristotle 640 B.C.–322 B.C., the Ionians were not Greek citizens, but at first Egyptian subjects and later Persian subjects.

Zeller's Hist. of Phil.: p. 37; 46; 58; 66–83; 112; 127; 170172.

William Turner's Hist. of Phil.: p 34; 39; 45; 53.

Roger's Student Hist. of Phil.: p. 15.

B. D. Alexander's Hist. of Phil.: p. 13; 21.

Sandford's The Mediterranean World p. 157; 195–205.

A brief sketch of the ancient Egyptian Empire would also make it clear that Asia Minor or Ionia was the ancient land of the Hittites, who were not known by any other name in ancient days.

According to Diodorus and Manetho, High Priest in Egypt, two columns were found at Nysa Arabia; one of the Goddess Isis and the other of the God Osiris, on the latter of which the God declared that he had led an army into India, to the sources of the Danube, and as far as the ocean. This means of course, that the Egyptian Empire, at a very early date, included not only the islands of the Aegean sea and Ionia, but also extended to the extremities of the East.

We are also informed that Senusert I, during the 12th Dynasty (i.e., about 1900 B.C.) conquered the whole sea coast of India, beyond the Ganges to the Eastern ocean. He is also said to have included the Cyclades and a great part of Europe in his conquests.

Secondly, the "Amarna Letters" found in the government offices of the Egyptian King, Iknaton, testify to the fact, that the Egyptian Empire had extended to western Asia, Syria and Palestine, and that for centuries Egyptian power had been supreme in the ancient world. This was in the 18th Dynasty i.e., about 1500 B.C.

We are also told that during the reign of Tuthmosis III, the dominion of Egypt extended not only along the coast of Palestine: but also from Nubia to Northern Asia.

(Breadsted's Conquest of Civilization p. 84; Diodorus 128; Manetho; Strabo: Dicaearchus; John Kendrick's Ancient Egypt vol. I).

2. The Authorship of the Individual Doctrines Is Extremely Doubtful. As one attempts to read the history of Greek philosophy, one discovers a complete absence of essential information concerning the early life and training of the so-called Greek philosophers, from Thales to Aristotle. No writer or historian professes to know anything about their early education. All they tell us about them consists of (a) a doubtful date and place of birth and (b) their doctrines; but the world is left to wonder who they were and from what source they got their early education, and would naturally expect that men who rose to the position of a Teacher among relatives, friends and associates, would be well-known, not only by them, but by the whole community.

On the contrary, men who might well be placed among the earliest Teachers in history, who had grown up from childhood to manhood, and had taught pupils, are represented as unknown, being without any domestic, social or early educational traces.

This is unbelievable, and yet it is a fact that the history of Greek philosophy has presented to the world a number of men whose lives it knows little or nothing about: but expects the world to accept them as the true authors of the doctrines which are alleged to be theirs.

In the absence of essential evidence, the world hesitates to recognise them as such, because the truth of this whole matter of Greek philosophy points to a very different direction.

Stolen Legacy

The Book on nature entitled peri physeos was the common name under which Greek students interested in nature-study wrote. The earliest copy is said to date back to the sixth century B.C. and it is customary to refer to the remnants of peri physeos as the Fragments. (William Turner's History of Philosophy p. 62). We do not believe that genuine Initiates produced the Book on nature, since this was contrary to the rules of the Egyptian Mysteries, in connexion with which the Philosophical Schools conducted their work. Egypt was the centre of the body of ancient wisdom, and knowledge, religious, philosophical and scientific spread to other lands through student Initiates. Such teachings remained for generations and centuries in the form of tradition, until the conquest of Egypt by Alexander the Great, and the movement of Aristotle and his school to compile Egyptian teaching and claim it as Greek Philosophy. (Ancient Mysteries by C. H. Vail p. 16.)

Consequently, as a source of authority of authorships, peri physeos, is of little value, if any, since history mentions only four names as authors of it, namely, Anaximander, Heraclitus, Parmenides, Anaxagoras; and asks the world to accept their authorship of philosophy, because Theophrastus, Sextus, Proclus and Simplicius, of the school at Alexandria are said to have preserved small remnants of it (the Fragments). If peri physeos is the criterion to the authorship of Greek Philosophy, then it falls short in its purpose by a long way, since only four philosophers are alleged to have written this book, and to have remnants of their work. According to this idea all the other philosophers, who failed to write peri physeos and to have remnants of it, also failed to write Greek philosophy. This is the reductio ad absurdum to which peri physeos leads us.

The schools of philosophy, Chaldean, Greek and Persian, were part of the Ancient Mystery System of Egypt. They were conducted in secrecy according to the demands of the Osiriaca, whose teachings became common to all the schools. In keeping with the demands for secrecy, the writing and publication of teachings were strictly forbidden and consequently, Initiates who had developed satisfactorily in their training, and had been advanced to the rank of Master or Teacher, refrained from publishing the teachings of the Mysteries or philosophy.

Consequently any publication of philosophy could not have come from the pen of the original philosophers themselves, but either from their close friends who knew their views, as in the case of Pythagoras and Socrates, or from interested persons who made a record of those philosophical teachings that had become popular opinion and tradition. There is no wonder then, that in the absence of original authorship, history has had to resort to the strategy of accepting Aristotle's opinion as the sole authority in determining the authorship of Greek Philosophy (Introduction to Alfred Weber's History of Philosophy). It is for these reasons that great doubt surrounds the so-called Greek authorship of philosophy. (William Turner's History of Philosophy p. 35; 39; 47; 53; 62; 79; 210–211; 627. Ancient Mysteries by C. H. Vail p. 16. Theophrastus: Fragment 2 apud Diels. Introduction to Alfred Weber's History of Philosophy.)

3. The Chronology of Greek Philosophers Is Mere Speculation. History knows nothing about the early life and training of the Greek philosophers and this is true not only of the pre-Socratic philosophers: but also of Socrates, Plato and Aristotle, who appear in history about the age of eighteen and begin to teach at forty.

As a body of men they were undesirable to the state, (personae non gratae) and were consequently persecuted and driven into hiding and secrecy. Under such circumstances they kept no records of their activities and this was done in order to conceal their identity. After the conquest of Egypt by Alexander the Great, and the seizure and looting of the Royal Library at Alexandria, Aristotle's plan to usurp Egyptian philosophy, was subsequently carried out by members of his school: Theophrastus, Andronicus of Rhodes and Eudemus, who soon found themselves confronted with the problem of a chronology for a history of philosophy. (Introduction of Zeller's Hist. of Phil. p. 13).

Throughout this effort there has been much speculation concerning the date of birth of philosophers, whom the public knew very little about. As early as the third century B.C. (274–194 B.C.) Eratosthenes, a Stoic drew up a chronology of Greek philosophers and in the second century B.C. (140) Apollodorus also drew up another. The effort continued, and in the first century B.C. (60–70 B.C.) Andronicus, the eleventh Head of the Peripatetic school, also drew up another.

This difficulty continued throughout the early centuries, and has come down to the present time for it appears that all modern writers on Greek Philosophy are unable to agree on the dates that should be assigned to the nativity of the philosophers. The only exception appears to occur with reference to the three Athenian philosophers, i.e., Socrates, Plato and Aristotle, the date of whose

Stolen Legacy

nativity is believed to be certain, and concerning which there is general agreement among historians.

However, when we come to deal with the pre-Socratic philosophers, we are confronted with confusion and uncertainty, and a few examples would serve to illustrate the untrustworthy nature of the chronology of Greek Philosophers.

(1) Diogenes Laertius places the birth of Thales at 640 B.C., while William Turner's History of Philosophy places it as 620 B.C.; that of Frank Thilly at 624 B.C.; that of A. K. Rogers at early in the sixth century B.C.; and that of W. G. Tennemann at 600 B.C.

(2) Diogenes Laertius places the birth of Anaximenes at 546 B.C.; while W. Windelbrand places it at the sixth century B.C.; that of Frank Thilly at 588 B.C.; that of B. D. Alexander at 560 B.C.; while that of A. K. Rogers at the sixth century B.C.

(3) Parmenides is credited by Diogenes as being born at 500 B.C.; while Fuller, Thilly and Rogers omit a date of birth, because they say it is unknown.

(4) Zeller places the birth of Xenophanes at 576 B.C.; while Diogenes gives 570 B C.; and the majority of the other historians declare that the date of birth is unknown.

(5) With reference to Xeno, Diogenes who does not know the date of his birth, says that he flourished between B.C. 464–460; while William Turner places it at 490 B.C.; like Frank Thilly and B. D. Alexander; while Fuller, A. K. Rogers and W. G. Tennemann declare it is unknown.

(6) With references to Heraclitus, Zeller makes the following suppositions: if he died in 475 B.C. and if he was sixty years old when he died, then he must have been born in 535 B.C.; similarly Diogenes supposes that he flourished between B.C. 504–500; and while William Turner places his birth at 530 B.C.; Windelbrand places it at 536 B.C.; and Fuller and Tennemann declare that he flourished in 500 B.C.

(7) With reference to Pythagoras, Zeller who does not know the date of his birth supposes that it occurred between the years 580–570 B.C.; and while Diogenes also supposes that it occurred between the years 582–500 B.C.; William Turner, Fuller, Rogers, and Tennemann declare that it is unknown.

(8) With reference to Empedocles, while Diogenes places his birth at 484 B.C.; Turner, Windelbrand, Fuller, B. D. Alexander and Tennemann place it at 490 B.C.; while A. K. Rogers and others declare it is unknown.

(9) With reference to Anaxagoras, while Zeller and Diogenes place his birth at 500 B.C.: William Turner, A. G. Fuller, and Frank Thilly agree with them, while Alexander places it at 450 B.C. and A. K. Rogers and others declare it is unknown.

(10) With reference to Leucippus, all historians seem to be of the opinion that he has never existed.

(11) Socrates (469–399 B.C.), Plato (427–347 B.C.), and Aristotle (384–322 B.C.) are the only three philosophers the dates of whose nativity and death do not seem to have led to speculation among historians; but the reason for this uniformity is probably clue to the fact that they were Athenians and had been indicted by the Athenian Government who would naturally have investigated them and kept a record of their cases. (A. K. Roger's Hist. of Phil. p. 104).

N.B.

It must be noted from the preceding comparative study of the chronology of Greek philosophers that (a) the variation in dates points to speculation (b) the pre-Socratic philosophers were unknown because they were foreigners to the Athenian Government and probably never existed (c) it follows that both the pre-Socratic philosophers together with Socrates, Plato and Aristotle were persecuted by the Athenian Government tor introducing foreign doctrines into Athens. (d) In consequence of these facts, any subsequent claim by the Greeks to the ownership or authorship of the same doctrines which they had rejected and persecuted, must be regarded as a usurpation.

4. The Compilation of the History of Greek Philosophy Was the Plan of Aristotle Executed by His School. When Aristotle decided to compile a history of Greek Philosophy he must have made known his wishes to his pupils Theophrastus and Eudemus: for no sooner did he produce his metaphysics, than Theophrastus followed him by publishing eighteen books on the doctrines of the physicists. Similarly, after Theophrastus had published his doctrines of the physicists, Eudemus produced separate histories of Arithmetic, Geometry, Astronomy and also theology. This was an amazing

Stolen Legacy

start, because of the large number of scientific books, and the wide range of subjects treated. This situation has rightly aroused the suspicion of the world, as it questions the source of these scientific works.

Since Theophrastus and Eudemus were students under Aristotle at the same time, and since the conquest of Egypt by Alexander the Great, made the Egyptian Library at Alexandria available to the Greeks for research, then it must be expected that the three men, Aristotle who was a close friend of Alexander, Theophrastus and Eudemus not only did research at the Alexandrine Library at the sane time, but must also have helped themselves to books, which enabled them to follow each other so closely in the production of scientific works (William Turner's Hist. of Phil. p. 158–159), which were either a portion of the war booty taken from the Library or compilations from them. (Note that Aristotle's works reveal the signs of note taking and that Theophrastus and Eudemus were pupils attending Aristotle's school at the same time). William Turner's Hist. of Phil. p. 127.

Just here it might be as well to mention the names of Aristotle's pupils who took an active part in promoting the movement towards the compilation of a history of Greek philosophy:

(a) Theophrastus of Lesbos 371–286 B.C., who succeeded Aristotle as head of the peripatetic school. As elsewhere mentioned, he is said to have produced eighteen books on the doctrines of physicists. Who were these physicists? Greek or Egyptians? Just think of it.

(b) Eudemus of Rhodes a contemporary of Theophrastus with whom he also attended Aristotle's school. He is said to have produced histories of Arithmetic, geometry, astronomy and theology, as elsewhere mentioned. What was the source of the data of the histories of these sciences, which must have taken any nation thousands of years to develop? Greece or Egypt? Just think of it.

(c) Andronicus of Rhodes, an Eclectic of Aristotle's school and editor of his works (B.C. 70).

These men's works together with Aristotle's metaphysics, which contained a critical summary of the doctrines of all preceding philosophers, seem to form the nucleus of a compilation of what has been called, the history of Greek philosophy (Zeller's Hist. of Greek Phil.: Introduction p. 7–14).

The next movement was the organization of an association called "The learned study of Aristotle's Writings", whose members were Theophrastus and Andronicus, who were both closely connected with the school of Aristotle. The function of this association was to identify the literature and doctrines of philosophy with their so-called respective authors, and in order to accomplish this the alumni of Aristotle's school and its friends were encouraged to enter upon a research for Aristotle's works and to write commentaries on them.

In addition to this, the Learned Association also encouraged research for the recovery of what has been named Fragments or remnants of a book, which is supposed to have once existed, and to have borne the common title "Peri Physeos", i.e., concerning nature.

Here again those who went out in search of "peri physeos" or its remnants were the alumni of Aristotle's school and its friends: but their efforts to establish authorship was a failure.

(a) Theophrastus found only two lines of peri physeos, supposed to have been written by Anaximander.

(b) Sextus and Proclus of the fifth century A.D., and Simplicius of the sixth century A.D. are said to have found a copy of "peri physeos" supposed to have been produced by Parmenides.

(c) In addition, the name of Simplicius is also associated with a copy of "peri physeos", which is supposed to have been produced by Anaxagoras.

So much for "peri physeos and the Fragments," and so much for the attempt of "The Learned Association" for the study of Aristotle's works; which has failed because of lack of evidence, as has elsewhere been pointed out.

The recovery of two copies and two lines of "peri physeos" is not proof that all Greek Philosophers wrote "peri physeos", or even that the names assigned to them were their bona fide authors. It certainly would appear that the object of the Learned Association was to beat Aristotle's own drum and dance. It was Aristotle's idea to compile a history of philosophy, and it was Aristotle's school and its alumni that carried out the idea, we are told.

CHAPTER II

So-called Greek Philosophy Was Alien To The Greeks And Their Conditions Of Life.

1. The Period of Greek Philosophy (640–322 B.C.) Was A Period of Internal and External Wars, and Was Therefore Unsuitable For Producing Philosophers. History supports the fact that from the time of Thales. to the time of Aristotle, the Greeks were victims of internal disunion, on the one hand, while on the other, they lived in constant fear of invasion from the Persians who were a common enemy to the city states.

Consequently when they were not fighting with one another they found themselves busy fighting the Persians, who soon dominated them and became their masters. From the 6th century B.C. the territory from the coast of Asia Minor to the Indus Valley became united under the single power of Persia, whose central territory Iran has survived as a national unit to the present day. Persian expansion was like a nightmare to the Greeks who dreaded the Persians on account of their invulnerable navy, and organized themselves into Leagues and Confederacies in order to resist their enemy. (C. 12 P. 195; Sandford's Mediterranean World). There are three sources which throw light on the chaotic and troublesome conditions of this period in Greek history. (A) The Persian Conquests (B) The Leagues and (C) Peloponnesian wars.

A. The Persian Conquests

After the Persians had conquered the Ionians (possibly ancient Hittites), and made them their subjects, Polycrates (539–524 B.C.) seized the Island of Samos and made it a famous city. (Sandford's Mediterranean World c. 9). Between 499 and 494 B.C. the Ionians revolted against the Persians, who defeated them at Lade, while Cyprus and Miletus were also captured. (Sandford's Mediterranean World c. 12). In the summer of 490 B.C. Greek and Persian forces met at Marathon, but after a hand to hand fight, both belligerents withdrew, only to prepare stronger forces in order to renew the conflict. Accordingly, after ten years had elapsed a Hellenic League was organized against the Persians, and the Spartan King Leonides was sent with an army to hold the pass at Thermopylae, until the fleet should win a decisive victory. (C. 12, P. 202; Sandford's Mediterranean World). Accordingly, during the month of August 481 B.C. Persian ships under the command of Xerxes anchored in the gulf of Pagasae, while the Greeks anchored off Cape Artemisium. Both sides awaited a favorable opportunity to attack. The Persians began to force the pass while simultaneously one of their detachments was secretly aided by a Greek traitor, along a steep mountain pass to the rear of the Greek position. Having been taken by surprise, the Greek guards immediately withdrew without resistance. The Spartans who were guarding Thermopylae were all slain and the pass captured by the Persians. (Sandford's Mediterranean World C. 12 P. 202). Having been defeated at Thermopylae, the Greeks withdrew to Salamis, where again they encountered a naval engagement with the Persians. It was late in September 481 B.C., and the result was a wanton destruction of ships on both sides, without any decision. Both belligerents withdrew: The Persians to Thessaly, and the Greeks to Attica. (Sandford's Mediterranean World C. 12 P. 203).

With the persistent aim of freedom from Persian domination, Athens, together with the island and coast cities (of the Aegean and Ionia) renewed their resistance of Persian rule. This was the confederacy of Delos, which undertook several naval engagements, but with little or no success. In 467 B.C. the battle of Eurymedon River was fought and lost with a great number of ships. Eighteen years later (449 B.C.) another naval engagement took place off the island of Cyprus, but again without decision, and consequently Persian sovereignty over the Greeks remained. (Sandford's Mediterranean World C. 12 P. 205). In the meantime Sparta, under the terms of the Treaty of Miletus (413 B.C.) obtained subsidies from Persia, for naval construction, on condition that she recognize Persian sovereignty over the Ionians and their allies. This was done by Sparta as a threat to Athenian ambitions.

However, it was not long after the Treaty of Miletus, that the Greeks themselves submitted to the authority and dominance of the Persians. During the winter 387–386 B.C., the individual Ionian cities, signed the peace terms of the Persian King, and finally accepted Persian rule. This Treaty was negotiated by a Spartan envoy who was authorized by the Persian King to enforce its provisions. (Sandford's Mediterranean World C. 13 and 15, P. 225 and 255).

B. The Leagues

Stolen Legacy

Apart from the resistance of a common foe, the Persians, a study of the function of the Leagues, reveals the enmity and spirit of aggression which were characteristic of the relationship which existed between the Greek city states themselves.

Accordingly in 505 B.C., the Peloponnesian states signed treaties among themselves, pledging warfare against Sparta who had absorbed them under her influence. Meanwhile, Aristogoras revived the Ionian League (499–494 B.C.) to resist Persian aggression, and friendship between Athens and Aegina was restored by the Hellenic League (481 B.C.) which was afterward converted into the Confederacy of Delos (478 B.C.) as mentioned elsewhere. In like manner, Thebes also fell in line with the general temper of the age and organized the Boeotian League, a federation of city states, for self-protection and aggression. (Sandford's Mediterranean World C. 9, P. 150; C. 12, P. 201).

In 377 B.C. a second Athenian Confederacy was organized, but this was to frustrate the aims of the Lacedaemonians and to compel them to respect the right of the Athenians and their allies (Sandford's Mediterranean World C. 15, P. 260). Likewise in 290 B C., the Aetolian League, made up of the States of central Greece, gained control of Delphi, and frequently violated Achaean rights in the Peloponnesus, while in 225 B.C. Antigonus Doson organized another Hellenic League, with the purpose of obstructing the ambitions of Sparta and her Aetolian allies. (Sandford's Mediterranean World C. 18, P. 317 and 319).

(W. H. Couch's Hist. of Greece, p. 206–209, c. 11. Botsford & Robinson's Hellenic Hist., p. 115–121; 127–142. T. B. Bury's Hist. of Greece, p. 216–229; 240–241; 259–269; 471472. The Tutorial Hist. of Greece by W. J. Woodhouse, c. 18, 20 and 21).

C. The Peloponnesian Wars 460–445 B.C. and 431–421 B.C.

Owing to the ambitions of Athens to dominate the Ionians and other neighboring peoples, Pericles launched a campaign of alliances and conquests extending from Thessaly to Argos, and from Euboea to Naupactus, Achaea and the chief islands of the Ionian Sea.

The net results were as follows: (a) Athens established alliances with Boeotia, Phocis and Locris, in spite of Sparta's opposition. (b) In 456 B.C. Aegina was captured and made tributary. (c) In 450 B.C. Athens failed in her attempt to invade Corinth. (d) In 451 friendship between Athens and Sparta was restored through the instrumentality of Cimon, on the condition that Athenian alliance with Argos was dissolved. (e) In 447 B.C. the exiled Oligarchs of Thebes defeated the Athenians at Coronea, and reestablished the Boeotian League under Theban leadership. (f) In 445 B.C. the 30 years peace was signed and after the revolt of Euboea and Megara, Sparta invaded Attica and Pericles sued for peace. Athens lost all her continental holdings. (Sandford's Mediterranean World C. 13, P. 220).

The second Peloponnesian war (431–421 B.C.) like that of the first arose through a general spirit of rebellion among the Greek city states against Athenian imperialism, Sparta being the chief enemy.

The net results were as follows: (a) In 435 B.C. war between Corcyra and Corinth, Corcyra being aided by Athens.

(b) In 432 B.C.

(1) Athens blockaded Potidaea, because she refused to dismantle her Southern walls, and dismiss her Corinthian Magistrates.

(2) Megara was excluded from Greek Markets, in order to reduce her to subjection.

(3) The Peloponnesian League planned war against Athens and Boeotia. Phocis and Locris were to fight against Athens, Corcyra and a few Northern states.

(c) In 431 B.C.

(1) Thebes attacked Plataea, and while a Peloponnesian army occupied Attica, the Athenian fleet raided Peloponnesus.

(2) Pericles being unable to defend Attica adequately transferred the civil population every Spring to the area between the walls of Athens and the Peiraeus. In the meantime the Athenian fleet operated against Potidaea, the Peloponnesian coast and Corinthian commerce.

(d) In 428 B.C.

(1) Mitylene and all the cities of Lesbos revolted.

(2) A brutal massacre of Oligarchs took place at Corcyra.

(e) In 425 B.C.

(1) A Laconian force at Pylos was captured and a fort was established through Demosthenes and Cleon.

(2) Cythera and other stations were fortified against the Peloponnesians.

(3) Amphipolis was captured by Brasidas a Spartan, who had instigated rebellion among the Athenian allies, and after Brasdias and Cleon had been killed in battle (422 B.C.), Athens authorized Nicias to sue for peace. (Sandford's Mediterranean World C. 13, P. 220–221).

It is obvious from a study of the causes and effects of the Peloponnesian wars that

(a) The Greek states were envious of each other and

(b) The desire for power and expansion led to constant aggression and warfare among themselves.

(c) The condition of constant warfare between the city states was unfavourable for the production of philosophers.

Before passing on to consider my next proposition I would like to say that it is an accepted truth that the development of philosophical thought requires an environment which is free from disturbance and worries. The period commonly assigned to Greek philosophy (i.e. Thales to Aristotle) was exactly the opposite to one of peace and tranquility, and therefore it could not be expected to produce philosophy. The obstacles against the origin and development of Greek philosophy, were not only the frequency of civil wars; and the constant defense against Persian aggression; but also the threat of extermination from the Athenian government, its worst enemy.

D. Philosophy Requires a Suitable Environment.

I must now add the following quotation which depicts this period. "For although the natural ills that beset mankind are many, we ourselves have added to them by wars and civil strife against one another, so that some have been unjustly put to death in their own cities, others driven into exile with their wives and children, and many have been compelled, for the sake of their daily bread, to die fighting against their own people, for the sake of the enemy". (Isocrates)

(Botsford & Robinson's Hellenic Hist., c. XIII. Couch's Hist. of

Greece, c. XXII. Bury's Hist. of Greece, c. X. The Tutorial Hist. of Greece by W. J. Woodhouse, c. 27, 28 and 29).

Stolen Legacy

CHAPTER III

Greek Philosophy Was the Offspring of The Egyptian Mystery System.

1. The Egyptian Theory of Salvation Became the Purpose of Greek Philosophy. The earliest theory of salvation is the Egyptian theory. The Egyptian Mystery System had as its most important object, the deification of man, and taught that the soul of man if liberated from its bodily fetters, could enable him to become godlike and see the Gods in this life and attain the beatific vision and hold communion with the Immortals (Ancient Mysteries, C. H. Vail, P. 25).

Plotinus defines this experience as the liberation of the mind from its finite consciousness, when it becomes one and is identified with the Infinite. This liberation was not only freedom of the soul from bodily impediments, but also from the wheel of reincarnation or rebirth. It involved a process of disciplines or purification both for the body and the soul. Since the Mystery System offered the salvation of the soul it also placed great emphasis upon its immortality. The Egyptian Mystery System, like the modern University, was the centre of organized culture, and candidates entered it as the leading source of ancient culture. According to Pietschmann, the Egyptian Mysteries had three grades of students (1) The Mortals i.e., probationary students who were being instructed, but who had not yet experienced the inner vision. (2) The Intelligences, i.e., those who had attained the inner vision, and had received mind or nous and (3) The Creators or Sons of Light, who had become identified with or united with the Light (i.e., true spiritual consciousness). W. Marsham Adams, in the "Book of the Master", has described those grades as the equivalents of Initiation, Illumination and Perfection. For years they underwent disciplinary intellectual exercises, and bodily asceticism with intervals of tests and ordeals to determine their fitness to proceed to the more serious, solemn and awful process of actual Initiation.

Their education consisted not only in the cultivation of the ten virtues, which were made a condition to eternal happiness, but also of the seven Liberal Arts which were intended to liberate the soul. There was also admission to the Greater Mysteries, where an esoteric philosophy was taught to those who had demonstrated their proficiency. (Ancient Mysteries C. H. Vail P. 24–25). Grammar, Rhetoric, and Logic were disciplines of moral nature by means of which the irrational tendencies of a human being were purged away, and he was trained to become a living witness of the Divine Logos. Geometry and Arithmetic were sciences of transcendental space and numeration, the comprehension of which provided the key not only to the problems of one's being; but also to those physical ones, which are so baffling today, owing to our use of the inductive methods. Astronomy dealt with the knowledge and distribution of latent forces in man, and the destiny of individuals, laces and nations. Music (or Harmony) meant the living practice of philosophy i.e., the adjustment of human life into harmony with God, until the personal soul became identified with God, when it would hear and participate in the music of the spheres. It was therapeutic, and was used by the Egyptian Priests in the cure of diseases. Such was the Egyptian theory of salvation, through which the individual was trained to become godlike while on earth, and at the same time qualified for everlasting happiness. This was accomplished through the efforts of the individual, through the cultivation of the Arts and Sciences on the one hand, and a life of virtue on the other. There was no mediator between man and his salvation, as we find in the Christian theory. Reference will again be made to these subjects, as part of the Curriculum of the Egyptian Mystery System.

Now that we have outlined the Egyptian theory of salvation and its purpose, let us examine Greek philosophy and its purpose in order to discover whether there is an agreement between the two systems, or not.

2. Circumstances of identity between the Egyptian and Greek Systems. A. The Indictment and Prosecution of Greek Philosophers.

The indictment and prosecution of Greek philosophers is a circumstance which is familiar to us all. Several philosophers, one after another, were indicted by the Athenian Government, on the common charge of introducing strange divinities. Anaxagoras, Socrates, and Aristotle received similar indictments for a similar offence. The most famous of these was that against Socrates which reads as follows. "Socrates commits a crime by not believing in the Gods of the city, and by introducing other new divinities. He also commits a crime by corrupting the youth". Now, in order to find out what these new divinities were, we must go back to the popular opinion which Aristophanes (423 B.C.) in the Clouds, aroused against him. It runs as follows: "Socrates is an evildoer, who busies himself with investigating things beneath the earth and in the sky, and who makes the worse appear the better reason, and who teaches others these same things (Plato's Apology C. 1–10; Aristophanes' Frogs, 1071; Apology 18 B.C., 19 C. Apology 24 B).

It is clear then that Socrates offended the Athenian government simply because he pursued the study of astronomy and probably that of geology; and that the other philosophers were persecuted for the same reason. But the study of science was a required condition to membership in the Egyptian Mystery System, and its purpose was the liberation of the Soul from the ten bodily fetters, and if the Greek philosophers studied the sciences, then they were fulfilling a required condition to membership in the Egyptian Mystery System and its purpose: either through direct contact with Egypt or its schools or lodges outside its territory.

B. A Life of Virtue was a Condition Required by the Egyptian Mysteries as Elsewhere Mentioned.

The virtues were not mere abstractions or ethical sentiments, but were positive valours and virility of the soul. Temperance meant complete control of the passional nature. Fortitude meant such courage as would not allow adversity to turn us away from our goal. Prudence meant the deep insight that befits the faculty of Seership. Justice meant the unswerving righteousness of thought and action.

Furthermore, when we compare the two ethical systems, we discover that the greater includes the less, and that it also suggests the origin of the latter. In the Egyptian Mysteries the Neophyte was required to manifest the following soul attributes:—

(1) Control of thought and (2) Control of action, the combination of which, Plato called Justice (i.e., the unswerving righteousness of thought and action). (3) Steadfastness of purpose, which was equivalent to Fortitude. (4) Identity with spiritual life or the higher ideals, which was equivalent to Temperance an attribute attained when the individual had gained conquest over the passional nature. (5) Evidence of having a mission in life and (6) Evidence of a call to spiritual Orders or the Priesthood in the Mysteries: the combination of which was equivalent to Prudence or a deep insight and graveness that befitted the faculty of Seership.

Other requirements in the ethical system of the Egyptian Mysteries were:—

(7) Freedom from resentment, when under the experience of persecution and wrong. This was known as courage. (8) Confidence in the power of the master (as Teacher), and (9) Confidence in one's own ability to learn; both attributes being known as Fidelity. (10) Readiness or preparedness for initiation. There has always been this principle of the Ancient Mysteries of Egypt: "When the pupil is ready, then the master will appear". This was equivalent to a condition of efficiency at all times for less than this pointed to a weakness. It is now quite clear that Plato drew the four Cardinal virtues from the Egyptian ten; also that Greek philosophy is the offspring of the Egyptian Mystery System.

C. (i) There was a Grand Lodge in Egypt which had associated Schools and Lodges in the ancient world.

There were mystery schools, or what we would commonly call lodges in Greece and other lands, outside of Egypt, whose work was carried on according to the Osiriaca, the Grand Lodge of Egypt. Such schools have frequently been referred to as private or philosophic mysteries, and their founders were Initiates of the Egyptian Mysteries; the Ionian temple at Didyma; the lodge of Euclid at Megara; the lodge of Pythagoras at Crotona; and the Orphic temple at Delphi, with the schools of Plato and Aristotle. Consequently we make a mistake when we suppose that the so-called Greek philosophers formulated new doctrines of their own; for their philosophy had been handed down by the great Egyptian Hierophants through the Mysteries. (Ancient Mysteries C. H. Vail P. 59). In addition to the control of the mysteries, the Grand Lodge permitted an exchange of visits between the various lodges, in order to ensure the progress of the brethren in the secret science.

We are told in the Timaeus of Plato, that aspirants for mystical wisdom visited Egypt for initiation and were told by the priests of Sais, "that you Greeks are but children" in the Secret Doctrine, but were admitted to information enabling them to promote their spiritual advancement. Likewise, we are told by Jamblichus of a correspondence between Anebo and Porphyry, dealing with the fraternal relations, existing between the various schools or lodges of instructions in different lands, how their members visited, greeted and assisted one another in the secret science, the more advanced being obliged to afford assistance and instruction to their brethren in the inferior Orders. (Jamblichus: correspondence between Anebo and Porphyry) (Plato's Timaeus) (W. L. Wilmshurst on meaning of Masonry).

Having stated that the Grand Lodge of ancient mysteries was situated in Egypt, with jurisdiction over all lodges and schools of the ancient world, it now remains to show that such a Grand Lodge, did actually and physically exist. In doing so, two things are necessary: first, a description of the Egyptian temple, of which our modern mystery lodges (called by different names) are copies, and second, a description of the actual remains of the Grand and Sublime Lodge of Ancient Egypt.

C. (ii) A description of the Egyptian temple.

Here I quote two authorities on the Egyptian temple, the first, C. H. Vail, on Ancient Mysteries P. 159 who says "that the Egyptian temples were surrounded with pillars recording the number of the constellations and the signs of the Zodiac or the cycles of the planets. And each temple was supposed to be a microcosm or a symbol of the temple of the Universe or of the starry vault called temple". The next authority is Max Muller, who in his Egyptian Mythology P. 187–193, has described Egyptian temples as follows:—

"Egyptian temples were made of stone, the outer courts of mud bricks. Wide roads led to the temples for the convenience of processions, while the immediate entrance was lined with statues, consisting of sphinxes and other animals. The front wall formed two high tower like buildings, called pylons, before which stood two granite obelisks. Immediately behind the pylons came a large court where the congregation assembled and watched the sacrifices. Immediately next to the hall of the congregation, came the hall of priests, and immediately following the hall of the priests came the final chamber, called the Adytum, i.e., the Holy of Holies, which was entered only by the high Priest. This was the place of the shrine and the abode of the God. Each temple was a reproduction of the world. The ceilings were painted to represent the sky and the stars, while the floor was green and blue like the meadows. Ceremonial cleanliness was at all times imperative, and the people before entering the temple must carefully purify themselves in a nearby stream. In later times, this became a ceremony of sprinkling with holy water before entrance into the temple".

It is clear from the foregoing description that not only the modern masonic lodges, are copies of the Egyptian temple, but also the ancient ones, for there is complete identity in their internal decoration. But the minor or lower lodges including those outside of Egypt, must have had a governing body, and so now, I proceed to quote C. H. Vail, who in his Ancient Mysteries, pages 182 and 183, describes fully the location and remains of the famous Grand Lodge of Luxor, as follows:—

C. (iii) The location of the Masonic Grand Lodge of Antiquity.

"At a short distance from Danderah, now called Upper Egypt, is the most extraordinary group of architectural ruins presented in any part of the world, known as the Temples of the ancient city of Thebes. Thebes in its prime occupied a large area on both sides of the Nile. This city was the centre of a great commercial nation of Upper Egypt ages before Memphis was the capital of the second nation in Lower Egypt; and however grand the architectural monuments of the latter may have been those of the former surpassed them. The portrayal by pencil or brush can convey but a faint idea of the perfected city. As the city stands today, it is like a city of giants, who after a long conflict have been destroyed, leaving the ruins of their various temples, as the only proof of their existence

"The Temple of Luxor (it was in this temple that the Grand Lodge of Initiates always met), stands on a raised platform of brickwork covering more than two thousand feet in length and one thousand feet in breadth (note the oblong shape. which became the pattern for all lodges and churches in the ancient world). It is the one that interests the members of all Ancient Orders, especially so, all the members of those Orders that worshipped at the Shrine of the Secret Fire, more than perhaps any other, and stands on the eastern bank of the Nile. It is in a very ruined state: but records say the stupendous scale of its proportions almost takes away the sense of its incompleteness. Up to about a quarter of a century ago, the greater part of its columns in the interior and outer walls had been removed, after falling, for use elsewhere. This temple was founded by the Pharaoh Amenothis III, who constructed the southern part, including the heavy colonnade overlooking the river; but destruction unfortunately conceals this fact. The chief entrance to the Temple looked to the east; while the Holy Chambers at the upper end of the plain approached the Nile. As mighty as the Temple of Luxor was, it was exceeded in magnitude and grandeur by that of Carnak. The distance between these two great structures was a mile and a half. Along this avenue was a double row of Sphinxes, placed twelve feet apart, and the width of the avenue was sixty feet. When in perfect state this avenue presented the most extraordinary entrance that the world has ever seen. If we had the power to picture from the field of imagination the grand processions of Neophytes constantly passing through and taking part in the ceremonies of Initiation, we would be powerless to produce the grandeur of the surroundings, and the imposing sight of colour and magnificent trappings of those who took part. Neither can we produce the music that kept the vast number of people in steady marching order. Crude it might have been to the cultivated ear of the 20th century. But could not the palpitating strain sung by massed voices on the lapse of time, whose history launches the profoundest aspirations of the human heart, like the trend of a mighty river, because the grand currents of Universal Law, imparting the desire to that Shadowy Past, as it steps forth from the pages of history, dim with age? Egypt must have been, when these Temples were built, a martial nation for records of her warlike deeds are perpetuated in deeply engraved tablets which even now, excite the admiration of the best Judges of archaeological remains. She was also a highly civilized nation, and of a nature that could bear the expenditure which always attends the culture of the Arts. She surpassed in her astonishing architecture, all other nations that have existed upon the earth."

I am fully convinced by these references and quotations that an Egyptian Grand Lodge of Ancient Mysteries actually existed some five thousand years ago or more, on the banks of the Nile in the city of Thebes, and that it was the only Grand Lodge of the Ancient World whose ruins have been found in Egypt, and that it was the governing body which necessarily controlled the Ancient Mysteries together with the philosophical Schools and minor Lodges wherever they happened to have been organized.

C. (iv) The rebuilding of the temple of Delphi.

The temple of Delphi was burnt down in 548 B.C. and it was King Amasis of Egypt, who rebuilt it for the brethren, by donating three times as much as was needed, in the sum of one thousand talents, and 50,000 lbs. of alum. According to information at hand, the temple had organized its members into an amphictyonic league for protection against political and other forms of violence; but they were too poor to raise sufficient funds from the membership, and they decided upon a public contribution from the citizens of Greece.

Accordingly they wandered throughout the land soliciting aid, but failed in their efforts. Having decided to visit the brethren in Egypt, they approached King Amasis, who as Grand Master, unhesitatingly offered to rebuild the Temple, and donated more than three times as much as was needed for the purpose.

N.B. Here it would be well to note that

(1) The Greeks regarded the Temple of Delphi as a foreign institution, hence

(2) They were unsympathetic towards it and for the same reason destroyed it by fire.

(3) Clearly, the Temple of Delphi was a branch of the Egyptian Mystery System, projected in Greece. Sandford's Mediterranean World p. 135; 139.

John Kendrick's Ancient Egypt Bk. II. P. 363.

3. The abolition of Greek Philosophy together with the Egyptian Mysteries. From the conquest of Egypt by Alexander the Great, the Greeks, who were always attracted by the mysterious worship of the Nile-land, began to imitate the Egyptian religion in its entirety; and during the Roman occupation, the Egyptian religion spread not only to Italy: but throughout the Roman Empire, including Brittany.

This assimilation of the Egyptian religion was confined to the Gods of the Osirian cycle and the Graeco-Egyptian Serapis, and aimed at a close imitation of the ancient traditions of the Nileland. Owing to the splendour of architecture, the hieroglyphs of the temples, the obelisks and sphinxes before the shrines, the linen vestments and the shaven heads and faces of the priests, the endless and obscure ritual, filled the Greeks with awe, and wonderful mysteries were consequently believed to have underlain these incomprehensibles, and the Egyptian religion stood in the way of the rising Christianity.

The success of the Egyptian religion was due no doubt, on the one hand to its conservatism; while on the other to the shadowy philosophical abstractions which constituted Graeco-Roman religion, so that the staunch faith of the Egyptians, together with their mysterious forms of worship, led to the universal conviction among the Ancients, that Egypt was not only the Holy Land but the Holiest of lands or countries, and that indeed, the Gods dwelt there.

The Nile became a centre for pilgrimages in the ancient world, and the pilgrims who went there and experienced the marvellous

Stolen Legacy

revelations and spiritual blessings which it afforded them, returned home with the conviction that the Nile was the home of the most profound religious knowledge.

The Greeks failed to imitate Egyptian conservatism and not only in Egyptian cities, with large Greek population, but in Europe, Egyptian divinities were corrupted with Greek and Asiatic names and mythologies and reduced to vague pantheistic personalities, so that Isis and Osiris had retained very little of their Egyptian origin. (Max Muller p. 241–43; Egyptian Mythology). Consequently, as they failed to advance Egyptian Philosophy, so they also failed to advance Egyptian religion.

During the first four centuries of the Christian era, the religion of Egypt continued unabated and uninterrupted, but after the Edict of Theodosius at the end of the fourth century A.D., ordering the close of Egyptian temples, Christianity began to spread more rapidly and both the religion of Egypt and that of Greece began to die. In the island of Philae, in the first cataract of the Nile, however, the Egyptian religion was continued by its inhabitants, the Blemmyans and Nobadians, who refused to accept Christianity and the Roman government fearing a rebellion, paid tribute to them as an appeasement.

During the sixth century A.D., however, Justinian issued a second edict which suppressed this remnant of Egyptian worshippers and propagated Christianity among the Nubians. With the death of the last priest, who could read and interpret "the writings of the words of the Gods" (the hieroglyphics) the Egyptian faith sank into oblivion. It was only in popular magic that some practices lingered on as traces of a faith that became a universal religion, or the survival of a statue of Isis and Horus, which were regarded as the Madonna and Child.

A sentiment of admiration and awe for this strangest of all religions still survived, but the information from classical writers concerning this faith has been incomplete. Napoleon's invasion of Egypt brought a revival of interest from the West to decipher her inscriptions and papyri with a view to an understanding and appreciation of this most ancient of civilizations.

(Mythology of Egypt by Max Muller C. XIII p. 241–245; The Mediterranean World by Sandford, p. 508, 548, 552–558, 568).

We learn the following facts from the above quotations:—(i)

The Egyptian Mysteries had become the Ancient World Religion, spreading throughout the Roman Empire and including Italy, Greece, Asia Minor, and various parts of Europe including Brittany. This continued under different names, long after Justinian's Edict of toleration granted to the Christians. (ii) Egypt was the Holy Land of the ancient world, that pilgrimages were made to that land because of the marvellous revelations and spiritual blessings which it afforded the ancient peoples, and because of the universal conviction among the Ancients that Egypt was the land of the Gods. (iii) The Edicts of Theodosius in the fourth century A. D,. and that of Justinian in the sixth century A.D. abolished alike not only the Mystery system of Egypt, but also its philosophical schools, located in Greece and elsewhere, outside Egypt.

(iv) The abolition of the Egyptian Mysteries was to create an opportunity for the adoption of Christianity. This was the problem: the Roman government felt that Egypt was now conquered in arms and reduced to her knees, but in order to make the conquest complete, it would be necessary to abolish the Mysteries which still controlled the religious mind of the ancient world. There must be a New World Religion to take the place of the Egyptian religion. This New Religion, which should take the place of the Mysteries, must be equally powerful and universal, and consequently everything possible must be done in order to promote its interests. This explains the rapid growth of Christianity following Justinian's Edict of toleration.

(v) Since the Edicts of Theodosius and Justinian abolished both the Mysteries of Egypt and the schools of Greek philosophy alike, it shows that the nature of the Egyptian Mysteries and Greek philosophy was identical and that Greek philosophy grew out of the Egyptian Mysteries.

4. How the African Continent gave its Culture to the Western World. As mentioned elsewhere, the Egyptian Mysteries and the philosophical schools of Greece were closed by the edicts of Theodosius in the 4th century A.D. and that of Justinian in the 6th century A.D. (i.e., 529); and as a consequence, intellectual darkness spread over Christian Europe and the Graeco-Roman world for ten centuries; during which time, knowledge had disappeared. As stated elsewhere, the Greeks showed no creative powers, and were unable to improve upon the knowledge which they had received from the Egyptians (Hist. of Science by Sedgwick and Tyler p. 141; 153; Zeller's Hist. of Phil. Introduction p. 31).

During the Persian, Greek and Roman invasions, large numbers of Egyptians fled not only to the desert and mountain regions, but also to adjacent lands in Africa, Arabia and Asia Minor, where they lived, and secretly developed the teachings which belonged to their mystery system. In the 8th century A.D. the Moors, i.e., natives of Mauritania in North Africa, invaded Spain and took with them, the Egyptian culture which they had preserved. Knowledge in the ancient days was centralized i.e., it belonged to a common parent and system, i.e., the Wisdom Teaching or Mysteries of Egypt, which the Greeks used to call Sophia.

As such, the people of North Africa were the neighbours of the Egyptians, and became the custodians of Egyptian culture, which they spread through considerable portions of Africa, Asia Minor and Europe. During their occupation of Spain, the Moors displayed with considerable credit, the grandeur of African culture and civilization. The schools and libraries which they established became famous throughout the Mediaeval world; Science and learning were cultivated and taught; the schools of Cordova, Toledo, Seville and Saragossa attained such celebrity, that they, like their parent Egypt, attracted students from all parts of the Western world; and from them arose the most famous African professors that the world has ever known, in medicine, surgery, astronomy and mathematics. But these people from North Africa did more than merely distinguish themselves in Spain. They were really the recognized custodians of African culture, to whom the world looked for enlightenment. Consequently, through the medium of the ancient Arabic language, philosophy and the various branches of science were disseminated: (a) all the so-called works of Aristotle in Metaphysics, moral philosophy and natural science (b) translations by Leonardo Pisano in Arabic mathematical science (c) translation by Gideo a Monk of Arezzo in musical notation. (Sedgwick and Tyler's Hist. of Science C. IX.)

In addition, the Moors kept up constant contact with mother Egypt: for they had established Caliphates not only at Baghdad and Cordova, but also at Cairo in Egypt. (Europe in the Middle Ages by Ault p. 216–219). Just here it would be well to mention that all the great leaders of the great religions of antiquity were Initiates of the Egyptian Mystery System: from Moses, who was an Egyptian Hierogrammat, down to Christ.

It should also be of interest to know that European scientists like Roger Bacon, Johann Kepler, Copernicus and others obtained their science through Arab or Berber sources. It is also noteworthy that throughout the Middle Ages, European knowledge of medicine came from these same sources.

(History of The Arabs, by Hitti pages 370, 629, 665 and 572).

(Philo: Esoteric Christianity by Annie Besant p. 107; 128–129; Ancient Mysteries by C. H. Vail p. 59; 61; 74–75; 109).

CHAPTER IV

The Egyptians Educated the Greeks

1. The Effects of the Persian Conquest. A. Immigration restrictions against the Greeks are removed and Egypt is thrown open to Greek research.

Owing to the practice of piracy, in which the Ionians and Carians were active, the Egyptians were forced to make immigration laws restricting the immigration of the Greeks and punishing their infringement by capital punishment, i.e., the sacrifice of the victim. Before the time of Psammitichus, the Greeks were not allowed to go beyond the coast of Lower Egypt, but during his reign and that of Amasis, those conditions were modified. For the first time in Egyptian history Ionians and Carians were employed as Mercenaries in the Egyptian Army (670 B.C.), interpretation was organized through a body of interpreters, and the Greeks began to gain useful information concerning the culture of the Egyptians.

In addition to these changes, King Amasis removed the restrictions against the Greeks and permitted them to enter Egypt and settle in Naucratis. About this same time, i.e., the reign of Amasis, the Persians, through Cambyses invaded Egypt, and the whole country was thrown open to the researches of the Greeks.

B. The Genesis of Greek Enlightenment.

The Persian invasion, did not only provide the Greeks with ample research, but stimulated the creation of prose history in Ionia. Heretofore, the Greeks had little or no accurate knowledge of Egyptian culture: but their contact with Egypt resulted in the genesis of their enlightenment. (Ovid Fasti III 338; Herodotus Bk. II p. 113; Plutarch p. 380; Eratosthenes ap Strabo 801–802; Diogenes Bk. IX 49).

C. Students from Ionia and the Islands of the Aegean visit Egypt for their Education.

Just as in our modern times, countries like the United States, England, and France are attracting students from all parts of the world, on account of their leadership in culture: so was it in ancient times. Egypt was supreme in the leadership of civilization, and students from all parts, flocked to that land, seeking admission into her mysteries or wisdom system.

The immigration of Greeks to Egypt for the purpose of their education, began as a result of the Persian invasion (525 B.C.), and continued until the Greeks gained possession of that land and access to the Royal Library, through the conquest of Alexander the Great. Alexandria was converted into a Greek city, a centre of research and the capital of the newly created Greek empire, under the rule of Ptolemies. Egyptian culture survived and flourished, under the name and control of the Greeks, until the edicts of Theodosius in the 4th century A.D., and that of Justinian in the 6th century A.D., which closed the Mystery Temples and Schools, as elsewhere mentioned. (Ancient Egypt by John Kendrick Bk. II p. 55; Sandford's Mediterranean World p. 562; 570).

Concerning the fact that Egypt was the greatest education centre of the ancient world which was also visited by the Greeks, reference must again be made to Plato in the Timaeus who tells us that Greek aspirants to wisdom visited Egypt for initiation, and that the priests of Sais used to refer to them as children in the Mysteries.

As regards the visit of Greek students to Egypt for the purpose of their education, the following are mentioned simply to establish the fact that Egypt was regarded as the educational centre of the ancient world and that like the Jews, the Greeks also visited Egypt and received their education. (1) It is said that during the reign of Amasis, Thales who is said to have been born about 585 B.C., visited Egypt and was initiated by the Egyptian Priests into the Mystery System and science of the Egyptians. We are also told that during his residence in Egypt, he learnt astronomy, land surveying, mensuration, engineering and Egyptian Theology. (See Thales in Blackwell's source book of Philosophy; Zeller's Hist. of Phil.; Diogenes Laertius and Kendrick's Ancient Egypt).

(2) It is said that Pythagoras, a native of Samos, travelled frequently to Egypt for the purpose of his education. Like every aspirant, he had to secure the consent and favour of the Priests, and we are informed by Diogenes that a friendship existed between Polycrates of Samos and Amasis King of Egypt, that Polycrates gave Pythagoras letters of introduction to the King, who secured for him an introduction to the Priests; first to the Priest of Heliopolis, then to the Priest of Memphis, and lastly to the Priests of Thebes, to each of whom Pythagoras gave a silver goblet. (Herodotus Bk. III 124; Diogenes VIII 3; Pliny N. H., 36, 9; Antipho recorded by Por-

Stolen Legacy

phyry).

We are also further informed through Herodotus, Jablonsk and Pliny, that after severe trials, including circumcision, had been imposed upon him by the Egyptian Priests, he was finally initiated into all their secrets. That he learnt the doctrine of metempsychosis; of which there was no trace before in the Greek religion; that his knowledge of medicine and strict system of dietetic rules, distinguished him as a product of Egypt, where medicine had attained its highest perfection; and that his attainments in geometry corresponded with the ascertained fact that Egypt was the birth place of that Science. In addition we have the statements of Plutarch, Demetrius and Antisthenes that Pythagoras founded the Science of Mathematics among the Greeks, and that he sacrificed to the Muses, when the Priests explained to him the properties of the right angled triangle. (Philarch de Repugn. Stoic 2 p. 1089; Demetrius; Antisthenes; Cicero de Natura Deorum III, 36). Pythagoras was also trained in music by the Egyptian priests. (Kendrick's Hist. of Ancient Egypt vol. I. p. 234).

(3) According to Diogenes Laertius and Herodotus, Democritus is said to have been born about 400 B.C. and to have been a native of Abdera in Miletus. We are also told by Demetrius in his treatise on "People of the Same Name", and by Antisthenes in his treatise on "Succession", that Democritus travelled to Egypt for the purpose of his education and received the instruction of the Priests. We also learn from Diogenes and Herodotus that he spent five years under the instruction of the Egyptian Priests and that after the completion of his education, he wrote a treatise on the sacred characters of Meroe.

In this respect we further learn from Origen, that circumcision was compulsory, and one of the necessary conditions of initiation to a knowledge of the hieroglyphics and sciences of the Egyptians, and it is obvious that Democritus, in order to obtain such knowledge, must have submitted also to that rite. Origen, who was a native of Egypt wrote as follows:—

"Apud Aegyptios nullus aut geometrica studebat, aut astronomiae secreta remabatur, nisi circumcisione suscepta." (No one among the Egyptians, either studied geometry, or investigated the secrets of Astronomy, unless circumcision had been undertaken).

(4) Concerning Plato's travels we are told by Hermodorus that at the age of 28 Plato visited Euclid at Megara in company with

other pupils of Socrates; and that for the next ten years he visited Cyrene, Italy and finally Egypt, where he received instruction from the Egyptian Priests.

(5) With regards to Socrates and Aristotle and the majority of pre-Socratic philosophers, history seems to be silent on the question of their travelling to Egypt like the few other students here mentioned, for the purpose of their education. It is enough to say, that in this case the exceptions have proved the rule, that all students, who had the means, went to Egypt to complete their education. The fact that history fails to supply a fuller account of this type of immigration, might be due to some or all of the following reasons:

(a) The immigration laws against the Greeks up to the time of King Amasis and the Persian Invasion, (b) Prose history was undeveloped among the Greeks during the period of their educational immigration to Egypt. (c) The Greek authorities persecuted and drove students of philosophy into hiding and consequently, (d) Students of the Mystery System concealed their movements.

Let us remember that Anaxagoras was indicted and imprisoned; that he escaped and fled to his home in Ionia, that Socrates was indicted, imprisoned and condemned to death; and that both Plato and Aristotle fled from Athens under great suspicion (William Turner's Hist. of Phil. p. 62; Plato's Phaedo; Zeller's Hist. of Phil. p. 84; 127; Roger's Hist. of Phil. p. 76; William Turner's Hist. of Phil. p. 126).

2. The Effects of the Conquest of Egypt by Alexander the Great.
A. The Royal Library and Museum together with Temples and other Libraries are Looted.

As elsewhere mentioned, it was an ancient custom of invading armies to loot libraries and temples in order to capture books and manuscripts, which were regarded as great treasures. A few instances would be enough to verify this custom: (a) we are informed that during the Persian Invasion beginning with Cambyses, the temples of Egypt were not only stripped of their gold and silver, but rifled for their ancient records. Every Egyptian Temple carried a secret library with secret manuscripts and books. (b) We are also informed that when Athens was captured by the Romans in 84 B.C. the library of books said to have belonged to Aristotle was also captured and taken to Rome. (William Turner's Hist. of Phil. p. 128; John Kendrick's Ancient Egypt vol. II p. 432).

Stolen Legacy

Just as in the invasion of Egypt by the Persians, the invading armies stripped the temples of their gold, silver and sacred books; and just as in the capture of Athens by the Romans Sulla carried off the only library of books which he found; so it is to be expected of Alexander the Great, in his invasion of Egypt. One of the first things that he and his companions and armies would do, would be to search for the treasures of the land and capture them. These were kept in temples and libraries and consisted of gold and silver out of which the gods and ceremonial vessels were made, and sacred books and, manuscripts kept both in libraries and in the "Holy of Holies" of Temples.

It is my firm belief that this indeed was the great opportunity which Alexander gave Aristotle and enabled him and his pupils to carry off as many books as they wanted from the Royal Library and to convert it into a research centre. Apart from the Royal Library at Alexandria, there was also another famous library near by: The "Royal Library of Thebes"; "The Menephtheion", which was founded by Pharaoh, Setei. The Menephtheion was completed by Rameses II; but little occurs in history about this greatest of Egyptian Royal Libraries.

However, any invading army would first loot the Royal Library of Alexandria and then would turn their attention to the Menephtheion at Thebes. They would also visit the cities of Memphis and Heliopolis and likewise loot their libraries and temples. This was the ancient custom and certainly one of the ways in which the Greeks received their education from Egyptians. (Egyptian Mythology by Max Muller p. 187–189; 205; Diodorus 16, 51; Bunsen I p. 27; Ancient Egypt by John Kendrick vol. II 56; 432–433).

It is therefore an erroneous belief that the Greeks, on Egyptian soil, and through their own native ability, set up a great university at Alexandria and turned out great scholars. On the other hand, since it is a well known fact that Egypt was the land of temples and libraries, we can see how comparatively easy it was for the Greeks to strip other Egyptian libraries of their books in order to maintain the new Library at Alexandria, after it had been already looted by Aristotle and his pupils. The Greeks (i.e., Alexander the Great, Aristotle's school and the succeeding Ptolemies) converted the Royal Library of Alexandria into a research centre, by transferring Aristotle's school and pupils from Athens to this great Egyptian Library, and therefore the students who studied there received instructions from Egyptian priests and teachers, until they died out.

The difficulty of language and interpretation made it imperative for the Greeks to use Egyptian teachers.

The Greeks did not carry culture and learning to Egypt, but found it already there, and wisely settled in that country, in order to absorb as much as possible of its culture.

B. The Royal Library of Thebes: The Menephtheion is described. It was also looted by invading armies.

But when we read a brief sketch of the magnificence of the Theban Royal Library; The Menephtheion, we even see a better picture and are bound to admit that Egypt was the store house of ancient culture and that that culture was preserved in the form of literature stored away in her great libraries and temples. Great as the Royal Library of Alexandria might have been, we see in the Theban Royal Library something far more magnificent and far more representative of the true greatness of our Ancient Egypt.

On the left of the steps leading to the second court, there is still seen the pedestal of the enormous granite statue of Rameses: the largest, that ever existed in Egypt, according to Diodorus. Its height has been calculated at fifty-four feet, and its weight, at 887¼ tons; a marvel to the modern mind. The interior face of the wall of the pylon represents the wars of Rameses III. The Osiride pillars of the second court, are the monolithal figures, sixteen cubits in height, supplying the place of columns, and at the foot of the steps leading from the court to the next hall beyond, there were two sitting statues of the King. The head of one of these was of red granite, known by the name of "Young Memon", was taken away by Belzoni, and is now a principal ornament of the British Museum.

Beyond this are the remains of a hall 133 feet broad by 100 feet long, supported by 48 columns, twelve of which are thirty-two feet in height and 21 feet in circumference. On different parts of the columns, and the walls are represented acts of homage by the king to the principal Deities of the Theban Pantheon, and the gracious promises which they make him in return.

In another sculpture the two chief Divinities of Egypt invest him with the emblems of military and civil dominion, i.e., the Scimitar, the Scourge and the Pedum. Beneath, the twenty-three sons of Rameses appear in procession, bearing the emblems of their respective high offices in the state, their names being inscribed above them. Nine smaller apartments, two of them still preserved, and

Stolen Legacy

supported by columns, lay behind the hall. On the jambs of the first of these apartments are sculptured Thoth: the Inventor of Letters, and the Goddess Saf, with the title of 'Lady of Letters'; and 'President of the Hall of Books', accompanied the former with an emblem of the sense of sight, and the latter of hearing.

There is no doubt that this is the "Sacred Library" which Diodorus describes as the inscribed "Dispensary of the Mind". It had an astronomical ceiling, in which the twelve Egyptian months are represented, with an inscription from which important inferences have been drawn respecting the chronology of the reign of Rameses III.

On the walls is a procession of priests, carrying the Sacred Arts, and in the next apartment, the last that now remains, the king is presenting offerings to the various Divinities. (Ancient Egypt by J. Kendrick Bk. I p. 128–131. Report of French Commission).

C. Museum and the Library of Alexander were used as a University.

The Museum and Library of Alexandria were so famous in ancient times, that we wonder why more information concerning this centre of learning, has not come down to us. A few references to authoritative sources might no doubt help to enlighten us on this matter.

From Sedgwick's and Tyler's History of Science, chapter 5 pages 87–119, we learn that the subjugation of Egypt by Alexander the Great in 330 B.C. had checked the further development of Greek civilization on its native soil.

That after the death of Alexander the Great in 323 B.C., his vast empire was divided among his generals, and that Alexandria, the new Egyptian capital fell to Ptolemy. That the city, barely ten years old, soon became the centre of the learned world, and that by 300 B.C., the Museum (i.e., the seat of the Muses), was founded, and became a veritable university of Greek learning.

That to the Museum was attached a great library, with a dining hall and lecture rooms for professors, and this became a school of philosophers, mathematicians and astronomers. Here for the next 700 years, science had its chief abiding place.

Here however, it should be remembered that the above statement of Sedgwick and Tyler is misleading, since the Greeks did not carry a civilization of their own to Egypt, but on the contrary found a very highly developed Egyptian culture, the survival of which was maintained by the use of Egyptian Priests and Scholars as teachers.

D. A Military Policy of the Greeks to Commandeer Information From the Egyptians was put in operation.

One of the military policies adopted by the Greek military authorities at Alexandria was the issue of commands to the leading Egyptian Priests for information concerning the Egyptian history, philosophy and religion. As a custom this is no less ancient than modern, since it is also a custom in modern times for victorious armies to confer with the men of science of an invaded country, in order to discover whether or not, there is anything new in the field of science, which they might possess. We would recall how at the end of World War II, the American scientists conferred with the Japanese scientists at Tokio. Accordingly, we are told that Ptolemy I Soter, in order to elicit the secrets of Egyptian wisdom or mystery system, ordered Manetho, the High Priest of the temple of Isis at Sebennytus in Lower Egypt, to write the philosophy, and the history of the religion of the Egyptians.

Accordingly, Manetho published several volumes concerning these respective fields, and Ptolemy issued an order prohibiting the translation of these books which had to be kept on reserve in the Library, for instruction of the Greeks by the Egyptian Priests. Here it becomes quite clear that the first professors of the Alexandrine School were the Egyptian Priests, and that the Scholarchs and pupils of Aristotle's transferred school, received their training directly from the Egyptian Priests. It is also well to note that the chief text books of the Alexandrine School were Manetho's books.

We are told by Apollodorus from whom Syncellus drew his information, that Ptolemy II ordered Eratosthenes, the Cyrenean (i.e., a black man and native of Cyrene) and librarian of the Alexandrine Library, to write a chronology of the Theban Kings, and that Eratosthenes did so with the aid of the Egyptian Hierophants at Thebes (Ancient Egypt by John Kendrick vol. II p. 81; Apollodorus; Syncellus; Clinton, Fasti Hellenici, sub anno).

Furthermore, it became the custom during the Greek and Roman occupation to use the services of Egyptian Priests and Scholars, as professors at the Alexandrine School. We are told that during the reign of Theodosius (378–395 A.D.), the Egyptian Professor

Horapollo wrote a system of the Egyptian hieroglyphics: The Hieroglyphica of Horapollo, which has been regarded as the best that has come down to modern times. We are also told that this professor taught not only at the Alexandrine School, but also at that of Constantinople.

(John Kendrick's Ancient Egypt Bk. I p. 242: Leeman's Amstelod, 1935 translated by Cory).

3. The Egyptians Were the First to Civilize the Greeks. Greece was first civilized by colonies from Egypt, then from Phoenicia and Thrace. These were under the government of wise men, who not only subdued the ferocity of an ignorant populace by civil institutions, but also cast about them the strong chain of religion and the fear of the gods. Whatever dogmas they had been taught in their respective countries, concerning things divine and human, they delivered to these newly formed societies, with the object of bringing them under the restraint of virtuous discipline. Phoroneus and Cecrops were Egyptians, Cadmus a Phoenician and Orpheus a Thracian, and each of them, through their colonies carried into Greece the religious and philosophical tenets of his respective country.

The practice of teaching the doctrines of religion to people under the guise of myths originated from the Egyptians and was adopted by the Phoenicians and Thracians, and subsequently introduced to the Greeks.

According to Strabo, it was not possible in ancient times to lead a promiscuous multitude to religion and virtue by philosophical harangues. This could be effected only by the aid of superstition, by prodigies and fables. The thunder bolt, the aegis, the trident, the spear, torches and snakes were the instruments made use of by the founders of States, to terrify the ignorant and vulgar into subjection. These references must speak for themselves.

Cheops and Cecrops were the names which the Greeks used for the Egyptian Khufu, who belonged to the 4th Dynasty of the Egyptians or the pyramid age, i.e., 2800 B.C.

(Strabo Bk. I; Brucker's Historia Critica Philosophiae with translation by Wm. Enfield: Bk. II p. 62).

4. Alexander Visits the Oracle of Ammon in the Oasis of Siwah. No discussion on Alexander's invasion of Egypt would be complete without reference to his famous visit to the Oracle of Ammon, situated in the Oasis of Siwah. Alexander had placed a garrison in Pe-

lusium, whence he marched through the desert along the eastern bank of the Nile to Heliopolis where he crossed the river to Memphis, where his fleet had been awaiting him, and where he was welcomed by the Egyptians and crowned as Pharaoh. Having sacrificed to Apis and other Gods, Alexander descended the Nile by the Canopic branch and set out on his journey to the Oracle of Ammon in the Oasis of Siwah. His route was along the coast of Libya, as far as Paraetonium, whence he marched through the desert to the Oasis of Siwah. What do we suppose was Alexander's motive for visiting the Temple of Ammon? Perhaps a brief description of the religious and economic importance of Heliopolis, Memphis, Thebes and Ammonium might help us to determine what it was.

In the first place these cities were strongholds of the Egyptian religion, where there were many rich temples, schools and Priests, and therefore were representative of the Egyptian religious life. In the second place these cities were centres of education, and after the Persian invasion, Greek students who travelled to Egypt for the purpose of their education, received their training from the Priests of one or all of these cities, as elsewhere mentioned.

When Pythagoras went to Egypt, he carried a letter of introduction from Polycrates of Samos to King Amasis, who in turn gave him letters of introduction to the Priests of Heliopolis, Memphis, and Thebes. As centres of education, the temples and libraries of these cities contained very valuable books: and in the third place, these regions had previously been captured by the Persians for the very fact of their wealth. This should explain why they included these districts in their Satrapy which paid them an enormous annual tribute amounting to 700 talents of gold, together with the produce of the fisheries of Lake Moeris which amounted to a talent a day, during the six months that the water flowed in from the Nile; and a third part of that sum, during the afflux. In addition Egypt furnished 120 thousand medicini of corn as rations for the Persian troops who were stationed in the White Fort of Memphis.

The equivalent of this tribute was 170 thousand pounds sterling, and shows the underlying motive not only of the Persian invading armies, but also of all invading armies of antiquity. In the case of Alexander there is no exception.

According to history, the Persians were in occupation of Egypt, and Alexander having mustered superior forces, went there and drove them out and took possession himself. May I ask this question: was this a joke, or was there a motive? And if there was a motive, what else could it have been but that Alexander wanted the wealth in books, gold, silver, ivory, slaves, and tribute which the Persians were extorting from the unfortunate Egyptians?

In ancient times, the Oracle of Ammon at Siwah was the most celebrated, and Heliopolis, Memphis and Thebes were representatives of the best of Egyptian culture.

(John Kendrick's Ancient Egypt Book II P. 433–435; Diodorus 15, 16. Herodotus Book III P. 124; Diogenes Laertius Book VIII; Timaeus of Plato; Pliny N. H. XXXVI 9; Antiphon recorded by Porphyry).

CHAPTER V

The Pre-Socratic Philosophers and the Teachings Ascribed to Them. N.B.

It is absolutely necessary here in chapters V and VI to mention the doctrines of the so called Greek philosophers in order to convince my readers of their Egyptian origin which is shown in the summaries of conclusions which follow these teachings. It is also necessary to mention them so as to serve the purpose of reference and to meet the convenience of readers.

I. The Earlier Ionian School. This Group consisted of (i) Thales (ii) Anaximander and (iii) Anaximenes.

(i) Thales, supposed to have lived 620–546 B.C. and a native of Miletus, is credited by Aristotle, with teaching that—

(a) water is the source of all living things.

(b) all things are full of God.

Both history and tradition are silent as to how Thales arrived at his conclusions, except that Aristotle attempts to offer his opinion as a reason: that is that Thales must have been influenced by the consideration of the moisture of nutriment, and based his conclusion on a rationalistic interpretation of the myth of Oceanus. This however is regarded as mere conjecture on the part of Aristotle. (Turner's History of Philosophy, p. 34).

(ii) Anaximander, supposed to have been born 610 B.C. at Miletus, is credited with the teaching that, the origin of all things is "the Infinite", or the Unlimited (i.e., apeiron), or the Boundless.

The Apeiron is regarded as equivalent to the modern notion of space, and the mythological notion of chaos.

Both history and tradition are silent as to how Anaximander arrived at his conclusion: but here again we find Aristotle offering his opinion as a reason, i.e., that Anaximander must have supposed that change destroys matter, and that unless the substratum of change is limitless, change must at sometime cease. This opinion, is of course, mere conjecture, on the part of Aristotle. (Turners History of Philosophy, p. 3536).

(iii) Anaximenes, also a native of Miletus, and supposed to

have died in 528 B.C., is credited with the teaching that all things originated from air.

Both history and tradition are silent as to how Anaximenes arrived at his conclusion; and all attempts to furnish a reason are regarded as mere conjecture. (Turner's History of Philosophy, p. 37–38).

2. Pythagoras. Born in the Aegean Island of Samos, supposedly in 530 B.C.; the following doctrines have been attributed to Pythagoras:—

(i) Transmigration, the immortality of the soul and salvation.

This salvation is based upon certain beliefs concerning the soul. True life is not to be found here on earth, and what men call life is really death, and the body is the tomb of the soul.

Owing to the contamination caused by the soul's imprisonment in the body, it is forced to pass through an indefinite series of re-incarnations: from the body of one animal, to that of another, until it is purged from such contamination.

Salvation, in this sense, consists of the freedom of the soul from the "cycle of birth, death and rebirth", which is common to every soul, and which condition must remain until purification or purgation is completed.

Being liberated from the ten chains of the flesh, and also from successive re-incarnations, the soul now acquires her pristine perfection, and the eligibility to join the company of the Gods, with whom she dwells for ever.

This was the reward which the Pythagorean System offered its initiates.

(ii) The doctrines of (a) Opposites, (b) the Summum Bonum, or Supreme Good, and (c) the process of purification.

(a) THE UNION OF OPPOSITES creates harmony in the universe. This is true in the case of musical sounds, such as we find in the lyre: where the harmony produced is the result of the mean proportional relation between the length of the two middle strings to that of the two extremes. This is also true in natural phenomena, which are identified with number, whose elements consist of the odd and the even. The even is unlimited, because of its quality of unlimited divisibility, and the odd indicates limitation; while the product of both is the unit or harmony.

Similarly, do we obtain harmony in the union of positive and negative; male and female; material and immaterial; body and soul.

(b) THE SUMMUM BONUM OR SUPREME GOOD in man, is to become godlike. This is an attainment, or transformation which is the harmony resulting from a life of virtue. It consists in a harmonious relationship between the faculties of man, by means of which his lower nature becomes subordinated to his higher nature.

(c) THE PROCESS OF PURIFICATION

The harmony and purification of the soul is attained, not only by virtue, but also by other means, the most important among them being the cultivation of the intellect through the pursuit of scientific knowledge and strict bodily discipline.

In this process, music also held an important place. The Pythagoreans believed and taught that just as medicine is used to cure the body, so music must be used to cure the soul.

Here it might be appropriate to insert the doctrine of the "Three Lives", since it is also a method and means of purification:—

"Mankind is divided into three classes: Lovers of wealth; lovers of honour, and lovers of wisdom (i.e. philosophers); this last, being highest." According to Pythagoras, philosophy determined the purification, which led to the final salvation of the soul.

(iii) The Cosmological Doctrine

All things are numbers, that is to say not only every object, but the entire universe is an arrangement of numbers. This means that the characteristic of any object is the number by which it is represented.

(a) Since the universe consists of ten bodies, namely, the five stars, the earth and the counter earth, then the universe must be represented by the perfect number ten.

(b) Applied to the space around us, but called by Pythagoreans the Boundless or Unlimited, it must be taken to mean, the measuring out of this Boundless, into a balanced and harmonious universe, so that everything might receive its proper proportion of it. No more, no less.

(c) This arrangement seems to suggest the notion of forms capable of receiving a mathematical expression, i.e., a doctrine which later appeared in Plato, as the theory of Ideas.

(d) In the centre of the universe there is a central fire around which the heavenly bodies fixed in their spheres, revolve from West to East, while around all there is the peripheral fire.

This motion of the heavenly bodies is regulated in the velocity, and produces the harmony of the spheres.

(Roger's Students' History of Philosophy p. 14–22).

(Bakewell's Source Book of Philosophy) (Life and Tenets of Pythagoras).

(Ruddick's History of Philosophy) (Life and Tenets of Pythagoras).

(Fuller's History of Philosophy) (Life and Tenets of Pythagoras).

(Turner's History of Philosophy: p. 40–43).

(History of Ancient Egypt by John Kendrick vol. I p. 401-402)

(Plato's Phaedo, 85E).

(Aristotle's Metaphysics I 5; 985b, 24; and I 5; 986a, 23).

3. The Eleatic Philosophers. The Eleatic Philosophers include (a) Xenophanes, (b) Parmenides, (c) Zeno and (d) Melissus. They deal with the problem of change, and are credited with introducing the notions of Being and Becoming. The term Eleatic is derived from Elea, a city in Southern Italy, where these men are said only to have visited.

(a) XENOPHANES

Born at Colophon, in Asia Minor, about 370 B.C., Xenophanes is credited with the following doctrines:—

(i) THE UNITY OF GOD

Men err when they ascribe their own characteristics to the gods: for God is all eye, all ear, and all intellect. Again, since there is no Becoming, and since Plurality depends upon Becoming, therefore there is no Plurality. Consequently all is one and one is all.

(ii) TEMPERANCE

Against the artificial culture of Greece, its luxuries, excess and fops; Xenophanes is credited with advocating Temperance i.e., plain living, simplicity, moderation, and pure thinking.

Roger's Students' History of Philosophy: p. 27–28.

Wm. Turner's History of Philosophy: p. 45–46.

Zeller's History of Philosophy: p. 58–60.

(b) PARMENIDES

Is said to have been born at Elea 540 B.C. and to have composed a poem concerning nature: peri physeos, which contains his doctrines.

A. THE POEM consists of three parts:—

(i) In part one, the Goddess of truth points out that there are two paths of knowledge: one leading to a knowledge of truth, and the other to a knowledge of the opinions of men.

(ii) In part two, the journey to truth is described and contains a metaphysical doctrine, and in part three, a cosmology of the apparent.

B. THE DOCTRINES are as follows:—

(i) The Physical Doctrine.

Though right reason (logos) holds that Being is one and immutable, the senses and common opinion (doxa) are convinced that plurality and change exist around us.

(ii) The Doctrine of Truth.

Truth consists of the knowledge that Being is, and that not-Being is not: and since not-Being is,not, then Being is one and alone.

Consequently, Being is unproduced and unchangeable. It is impossible for Being to produce Being; for under such circumstances Being must exist before it begins to exist.

(iii) The doctrine of the Cosmology of the Apparent.

Here Parmenides simply repeats the Pythagorean doctrine of opposites:—

All things are composed of light or warmth, and of darkness or cold, and according to Aristotle, the former of these opposites corresponds to Being, while the latter to not-Being.

These opposites are equivalent to the male and female principles in the cosmos.

(iv) The Doctrine of the Anthropology of the Apparent:—The life of the soul, i.e., perception and reflexion, depends upon the blending of opposites, i.e., of the light-warm and the dark-cold principles, each of which stands in a physical relation to a corresponding principle in the cosmos.

(Zeller's History of Philosophy p. 60–62).

(Roger's Students' History of Philosophy p. 29–30).

(William Turner's History of Philosophy p. 47–48). (B. D. Alexander's History of Philosophy p. 22–24).

(c) ZENO

Supposed to be born 490 B.C. at Elea was a pupil of Parmenides, according to Plato. (Parmenides 127B).

His doctrines were intended to be a contradiction of (i) Motion and (ii) Plurality and space.

(i) Arguments against motion:—

(a) A body, in order to move from one point to another, must move through an infinite number of spaces since magnitude is divisible ad infinitum.

(b) A body which is in one place is at rest. An arrow in its flight, is at each successive moment in one place therefore it is at rest.

(c) The race between Achilles and the tortoise, is intended to contradict the concept of motion. In such a race Achilles can never overtake the tortoise, because he must first reach the point at which the tortoise started; but in the meantime the tortoise will have gained more ground. Since Achilles must always reach first the position previously occupied by the tortoise, the tortoise must always keep ahead, at every point.

(ii) Arguments against Plurality and Space:—

(a) If a measure of corn produces a sound, then each grain

ought to produce a sound. (This argument is taken from Simplicus: but ascribed to Zeno.)

(b) If Being exists in space. then space itself must exist in space, and the process will have to go on ad infinitum. (This argument is also taken from Simplicus.)

(c) If magnitude exists, it must be infinitely great and infinitely small, at one and the same time, since it has an infinitude of parts which are indivisible. Therefore the idea of the manifold is contradictory.

(William Turner's History of Philosophy p. 49–50).

(Roger's Students' History of Philosophy p. 31–32).

(Zeller's History of Philosophy p. 63–64).

4. The Later Ionian School: (a) Heraclitus, (b) Anaxagoras, (c) Democritus.

(a) HERACLITUS

Believed to have been born B.C. 530. and to have died in 470 B.C. Heraclitus, a native of Ephesus, in Asia Minor, has been credited with the following doctrines:—

(i) THE DOCTRINE OF UNIVERSAL FLUX

There is no static Being, and no Unchanging element. Change is Lord of the Universe. The underlying element of the universe is Fire, and all things are changed for Fire, and Fire for all things.

(a) The change is not at random; but uniform, orderly and cyclic. Thus the heavenly Fires are transmuted successively, into vapour, water and earth; only to go through a similar process as they ascend again into Fire.

(b) It contains the elements both of the old and new, at any given moment in the process. Consequently, where night ends, there day begins; where summer begins, there spring ends; and where mortal life ends, there spiritual life begins.

(c) It also consists in the generation which results from the union of opposites (a doctrine. later to be found in Plato and Socrates).

Hence we observe that the union of male and female produces

Stolen Legacy

organic life; and that sharp and flat notes produce harmony.

(ii) THE THEORY OF KNOWLEDGE

Since sense-knowledge, or knowledge derived from the senses is illusion, it must be avoided, and true knowledge sought for in the perception of the underlying unity of the various opposites.

This is possible for man, who is part of the all comprehending Fire, which underlies the Universe.

But in the doctrine of the upward and downward paths, true knowledge comes from the upward path which leads to the eternal Fire: whereas folly and death are the result of following the downward path.

(iii) THE DOCTRINE OF THE LOGOS

That the hidden harmony of nature ever reproduces concord from oppositions, that the divine law (dikē) or universal reason (logos) rules all things; and that the primitive essence recomposes itself anew in all things according to fixed laws, and is again restored by them.

(Zeller's History of Philosophy p. 68).

(A. B. Turner's History of Philosophy p. 66–77). (Zeller's History of Philosophy p. 66–71).

(William Turner's History of Philosophy p. 53–58).

(b) THE LIFE AND TEACHINGS OF ANAXAGORAS

Anaxagoras, a native of Clazomenae, in Ionia, is supposed to have been born in 500 B.C. Like all the other philosophers, nothing is known about his early life and education. He comes into history through a visit to Athens, where he met and made the friendship of Pericles, and where he was charged with impiety. He however escaped from prison and fled back to his home in Ionia where he died in 430 B.C.

His doctrines included the following:—

(i) Nous i.e., mind alone is self-moved, and is the cause of motion in everything in the universe, and has supreme power over all things. (William Turner's History of Philosophy, p. 63); (Zeller's Hist. of Phil. p. 85; 86).

(ii) Sensation is produced by the stimulation of opposites. We experience the sensation of cold, because of the heat in us, and we experience a sweet taste because of the sour in us. (Wm. Turner's Hist. of Phil. p. 64; Theophrastus: de Sensu, Fragment 27: Zeller's Hist. of Phil. p. 86).

N.B.

These doctrines will be treated elsewhere, as regards their source and authorship.

(c) THE LIFE AND TEACHINGS OF DEMOCRITUS

(1) HIS LIFE

Democritus (420–316 B.C.) is said to have been the son of Hegesistratus, and also a native of Abdera, a city at Miletus, an island in the Aegean.

Both Aristotle and Theophrastus have regarded Leucippus as the founder of atomism, in spite of the fact that his existence is doubted. Like all the other Greek philosophers, nothing seems to be known about his early life and training. However he enters history as a magician and sorcerer.

(Burnet, op. cit. p. 350; Wm. Turner's Hist. of Phil. p. 65).

(2) HIS DOCTRINES

The name of Democritus has been associated with the following doctrines, summarized as atomism in his explanation of (i) the nature of the atoms, and their behavior in relation to the phenomena of (ii) creation (iii) life and death and (iv) sensation and knowledge

(i) The Description of the Atom

(a) The world-stuff. The atom is explained as a colorless, transparent and homogeneous powder, consisting of an infinite number of particles.

(b) Their Qualities: The atom is described as full or solid, invisible, indestructible, un-created and capable self-motion. The atoms differ in shape, order, position, quantity and weight.

(c) The Identity of the Atom with Reality: Every atom is equivalent to "that which is (i.e. To on); and the void is equivalent to "that which is not" (i.e., To mē on). Reality is the movement of "that which is," within that-which is not.

(ii) The Atom in Creation.

Owing to the difference in size, weight and mobility, and in particular to necessity, there is a resultant motion, by means of which the atoms combine themselves for the formation of the organic and inorganic worlds.

(iii) The Atoms in the Phenomena of Life and Death.

What we commonly call life and death, are due to a change in the arrangement of the atoms. When they are arranged in a certain way, life emerges; but when that arrangement is changed to another way, then death is the result.

In death, the personality disappears, the senses also disappear; but the atoms live on for ever. The heavier atoms descend to the earth: but the soul atoms, which are composed of fire, ascend to the celestial regions, whence they came.

(iv) The Atom in Sensation and Knowledge

(a) The Mind or Soul is composed of fire atoms, which are the finest, the smoothest, and the most mobile. These fire atoms are distributed throughout the whole universe; and in all animate things, and especially in the human body, where they are found in the largest numbers.

(b) External objects constantly give off emanations or minute images of themselves. These in turn impress themselves upon our senses, which set in motion our Soul atoms, and thereby create Sensation and Knowledge.

(Diogenes Laertius Book IX p. 443–455).

(Wm. Turner's History of Philosophy p. 65–70).

(Roger's Students History of Philosophy p. 40–42).

(Zeller's History of Philosophy p. 76–83).

(B. D. Alexander's History of Philosophy p. 37–41).

5. Summary of Conclusions Concerning the Pre-Socratic Philosophers and the History of the Four Qualities and Four Elements. I. The early Ionic philosophers have been given the credit of teaching the following doctrines (a) Thales, that all things originated from

water, (b) Anaximander, that all things originated from Primitive matter, i.e., the boundless (to apeiron), and (c) Anaximenes, that all things get their life from air. But these ideas were not new at the time when these men are supposed to have lived, i.e., between the sixth and fifth centuries B.C. The creation story, found in the book of Genesis, speaks of the elements of water, air and earth as the cosmic ingredients of the chaos out of which creation gradually developed. The date of the Pentateuch is placed at the eighth century B.C.; but the view of the Mosaic authorship of Genesis takes us still further back into antiquity, and many centuries before the time of the Ionian philosophers. We are told not only by the bible, but also by the historian Philo, that Moses was an Initiate of the Egyptian Mysteries and became a Hierogrammat; learned in all the wisdom of the Egyptian people. This was only possible by proper initiation and gradual advancement, when evidence of fitness was demonstrated by the Neophyte. The Egyptian name of Moses was given to all candidates at their baptism, and meant "saved by water".

The Exodus of the Israelites appears to have occurred in the 21st Egyptian Dynasty, i.e., 1100 B.C. in the reign of Bocchoris under the leadership of Moses, whose creation story of Genesis is clearly of Egyptian origin. It is clear that the early Ionic Philosophers drew their teachings from Egyptian sources.

(Chaeremon: Jos. C. Apion I, 32; Philo; Ancient Mysteries C. H. Vail p. 61; John Kendrick's Ancient Egypt vol. 2 p. 268–270; 303; See also Dr. Hasting's Bible Dictionary, on authorship and date of Pentateuch).

II. In the case of the Eleatic philosophers, history regards Zenophanes as a Satirist, not a philosopher, and Zeno as paradoxical concerning his treatment of the problems of plurality, space and motion, which ultimately leads to a reductio ad absurdum. Parmenides introduced no new teaching when he spoke of Being (To on) as that which exists; and Non-Being (To mē on) as that which does not exist. He only reemphasized the doctrine of opposites as a principle of nature: a doctrine taught not only by the Pythagoreans, but also the Athenian philosophers, chiefly Socrates. But the doctrine of opposites owes its origin to the Egyptian Mysteries which take us back to 4000 B.C. when it was demonstrated not only by double pillars in front of temples, but also by the pairs of Gods in the Mystery System, representing male and female, positive and negative principles of nature. It is also clear that the Eleatic Philosophers drew their teachings from Egyptian sources.

(Plato Phaedo; Memphite Theology: Intellectual Adventure of Primitive Man by Frankfort p. 55; 66–67; 51–60. Plutarch: Isis et Osiris, p. 364C; 355A; 371B; 868, Ancient Egypt: John Kendrick vol. I p. 339).

III. The later Ionic philosophers have been given credit for the following doctrines:

(1) Heraclitus, (a) that the world was produced by fire through a process of transmutation, and (b) since all things originate from fire, then Fire is the Logos: The Creator.

(2) Anaxagoras (a) the Nous or mind is the source of motion or life in the universe and that sensation is produced by the stimulation of opposites.

(3) Democritus (a) that atoms under-lie all material things, and (b) that the phenomena of life and death are merely changes in the mixture of the atoms, so that the atoms never die, because they are immortal.

These doctrines were by no means produced by the late Ionic philosophers, but could be shown to have originated from the Egyptian Mystery System. The Egyptians were fire worshippers, because they believed that fire was the creator of the universe, and built their great pyramids (pyr = fire) in order to worship the God of Fire, and the pyramid age goes back to something like 3300 B.C., several thousands of years before the Greeks were said to have come into the Mediterranean area.

According to Jamblichus the Egyptian God Ptah was the God of order and form in creation, an Intellectual Principle. This God was also recognized as the Divine Artificer who fashioned the universe out of fire.

Rosellini: mon del sults; John Kendrick's Ancient Egypt vol. I p. 318.

Furthermore, Swinburne Clymer in his Philosophy of Fire p. 18 has made the following statement "The study of the Mysteries of Isis and Osiris (Egyptian Goddess and God) quickly proves to the student that it was a pure Fire Philosophy. Zoroaster carried those mysteries into Greece, while Orpheus carried them into Thrace. In each of these places, these Egyptian mysteries assumed the names of different Gods in order to be adapted to local conditions. Hence in Asia they took the form of Mithra: in Samothrace, the form of the Mother of the Gods; in Boeotia, the form of Bacchus; in Crete, the form of Jupiter; in Athens, the forms of Ceres and Proserpine.

The most noted of these Egyptian imitations were the Orphic, Bacchic, Eleusinian, Samothracian, and Mithraic. All of these Fire Worshippers, believed that the universe originated from Fire, and they lived at a time which antedated the time of the late Ionic philosophers by thousands of years.

The other doctrines of the later Ionic philosophers together with those of Socrates, Plato and Aristotle will be treated under Summaries of Socrates, Plato and Aristotle and in Chapter VIII, and will include (1) Opposites (2) The nous or mind (3) The Logos, (4) The Atom, (5) The Theory of Ideas, (6) The Unmoved Mover, (7) Immortality.

IV. The Greek Philosophers practised plagiarism.

The teachings of Pythagoras seem to have been so comprehensive that nearly all his successors embraced and taught a portion of his doctrine, which we are told he obtained by frequent visits which he made to Egypt for the purpose of his education. Two things are at once obvious, (1) that the Greek philosophers practiced plagiarism and did not teach anything new and (2) the source of their teachings was the Egyptian Mystery System, either directly through contact with Egypt, or indirectly through Pythagoras or tradition. These facts can now be further demonstrated by an outline of the doctrines of Pythagoras, with the names of philosophers who repeated his doctrines:

1. The Doctrine of Opposites: the unit of number is composed both of odd and even elements; of the finite and infinite; and of the positive and negative. In this connection, we find (a) Heraclitus suggesting fire to be the source of creation, by means of the principle of strife which separates phenomena; and harmony which restores them to their original source. (William Turner's History of Philosophy p. 55; Zeller's Hist. of Phil. p. 67–68). (b) Parmenides, suggesting Being as existent and Non-Being as non-existent (Zeller's Hist. of Phil. p. 61; Turner's Hist. of Phil. p. 48). (c) Socrates, attempting to prove the immortality of the Soul by the doctrine of opposites (Plato Phaedo). (d) Plato, attempting to explain nature, used the Theory of Ideas which he based upon the principle of opposites. Consequently the Idea is true reality, i.e., Being (To

on); hence the concept is real; but the thing which is known by the concept is unreal. The noumen is real and perfect; but the phenomenon is unreal and imperfect (Parmenides 132D; Aristotle Meta 16, 987b9). (e) Aristotle in attempting to establish the existence of God, describes the divine attributes in terms of opposites. God is the First Mover that is unmoved (proton kinoûn akineton). Hence, we have a combination of motion and rest, as the attributes of Deity and Nature. (Aristotle's physics VIII 5, 256a; II 1; 192b 14; II 8, 199; de caelo I 4, 271a; Wm. Turner's Hist. of Phil. p. 141).

2. The Doctrine of Harmony, as a union of opposites, after being expounded by Pythagoras, appears also in the systems of (a) Heraclitus, who explains the phenomena of nature as passing successively through their opposites; (b) Socrates, who also defines harmony as the union of opposites; (c) Plato, who defines the harmony of the soul as the proper subordination of its parts, i.e., the higher and lower natures. (Turner's Hist. of Phil. p. 41; 56; Zeller's Hist. of Phil. p. 51; 69; Plato Phaedo C 15; Plato Republic); also (d) Aristotle, who defines the soul as a harmony in his de animo I. 2.

3. The Central and Peripheral Fires. Here Pythagoras attempts to show that fire under-lies creation, and this same notion is expressed by (a) Heraclitus, who speaks of the origin of the universe through the transformation of fire. Then we have (b) Anaxagoras (c) Democritus (d) Socrates and (e) Plato, each using the term mind (nous) as responsible for creation. Anaxagoras and Socrates who speak directly of mind (nous) as an Intelligence and purpose behind nature; while Democritus and Plato speak of mind (nous) indirectly as the World Soul, but further describe it as being composed of fire atoms floating throughout space. Clearly then, Mind (nous), no matter what other name or function we give it, is fire, since it is composed of fire atoms; and fire according to Pythagoras underlies creation. (Wm. Turner's Hist. of Phil. p. 42, 55, 63, 82; Zeller's Hist. of Phil. p. 53, 67, 76–83; Aristotle: Metaphysics I, 3, 984b, 17; Diogenes Laertius: Bk. X. p. 443–453; Xenophon Memorabilia I, 4, 2; Plato Timaeus: 30, 35; Roger's Student Hist. of Phil. p. 40–42; B. D. Alexander's Hist. of Phil. p. 43).

4. Immortality of the Soul. According to Pythagoras, the doctrine of the immortality of the Soul is implied in the doctrine of the Transmigration of the Soul:—

A. Socrates: The purpose of philosophy is the salvation of the Soul, whereby it feeds upon the truth congenial to its divine nature and thus escapes from the wheel of rebirth, and finally attains the consummation of unity with God. (Zeller's Hist. of Phil. p. 50–56; Roger's Hist. of Phil. p. 29 and 60: William Turner's Hist. of Phil. p. 41 and 48).

B. Plato's doctrines (1) Transmigration and (2) Recollection: (1) Transmigration: the souls of men go to the place of reward or punishment, and after one thousand years they are permitted to choose a new lot of life. He who has thrice chosen the higher life, gains after three thousand years, the home of the Gods in the kingdom of thought. Others wander about for thousands of years in various bodies; and many are destined to pursue their earthly life in lower animal forms. It is necessary to point out that in this doctrine of Transmigration, Plato describes the judgement scene in the Egyptian Book of the Dead. (2) Recollection: although the sense perceived world cannot lead us to a knowledge of Ideas, yet it reminds us of the Ideas which we saw in a previous existence.

(The allegory of the Subterranean Cavern; Plato's Republic C. X; The Allegory of the slave boy; Plato's Meno; Timaeus of Plato: 31B, 33B; 38E; The Phaedo of Plato: C 15; 29; 57; Wm. Turner's Hist. of Phil. P. 105–112; B. D. Alexander's Hist. of Phil. p. 55; 152–153).

5. Summum Bonum

According to Pythagoras. the supreme good in man is to become godlike. This transformation is to be accomplished by virtue which is a union of opposites in man's faculties, i.e., the subordination of man's lower nature to his higher nature. (Zeller's Hist. of Phil. p. 43). But the precise purpose of the Egyptian Mysteries was to make a man godlike by the purificatory agencies of education and virtue. Consequently it is clear that Pythagoras obtained this doctrine directly from the Egyptian Mysteries. Hence it also follows that philosophers who have taught this doctrine, must have obtained it, either directly from the Egyptian Mysteries, or indirectly, through the teachings of Pythagoras. (According to Sallust, Deification or becoming godlike was the purpose of the Egyptian Mysteries, and according to C. H. Vail in his Ancient Mysteries, the Egyptian Summum Bonum consisted of five stages, during which the Neophyte developed from a good man into a triumphant Master, attaining the highest spiritual consciousness by means of casting off the ten bodily fetters and becoming an adept like Horus or Buddha or Christ).

The philosophers, besides Pythagoras, who are given credit

with having taught the doctrine of the Supreme Good, are (a) Socrates, who defined it as an attainment in which man becomes godlike, through self-denial and the cultivation of the mind. (Xenophon Memorabilia I, 5, 4,) (b) Plato who defined it as happiness which is the attainment of the Idea of the Good, which is God. (Plato: Symposium 204E; Plato: Republic IV, 441, 443; Plato: Phaedo 64 sqq; Plato: Theaetetus 176 A). (c) Aristotle; who defined it as happiness which is based upon reason and which includes all the gifts of fortune. It should be noted however that Aristotle's definition of the Supreme Good marks the first departure from the concept of the Summum Bonum of the Egyptian Mysteries; and the same thing is true of the Hedonists, who defined it as pleasure. (Wm. Turner's Hist. of Phil. p. 153. Aristotle Ethics, Nic I, 6, 1097; Aristotle Ethics, Nic I, 9, 1099a, 31) The conception of a Supreme Good is Egyptian, from which source Pythagoras and other philosophers obtained the doctrine.

V. SUMMARY OF CONCLUSIONS CONCERNING DEMOCRITUS

Because of the importance of the doctrine of the atom, and the great suspicion of his great number of books like that of Aristotle, Democritus is treated separately, like each of the Athenian philosophers.

1. HIS LIFE:

The same thing might be said of Democritus as might be said of any of the men who were called Greek philosophers: nothing appears to be known about his early life and training. However he comes into history attracting public attention, as a sorcerer and magician. (Turner's Hist. of Phil. p. 65).

2. HIS DOCTRINES AND AUTHORSHIP:

(i) Authorship: The authorship of the doctrine of the atom is doubtful, from the standpoint or view of certain modern writers. The names of the Ionians Leucippus and Democritus have been associated with this doctrine, which according to the opinion of Aristotle and Theophrastus, originated through Leucippus, but was developed by Democritus.

As a matter of fact, the Ionians doubted the existence of Leucippus because he was unknown to them; and it seems proper that the opinion of the Ionians should receive credence rather than that of Aristotle and Theophrastus, who were Athenians, and who were compiling philosophy in the interest of their movement.

(Burnet op. cit. p. 350; Turner's Hist. of Phil. p. 65).

(ii) The doctrine concerning the Atom is eclectic.

The doctrine of the atom as explained by Democritus, is eclectic, and represents one of the many forms in which the ancient doctrine of opposites has been expressed. The Pythagoreans expressed it by the elements of number: odd and even.

Parmenides being unfamiliar with the law of generation, denied the existence of one opposite (not-Being), in order to affirm the existence of the other (being).

Socrates, being more acquainted with the law of generation than Parmenides, expressed it in several pairs of opposites, in an effort to prove the immortality of the soul: hence he spoke of unity and duality; of division and composition; of life and death.

In like manner Democritus expressed the doctrine of opposites, when he described Reality by the life of the atom, i.e., a movement of "that which is" (To on) within "that which is not" (To mē on).

The original source of this doctrine however, is the philosophy of the Mystery System of Egypt where we find the male and female principles of nature symbolized by (a) Osiris and Isis: the Egyptian God and Goddess, and (b) the Gods Homs and Seth, symbolizing a world in static equilibrium of conflicting forces, as they contend for dominion over Egypt.

(Memphite Theology: Kingship and the Gods by Frankfort C. 3, p. 25–26; 35: Herodotus I, 6–26; Ancient Egypt by John Kendrick Bk. I p. 339; Egyptian Religion by Frankfort, p. 64, 73 and 88; Zeller's Hist. of Phil. p. 61; Wm. Turner's Hist. of Phil. p. 41; Plato Phaedo C. 15, 16, 49).

The doctrine and philosophy of opposites is further demonstrated by the Egyptian Creation story, in which Order came out of Chaos and which was represented by four pairs of opposites i.e., male and female gods.

(a) Nun and Naunet i.e., primeval Matter and Space.

(b) Huk and Hauket i.e., Illimitable and the Boundless.

(c) Huh and Hauhet, i.e., Darkness and Obscurity.

Stolen Legacy

(d) Amon and Amaunet, i.e., the hidden and concealed ones (the Air, Wind).

Clearly the doctrine of opposites was a basic philosophy of the Egyptians, being connected with not only the Gods of their Mystery dramas, but with their Cosmology, and since this connection makes the doctrine one of the earliest in the development of Egyptian thought, it antedates the reign of Menes, and means that the Egyptians were familiar with it before 3000 B.C.

Under these circumstances and in consequence of these facts, the Egyptian Mystery System was the source of the doctrines (a) of the atom and (b) of opposites. Leucippus and Democritus taught nothing new and must have obtained their knowledge of the doctrines from the Egyptians, directly or indirectly.

(iii) The Doctrines of the universal distribution of fire atoms, and their emanation from external objects are derived from Magic:—

These doctrines are magical and express the magical principle "that the qualities of animals or things are distributed throughout all their parts." (Dr. Frazer's Golden Bough). Consequently within the universe contact is established between objects through emanations, and in the case of human beings, the result might be sensation or cognition; healing or contagion.

This principle is demonstrated not only by the cures such as were affected by the garment of Christ, and the handkerchiefs of St. Paul: but also by the modern scientific and medical practice of the preventive measure of quarantine. It must be remembered that magic was part of the education of the Egyptian priests: for the religious rites and ceremonies of the Egyptians were magical; and the priests were the custodians of the knowledge.

(iv) A fourth point is the fact that in the history and compilation of Greek philosophy by Aristotle and his followers, there are only two men whose names are associated with the authorship of an extraordinary number of scientific books; and the names of these men are Democritus himself and Aristotle.

(Diogenes Laertius Bk. 9 p. 445-461; Bk. 5 p. 465-467).

(v) A fifth point which deserves important mention is the fact that in the history and compilation of Greek philosophy by Aristotle and his followers, it has been discovered that wherever there has been the possession of a large collection of scientific books, there has also been direct or indirect association with Alexander the Great.

(vi) The association between Democritus and Alexander the Great is seen through the Democritean Circle; a succession of Teachers and students, from a common original Teacher:—Democritus (420–316 B.C.) is said to have taught Metrodorus of Chios, who in turn is said to have taught Anaxarchus, who is said to have flourished at the time of the 110th Olympiad (340–337 B.C.), and to have accompanied Alexander the Great on his campaign against Egypt 333 B.C.

Here, it is easy to see the tie between Democritus and Anaxarchus for these men were all Ionians, and members of the same school and were alive at the time of Alexander's Conquest of Egypt. (Zeller's Hist. of Phil. p. 83; Diogenes Laertius Bk. 2, p. 471).

On the other hand, Aristotle's contact with Alexander the Great is well known, since he was a tutor of the young prince, at the Macedonian palace. Roger's Student Hist. of Phil. p. 104).

(vii) Circumstantial evidence points to the fact that the books of Democritus were not written by him, nor did they contain his teachings. This is so, for the following reasons:—

(a) Leucippus, whom the Ionians did not know, and whose existence has been questioned, has been given credit by Aristotle for the origin of the doctrine of the atom. (Zeller's Hist. of Phil. p. 77; Burnet, op. cit. p. 350) (Wm. Turner's Hist. of Phil. P. 65; Diogenes Bk. X, 13).

(b) Apart from what was written on the Atom, the name of Democritus is, associated with a large list of books, dealing with over sixty different subjects, and covering all the branches of science known to the ancient world. In addition to this vast field of knowledge, the list also contains books on Military Science, Law and Magic. Clearly, the accumulation of such a vast range of knowledge, by a single individual, written in a single lifetime is impossible both physically and mentally. The method among the ancients of imparting knowledge was by gradual stages, followed by evidence of proficiency, which in turn was also followed by initiations, which marked every step in the progress of the Neophyte.

The progress of training was slow and no Neophyte could accomplish such knowledge in his life time as took the Egyptians over five thousand years to accumulate. These human limitations are as true today as they were among the ancients; for our great scientists of the Modern World are specialists only in single subjects.

(c) The question now remains: how did Democritus accumulate those books if he did not write them? We believe we have the answer because it has been noticed in the history of Greek philosophy that (a) wherever a Greek philosopher has had association, direct or indirect, with Alexander the Great, there was also the possession of a large collection of scientific books, and (b) this is true in the cases of Democritus and Aristotle. (c) Anaxarchus and Democritus were Ionians, who belonged to the same school and (d) Anaxarchus accompanied Alexander the Great on his campaign against Egypt. (The indirect association between Democritus and Alexander the Great now becomes obvious.) (e) It follows that since Alexander's conquest of Egypt had brought the Greeks their long hoped for opportunity, i.e., access to the Egyptian Library and Museum, we would naturally expect Alexander and his friends, and the invading armies to have helped themselves with the Egyptian books. We would also expect Anaxarchus upon his return to Ionia, to have sold, at least a portion of his loot, to Democritus, (nor do we expect Aristotle and Theophrastus to relate these facts to us), since under the rules of the Mysteries, knowledge (spoken or written,) could be diffused only by brethren among brethren. This we believe is the way Democritus came to possess such a large number of scientific books.

Again it must be stated that Democritus taught nothing new, but simply what he had learnt from the Egyptians, directly or indirectly.

His doctrine on the universal distribution of fire atoms is based upon a magical principle: if the atom is an ingredient of the world, then it would be universally distributed.

Furthermore, Democritus enters history as a magician, and since there is historical evidence that he visited the Egyptian priests, it is evident that magic was part of the training which he must have received from them.

(Antisthenes: Treatise on Succession; Herodotus; Origen; Diogenes Laertius: Bk. 9 p. 443; Zeller's Hist. of Phil. p. 77).

3. His Books are doubtful in authorship.

Several important facts must be noted in connection with the books which are said to have been written by Democritus:—

(a) A large number of books which appears in a list in the 9th Book of Diogenes, Laertius, does not appear elsewhere in the usual textbooks on the history of Greek Philosophy; while Zeller asserts that the genuineness of these books cannot be determined upon the evidence of the fragments. (Zeller's Hist. of Phil. p. 77). It seems that his list of publications remains doubtful in authorship.

(b) More than 60 different subjects are treated and they include Ethics, Physics, Astronomy, Botany, Zoology, Poetry, Medicine, Dialectics, Military Science, and Law; also books on Magic, including divination.

(c) We are informed by Diogenes Laertius that this large list of books was compiled by Thrasyllus (about 20 A.D.) who was a student of the school of Plato, and also a member of Aristotle's movement, which had for its purpose, the compilation of Greek philosophy. (Zeller's Hist. of Phil. p. 13–14) (Diogenes Laertius Bk. 9 p. 455–461).

VI. The Four Qualities and Four Elements.

The history of the following ancient theory of "The Four Qualities and Four Elements", provides the world with the evidence of the Egyptian origin of the doctrines of (a) Opposites or Contraries, (b) Change or Transmutation and (c) the life and function of the universe is due to either of four elements: fire, or water, or earth or air.

1. This ancient theory was expressed by a diagram formed by outer and inner squares.

2. The corners of the outer square carried the names of the elements: fire, water, earth and air.

3. The corners of the inner square, being at the mid points of the sides of the outer square, carried the four fundamental qualities, the hot, the dry, the cold and the wet.

4. The diagram explains that fire is hot and dry; earth is dry and cold; water is cold and wet; and air is wet and hot.

5. Accordingly water is an embodiment of cold and wet qualities, and when the cold quality is replaced by the hot quality, the element water is changed into the element air, with the wet and hot qualities.

6. Consequently, transmutation is definitely implied in the teaching of this symbol.

7. It is the oldest teaching of physical science and has been traced to the Egyptians, as far back as 5000 B.C.

8. It shows that Plato and Aristotle (who had been credited with the authorship of this teaching) derived their doctrines or portions of them from the Egyptians. (Rosicrucian Digest, May 1952, p. 175).

CHAPTER VI

The Athenian Philosophers.

1. Socrates: (i) His Life (ii) Doctrines (iii) Summary of Conclusions.
(i) LIFE OF SOCRATES (a) Date and place of birth.

Socrates was born in Athens, in the year 469 B.C. He was the son of Sophroniscus, a sculptor, and Phaenarete, a midwife. Very little is known about his early years; but we are told that he was brought up in the profession of his father, and that he called himself not only a pupil of Prodicus and Aspasia, (which statement suggests that he might have learnt from them, music, geometry and gymnastics): but also a self taught philosopher, according to Xenophon in the Symposium. Up to the age of 40, his life appears to be a complete blank: the first mention being made of him, when he served as an ordinary soldier in the sieges of Potidaea and Delium between (432–429) B.C. (Trial and Death of Socrates: F. J. Church: p. 15 of Introduction).

(b) His economic status and personality.

Socrates did not accept fees for what he taught, and he became so poor, that his wife Xanthippe became very dissatisfied with domestic conditions.

He believed that he possessed (Daimonion Ti) a divine something, i.e., a divine voice which advised and guided him in the great crises of his life. (Turner's Hist. of Phil. p. 78–79; and Plato's Apology).

(c) His Condemnation and death in 399 B.C.

After the accustomed speeches of the accusers: (Miletus, Anytus and Lycon); Socrates followed with his defense, at the conclusion of which, the judges voted 281 to 220, and Socrates was condemned to death.

As a parting word, he addressed himself both to those who voted against him, and those who voted in his favour. In the case of the former, he rebuked them by predicting that evil would befall them, in consequence of their crime in condemning him.

In the case of the latter, he not only consoled them with the assurance that no evil could come to a good man either in life or in death; but also expressed to them his idea about immortality.

"Death is either an eternal and dreamless sleep, wherein there is no sensation at all; or it is a journey to another, and a better world, where are the famous men of old". Whichever alternative be true, death is not an evil, but a good. His death is willed by the gods, and he is content. (Plato's Apology Chapters 25–28).

His death was delayed through a state religious ceremonial, and he remained in prison for 30 days. We are told that during this time, he was visited by his friends, who consisted of the inner circle, and also his wife Xanthippe; that this was the occasion of his discourse concerning the immortality of the soul; that he could have escaped from death if he wished; because his friends visited him before day-break and offered to set him free; but that he refused the offer. Accordingly Socrates drank the hemlock and died. (Plato Phaedo;) (Xenophon Memorabilia IV, 8, 2).

(d) Crito's account:

Crito, on the night before the death of Socrates, while he was in prison, on behalf of the company of visitors, made a final appeal to him to permit them to secure his escape, and spoke as follows:—

"O, my Socrates, I beseech you for the last time to listen to me and save yourself. For to me your death will be more than a single disaster: not only shall I lose a friend the like of whom I shall never find again, but many persons, who do not know you and me well, will think that I might have saved you, if I had been willing to spend money, but that I neglected to do so. And what character could be more disgraceful than the character of caring more for money than for one's friends? The world will never believe that we were anxious to save you, but that you yourself refused to escape.

"Tell me this Socrates. Surely you are not anxious about me and your other friends, and afraid, lest, if you escape, the informers should say that we stole you away, and get us into trouble, and involve us in a great deal of expense, or perhaps in the loss of all our property, and it may be, bring some other punishment upon us besides? If you have any fear of that kind, dismiss it.

"For of course we are bound to run those risks, and still greater risks than those if necessary, in saving you. So do not, I beseech you, refuse to listen to me."

Then Socrates replied: "I am anxious about that, Crito, and about much besides," and Crito continued the appeal:—

"Then have no fear on that score. There are men who, for no very large sum, are ready to bring you out of prison into safety, and then, you know, these informers are cheaply bought, and there will be no need to spend much on them.

"My fortune is at your disposal, and I think that it is sufficient, and if you have any feeling about making use of my money, there are strangers in Athens, whom you know, ready to use theirs, and one of them, Simmias of Thebes, who actually brought enough for the purpose. And Cebes and many others, are ready too.

"And therefore, I repeat, do not shrink from saving yourself, on that ground. And do not let what. you said in court (that if you went into exile, you would not know what to do with yourself), stand in your way: for there are many places for you to go to, where you will be welcomed.

"If you choose to go to Thessaly, I have friends there who will make much of you, and shelter you from any annoyance from the people of Thessaly.

"Consider then, Socrates; or rather the time for consideration is past; we must resolve, and there is only one plan possible. Everything must be done tonight. If we delay any longer, we are lost.

"O, Socrates, I implore you not to refuse to listen to me." (Plato's Crito C. 3–5).

(e) Phaedo's account of the final scene just before the death of Socrates.

In answer to another question from Echecrates, Phaedo replied: I will try to tell you the whole story:—

"On the previous days, I and the others had always met in the morning at the court, where the trial was held, which was close to the prison; and then we would go in to Socrates.

"We used to wait each morning until the prison was opened, conversing; for it was not opened early. When it was opened we used to go in to Socrates, and we generally spent the whole day with him. But on that morning we met earlier than usual, for the evening before we had learnt, on leaving the prison, that the ship had arrived from Delos. So we arranged to be at the usual place as early as possible. When we reached the prison, the porter, who generally let us in came out to us and bade us wait a little, and not to go in until he himself summoned us; for the 'Eleven' were releasing Socrates from his fetters and giving him directions for his death.

"In no great while he returned and bade us enter. So we went in and found Socrates just released. When Xanthippe saw us, she wailed aloud, and cried in her woman's way: 'This is the last time: Socrates, that you will talk with your friends, or they with you.' And Socrates glanced at Crito and said, 'Crito, let her be taken home'. So some of Crito's servants led her away; weeping bitterly and beating her breasts. And it was about sunset, and the servant of the Eleven after bidding Socrates farewell, gave him the instructions as to how to take the poison, and then handed it to him. Socrates took the cup, and drank the poison cheerfully, and then walked about until his legs felt heavy. And when he had lain down, he made his last request to Crito in the following words: I owe a cock to Asclepius, do not forget to pay it. By this time the poison took effect and he passed away." (Plato Phaedo C. 3 and 65).

(ii) THE DOCTRINES OF SOCRATES

i. The doctrine of Nous, i.e., mind or an Intelligent Cause, in order to account for God and Creation. He is credited with the teleological premise: whatever exists for a useful purpose is the work of an Intelligence. (Xenophon Memorabilia I, 4, 2; Wm. Turner's Hist. of Phil. p. 82).

ii. The doctrine of the Supreme Good:—

The Supreme good i.e., the summum bonum is equated both with happiness and with knowledge. This however is not merely eutuchia which depends upon external conditions and accidents of fortune; but is (eupraxia), a well-being, which is conditioned by good action. This is an attainment in which man becomes godlike through self denial of external needs and the cultivation of the mind: for happiness comes not through the perishable things of the external world, but through the things that endure, which are within us. (Xenophon Memorabilia I, 5, 4.) Wm. Turner's Hist. of Phil. p. 83).

iii. The doctrines of opposites and harmony:

(a) Odd and even are the elements of numbers. One is definite but the other is unlimited, and the unit is the product both of odd and even. Hence the universe consists of opposites: the finite and the infinite, the male and the female; the odd and the even; the left and right.

(b) Harmony is the union of opposites.

(Plato's Phaedo C. 15; Wm. Turner's Hist. of Phil. p. 41; 47).

(Zeller's Hist. of Phil. p. 61).

iv. The Doctrines Concerning the Soul:

(a) The immortality of the Soul

(b) The transmigration of the Soul

(c) The Salvation of the Soul:—

The purpose of philosophy is the salvation of the Soul, whereby it feeds upon the truth congenial to its divine nature, and thus escapes from the wheel of re-birth, and finally attains the consummation of unity with God. (Zeller's Hist. of Phil. p. 50–56; Roger's Hist. of Phil. p. 29 and 60; Wm. Turner's Hist. of Phil. p. 41 and 48).

(d) The body is the tomb of the Soul

(e) The aspirations of the Soul:—

There is a realm of true reality, which is above the world of sense. To this the Soul aspires.

v. The doctrine of Self-knowledge: Know thyself (seauton gnothi).

Self-knowledge is the basis of true knowledge. The Mysteries required as a first step, the mastery of the passions, which made room for the occupation of unlimited powers. Hence, as a second step, the Neophyte was required to search within himself for the new powers which had taken possession of him. The Egyptians consequently wrote on their temples: "Man, know thyself". (Zeller's Hist. of Phil. p. 105; S. Clymer's Fire Philosophy p. 203).

vi. Astrology and Geology:

There was a suspicion that Socrates was also engaged in the study of Astrology and Geology, and that he taught these subjects, for in his defense before the Athenian judges, he stated that the more formidable of his accusers tried to persuade them with lies, that one Socrates, a wise man, was speculating about the heavens and about things beneath the earth, and that he was capable of making the worse appear the better reason. (Plato's Apology C. 2).

Stolen Legacy

This suspicion is further supported by the indictment brought against Socrates, and which reads as follows:—"Miletus, the son of Miletus, of the deme Pitthis, on his oath, brings the following accusation against Socrates, the son of Sophroniscus, of the deme Alopece.

"Socrates commits a crime by not believing in the gods of the city, and by introducing new divinities. He also commits a crime by corrupting the youth. Penalty, death."

(Plato's Apology C. 24; C. 18 and 19).

There is still a third source from which the suspicion arose that Socrates was engaged also in Astrology and Geology. This was the caricature of Socrates, published by Aristophanes in his comedy: the Clouds, as follows:—

"Socrates is a miserable recluse, who speaks a great deal of absurd and amusing nonsense about Physics, and declares that Zeus is dethroned, that Rotation reigns in his stead, and that the new divinities are Air, which holds the earth suspended, Ether, the Clouds and Tongue.

"He professes to possess the power of Belial, which enables him to make the worse appear the better reason, and his teachings cause children to beat their parents."

(Aristophanes Clouds, 828 and 380; Life and Trial of Socrates; F. J. Church: Introduction p. 18).

(iii) Summary of Conclusions.

1. Life and Personality of Socrates.

There are two circumstances in the life of Socrates which demand our attention: (a) he is said to have been completely unknown up to the age of 40 and (b) to have lived a life of poverty. These circumstances point to secrecy in training, and poverty as conditions of his life; and as such, they coincide with the requirements of the Mystery System of Egypt, and her secret schools, whether in the land of Egypt or abroad, which exacted the vows of secrecy and poverty from all Neophytes and Initiates. All aspirants of the Mysteries had to receive secret training and preparation, and Socrates was no exception. He alone of the three Athenian philosophers deserves the appellation of a true Master Mason. Plato was a great coward and Aristotle was greater still. At the execution of Socrates,

Plato fled to Megara to the lodge of Euclid, and Aristotle when indicted fled in exile to Calchis.

(Clement of Alexandria: Stromata Bk. 5. C. 7 and 9; Plutarch on "Isis and Osiris" Sec. 9–11; Plato's Apology C. 8: 17; Phaedo C. 10: 13; 32; 63).

2. The Doctrines:—

(i) The doctrine of the Nous or an Intelligent Cause.

With reference to this doctrine, we find that it is also credited to Anaxagoras, who is said to have lived between 500 and 430 B.C. and who therefore antedated Socrates (469–399 B.C.) in expounding it (Wm. Turner's Hist. of Phil. p. 63; p. 82).

Secondly, further examination shows that the doctrine of the Nous is also a direct inference from the doctrine of Cognition, as credited to Democritus (460–360 B.C.), who is credited with stating that fire atoms are distributed through the universe, and that mind is composed of fire atoms.

Therefore it can be inferred (a) that mind fills or is distributed through the universe and (b) since only like can produce like, then the mind of the Universe must have been produced by a mind which is its source.

(Wm. Turner's Hist. of Phil. p. 68; Zeller's Hist. of Phil. p. 80).

Thirdly, this doctrine of the Nous, is a doctrine that originated from the Ancient Mysteries of Egypt, where the God Osiris was represented in all Egyptian temples by the symbol of an Open Eye. This symbol indicated not only sight that transcends time and space, but also the omniscience of God, as the Great Mind which created and which directs the Universe. This symbol is carried as a decoration in all modern Masonic lodges and has the same meaning. (Ancient Mysteries: C. H. Vail p. 189).

(ii) The doctrine of the Supreme Good:—

This doctrine of the Supreme Good or Summum Bonum is likewise a very ancient doctrine which takes us back to the Egyptian Mysteries.

As stated in the books on Greek philosophy and by Socrates, it is only in part, and consequently a mistaken notion of the original doctrine has resulted. To say that the supreme good is happiness, that happiness is well-being, that well-being is knowledge, and that knowledge is virtue, is the same thing as saying that the Supreme Good is virtue.

(Xenophon Memorabilia I 4, 5; Wm. Turner's Hist. of Phil. p. 81–83).

In the Egyptian Mysteries, however, the concept of the Supreme Good is expressed as the purpose of virtue, and that is the salvation of the Soul, by liberating it from the ten bodily fetters. This process of liberation is a process of purification both of mind and of body: the former by the study of philosophy and science, and the latter by bodily ascetic disciplines. This training was continued from the baptism of water, and was subsequently followed by the baptism of fire, when the candidate had made the necessary progress. This process transformed man and made him godlike, and fitted him for union with God.

The concept of the Supreme Good, which originally came from the Egyptian Mysteries is the earliest theory of salvation: and Socrates must have derived this doctrine from that source, or indirectly from the Pythagoreans.

(Plato's Phaedo C. 31; 33–34; Ancient Mysteries, C. H. Vail p. 24–25; Fire Philosophy, R. S. Clymer p. 19; 74; 80).

(iii) The following doctrines are generally admitted as having been derived from the Pythagoreans:

(a) Transmigration of the Soul

(b) The immortality of the Soul

(c) The tomb of the Soul is the body.

(d) The doctrines of opposites and harmony.

Since doctrines (a), (b), (c) and (d) originated from the Pythagoreans, and since the Pythagoreans derived them from the Egyptians, then their Egyptian origin, directly or indirectly becomes evident.

(Roger's Hist. of Phil. p. 29 and 60; Turner's Hist. of Phil. p. 41 and 48; Plato's Phaedo).

(iv) Astrology and Geology:

From (a) the indictment (b) his defense before the Athenian

Judges and (c) the caricature by Aristophanes in the Clouds, we discover that Socrates was suspected of being a student of Nature, and of introducing new divinities into Athens.

Again it must be stated, that under the Mystery System of Egypt, the study of Nature was a requirement, and since the Athenians prosecuted and condemned Socrates to death, for engaging in this study and spreading the knowledge, they must have regarded the new ideas as foreign or of Egyptian origin.

(Plato's Apology C. 24–28; Ancient Mysteries, C. H. Vail p. 24–25).

(v) The Doctrine of Self-knowledge:

The doctrine of self-knowledge, for centuries attributed to Socrates is now definitely known to have originated from the Egyptian Temples, on the outside of which the words "Man, know thyself" were written.

It is evident that Socrates taught nothing new, because his doctrines are eclectic containing elements from Anaxagoras, Democritus, Heraclitus, Parmenides and Pythagoras, and finally have been traced to the teachings of the Egyptian Mystery System.

(Fire Philosophy, S. R. Clymer p. 203).

vi) The importance of the farewell conversations of Socrates with his pupils and friends at the prison:

In examining what took place during the farewell conversations of Socrates with his pupils and friends, at least five points should be noted:—

(a) The subject of the Conversations

(b) The determination of his friends to smuggle him away

(c) His refusal to accept liberation

(d) His dying request, which was addressed to Crito, whom he asked to pay an important debt for him

(e) The value of those conversations, in their present form in literature.

Now the question arises, what is the meaning and significance of these five points? The answers and conclusions are as follows:—

(a) As the subject of the conversations dealt with the immortality and salvation of the Soul, we at once recognize the fact that this was the central theme of the Ancient Mysteries, and consequently that Socrates was acquainted with the doctrines.

Moreover, when we read the Phaedo and the doctrines, both of Opposites and Recollection which he had advanced in proof of immortality, we are convinced that he must have received his training from the Mystery System of Egypt, in connection with which there were Hierophants and qualified teachers.

(b) Secondly, in dealing with the behavior of his friends, in their determination to smuggle him away, we are dealing with their attempt to render help to a brother in distress.

This was the life that Initiates were expected to live, for brotherhood was another great principle upon which, the Egyptian Mysteries laid emphasis. Evidently, Socrates was a "Brother Initiate" of the Egyptian Mysteries, since it comprised one universal brotherhood.

(c) Thirdly, in dealing with the refusal of Socrates to accept liberation, again we are dealing with a type of behaviour, which singles him out as an advanced Initiate of the Ancient Mysteries of Egypt. In the paths to mastery and victory, the Mystery System regarded unselfishness or sacrifice as an advanced stage of attainment, which must be accomplished before unlimited power could be bestowed upon the candidate. It is true that Anaxagoras escaped for his life and in like manner Plato and Aristotle; but this only serves to show that Socrates had reached a higher degree in the Mysteries than all of them. This necessitated training and the training centre was Egypt.

(d) Fourthly, with reference to the dying request of Socrates, addressed to Crito, in which he asked him to pay a certain debt, we again encounter another of the great ideals essential to the life of an Initiate. This in the teaching of the Mysteries embraces the exercise of a cardinal virtue i.e., justice: a practice which the Candidate must adopt, in order that his sense of value might also develop.

Here again the action of Socrates reveals that he was a Brother Initiate, with a high sense of justice and honesty, since he did not wish to die without discharging all his obligations. Certainly, the dying request of Socrates reveals him as a loyal member of the

Mystery System of Egypt.

(e) Fifthly and finally, what value may we attach to the literature which deals with the farewell conversations of Socrates with his friends and pupils? Since this literature embraces a man whose beliefs and practices coincide with those of the Initiates of the Ancient Mysteries of Egypt, then we may regard the study of Xenophon's Memorabilia, Plato's Apology, the Phaedo, Euthyphro, Crito and Timaeus as valuable specimens of literature of the Mysteries, or Masonic World.

(Ancient Mysteries; C. H. Vail C. 24–25; also C. 32).

(The Phaedo of Plato; The Timaeus of Plato).

(R. S. Clymer; Fire Philosophy C. 44; 49; 67; 75).

2. Plato: (i) Early Life (ii) Travels (iii) Disputed Writings (iv) His Doctrines (v) Summary of Conclusions. (i) His Early Life:

Plato is said to have been born at Athens in 427 B.C., and that his father's name was Aristo, and his mother's name was Perictione, who was a relative of Solon.

Little information is known about his early life and training: but there is a supposition that because his parents were wealthy, he must have had such educational opportunities as were available to a wealthy youth. He is said to have studied the doctrines of Heraclitus under Cratylus, and to have been a pupil of Socrates for eight years. It is also said that he was a soldier. (Roger's Student Hist. of Philosophy p. 76) (Wm. Turner's Hist. of Philosophy p. 93) (Will. Durant's Story of Phil.)

(ii) (a) His Travels:

He was 28 years old, when Socrates died (i.e., 399 B.C.), and together with the other pupils of Socrates, he fled from Athens to Euclid at Megara for Safety. He kept away from Athens for 12 years, during which time, it is also said that apart from visiting Euclid, he travelled (a) to Southern Italy where he met the remnant of Pythagoreans, (b) to Syracuse in Sicily, where, through Dion, he met Dionysius to whom he became a Tutor: who subsequently caused him to be sold as a slave, and (c) to Egypt.

(Fuller's Hist. of Philosophy) (Roger's Student's Hist. of Philosophy) (Wm. Turner's Hist. of Phil. p. 94) (Diogenes Laertius Bk. III, p. 277).

Stolen Legacy

(ii) (b) His Academy

Plato is said to have returned to Athens in 387 B.C. when a middle aged man of 40 years and to have opened an Academy in a gymnasium on the western suburbs of Athens over which he presided for 20 years. He is said to have taught the following subjects (a) Political Science (b) Statesmanship (c) Mathematics (d) Dialectics, and it is said that the curriculum was based upon the educational principles advocated in the Republic.

(Fuller's Hist. of Philosophy: Plato's Life) (B. D. Alexander's Hist. of Philosophy p. 68) (Roger's Students Hist. of Philosophy p. 72) (Wm. Turner's Hist. of Philosophy p. 122 123).

(iii) His Writings are disputed and doubted by modern scholarship.

There are 36 dialogues and a number of letters, which Plato is supposed to have written: but which are disputed and doubted by modern scholarship.

(a) Grote states that Plato has written only those dialogues that bear his name.

(b) Schaarsmidt states that only nine of the 36 dialogues are genuine while

(c) Aristotle considered the Platonic dialogues as nine in number, namely The Laws, Timaeus, Phaedo, Symposium, Phaedrus, Georgias, Theaetus, Philebus and the Republic, which he thought are genuine.

(d) Of the remaining 27 dialogues some scholars contend that the youthful dialogues should be included with the genuine ones, and these are the Apology, Crito, Enthydemus, Laches, Lysis and Protagoras, and

(e) Of the remaining 21 dialogues scholars suggest that those which were not written by Plato must have been written by his pupils (B. D. Alexander's Hist. of Phil. p. 68).

(iv) THE DOCTRINES OF PLATO:

The doctrines attributed to Plato are scattered over a wide area of literature: being found in piecemeal throughout what are called dialogues: but particularly in connection with

(I) the theory of ideas and its application to natural phenomena which includes the doctrines of (a) the real and unreal (b) the Nous (mind) and (c) Creation.

(II) the ethical doctrines concerning (A) the highest good (B) definition of virtue and (C) the cardinal virtues.

(III) the doctrine of the Ideal State whose attributes are compared with the attributes of the soul and justice. Following this order, they are as follows:

(I) The Theory of Ideas

A. Definition of Ideas. This may be expressed in the following syllogism:

The idea (retaining its unity, unchangeableness and perfection) is the element of reality in a thing.

The idea is the concept by which a thing is known. Therefore the concept by which a thing is known is the element of reality in a thing (To on).

It follows also, that since the concept or idea of a thing is real, then the concrete thing itself is unreal.

(Timaeus 51) (Phaedrus 247).

B. The application of the theory of Ideas to natural Phenomena.

In view of the definition of the Idea, three doctrines have resulted:—

(a) The doctrine of the real and unreal.

The things which we see around us are the phenomena of nature, they belong to the earthly realm, they are only copies (Eidola) of their prototypes (paradeigmata), the Ideas and noumena, which dwell in the heavenly realm. The Ideas are real and perfect, but the phenomena are unreal and imperfect; and it is the function of philosophy to enable the mind to rise above the contemplation of the visible copies of Ideas, and advance to a knowledge of the Ideas themselves. (The Phaedrus 250).

There is however, something common between them, because the phenomena partake of the Idea (metechei). This participation is an imitation (mimesis), but it is so imperfect that natural phenomena fall far short of Ideas.

(Parmenides 132 D) (Aristotle's Metaphysics I, 6; 987b, 9).

(b) The doctrine of the Nous or World Soul.

This teaches that the universe are living animals and that they are endowed with the most perfect and intelligent souls; that if God had made the world as perfect as the nature of matter allowed, that He must have endowed it with a perfect soul. This soul acts as mediator between the Ideas and natural phenomena, and is the cause of life, motion, order, and knowledge in the universe. (Timaeus, 30, 35).

(c) The doctrine of a Demiurgos in Creation (Cosmology)

In the myth of creation found in the Timaeus, we find the doctrine on Creation, as it is ascribed to Plato's authorship, as follows:—

Out of chaos, which was ruled by necessity, God the Demiurgos or Creator, made order, by fashioning the phenomena of matter according to the eternal prototypes (i.e., the Ideas) in as perfect a manner, as the imperfection of matter would allow. He next created the Gods, and ordered them to fashion the body of man, while He himself, made the soul of man, from the same material as that of the world soul.

The soul of man is a self-moving principle and is responsible for life, motion and consciousness in the body.

(Myth of creation in Timaeus; Wm. Turner's Hist. of Philosophy, p. 109–110).

(II) The Ethical Doctrines

The ethical doctrines that have been attributed to Plato are (A) that of the highest good, i.e., the Summum Bonum (B) the connotation of virtue and (C) the reduction of the virtues to four and the place of wisdom among them (A) as something subjective, and as an earthly experience, the highest good is happiness: but as an objective attainment, it is the Idea of good, and consequently identified with God.

Therefore the purpose of man's life is freedom from the fetters of the body, in which the soul is confined, and the practice of virtue and wisdom, makes him like a God, even while on earth.

(B) and (C)

Virtue is the order, the health and the harmony of the soul.

There are many virtues, but the greatest is wisdom. All virtues may be reduced to the four cardinal virtues: wisdom, fortitude, temperance and justice.

(Symposium 204E): (Theaetetus 176A): (Phaedo 64 sqq.) (The Republic IV, 441, 443).

(III) The Ideal State (The Republic)

The doctrine attributed to Plato in the field of civics is the doctrine of the Ideal state whose attributes are compared with the attributes of the soul and justice.

In a state, virtue should be the chief aim, and unless philosophers become rulers, or rulers become thorough students of philosophy, there will be unceasing troubles for states and humanity at large. The Ideal state is modelled upon the individual soul, and just as the soul has three parts, so also should the state have three parts: the rulers, the warriors, and the workers.

(Republic VI, 490 sqq.; V, 478; III, 415).

Similarly, just as the harmony of the soul depends upon the proper subordination of its parts, so also does the state depend upon the proper subordination of its parts, in order to enjoy peace.

Here Plato introduces the allegory of the charioteer and the winged steeds, in order to show that virtue is to the soul as justice is to the state:—One horse is of noble origin: while the other is ignoble: and consequently they cannot agree. As the noble horse strives to mount up to the heavenly regions which are suitable to its nature: so the other tries to drag him down. Likewise in dealing with the soul, it is the proper subordination of its parts, that enables the noble in man to attain its excellence; so also in dealing with the state, it is justice, or the proper subordination of the different classes, that makes it an Ideal State.

(Roger's Students Hist. of. Phil. p. 83); (Plato's Republic).

(v) SUMMARY OF CONCLUSIONS.

The doctrines of Plato are eclectic and point to Egyptian origin.

1. The doctrine of the real and unreal to represent doctrine found in the comparison between natural phenomena and the Ideas, is only an instance of the application of the doctrine of opposites. Here the things of this world have their corresponding types in the heavenly realm; here the Ideas correspond to Being, while the natural phenomena correspond to not-Being. But the doctrine of opposites may be traced back not only to Socrates, Democritus, Parmenides and the Pythagoreans, but further back to its original source, i.e., the Egyptian Mystery System, where the principle of opposites was represented not only by pairs of male and female Gods, such as Osiris and Isis, but also by pairs of pillars in the front of all the Egyptian temples.

(Memphite Theology in Kingship and the Gods, by Frankfort, C. 3, p. 25–26 and 35).

(Herodotus I, 6–26) (Ancient Egypt by John Kendrick, Bk. I, p. 339).

(Egyptian Religion by Frankfort, p. 64, 73, 88). (Zeller's Hist. of Phil. p. 61).

(The Phaedo C. 15, 16, 49).

II. The doctrine of the Nous or World Soul is a principle of Egyptian magic:

Plato is credited with expressing this doctrine in the form of a simile, in which he compares the world to a living animal, which is composed of Souls. One being made perfect and responsible for the life, motion and knowledge of the animal or universe.

This doctrine may be traced not only to (a) Democritus who based his teaching about the fire atoms of the soul, and cognition upon the magical principle of the Egyptians: "that the qualities of an animal are distributed throughout its parts."

(Golden Bough by Frazer) (Hist. of Phil., B. D. Alexander, p. 40).

(Wm. Turner, Hist. of Phil., p. 68), but also to (b) Anaxagoras, who is said to have advanced the Nous (mind) as responsible for creating order out of chaos, and which is omnipotent and omniscient.

(History of Philosophy, Wm. Turner, p. 63).

The doctrine of the Nous as a matter of fact, originated from (c) the Mystery System of Egypt, in connection with which, the God Osiris was represented in all Egyptian temples, by the symbol of an Open Eye, referred to elsewhere.

This symbol indicated not only sight that transcended space and time: but also omniscience, as the Great Mind which created and which still directs the universe. This symbol also forms a part of the decoration of all Masonic lodges of the modern world and dates back to the Osirian or Sun worship of the Egyptians more than 5000 B.C. This same notion was also represented by the Egyptians by a God with eyes all over Him and was known as the "All seeing Eye."

(Zeller's Hist. of Phil., p. 809).

(The Ancient Mysteries, C. H. Vail, p. 189)

(Max Muller: Egyptian Mythology).

III. The doctrine of the Demiurge in Creation.

This doctrine which is ascribed to the authorship of Plato, did not by any means originate from Plato. It was not only a current doctrine at the time of Plato, but was well known among the Eastern Ancient nations and taught by them many centuries before his time (427–347 B.C.).

History tells us that the Persians taught this doctrine more than six centuries B.C. through their leader Zoroaster. History also tells us that Pythagoras (500 B.C.), taught the same doctrine expressed in terms of Monads. The universe consisted of two unities, i.e., (a) the Unity from which the series of numbers or beings is derived, being absolute Unity, which is the source of all, i.e., the Monad of Monads or the God of Gods and (b) the One, i.e., the first in the series of derived numbers or beings. It is opposed to and limited by plurality, and therefore it is relative unity, i.e., a created Monad or God (a Demiurge), consequently the opposition between the One and the many is the source of all the rest. Furthermore, history likewise tells us that the original source of the doctrine of a Demiurge in creation was Egypt, and it dates back to the creation story of Egypt 4000 B.C. which is to be found in the account given by the Memphite Theology: an inscription on a stone, now kept in the British Museum. It contains the theological and cosmological views of the Egyptians which date back to the very beginning of Egyptian history, when the first dynasties had made their new capital at Memphis, the city of the God Ptah, i.e., about 4000 B.C., or even earlier.

The Egyptian cosmology must be presented in three parts; each part being supplementary to the other, and presenting a complete philosophy by their combination. Part (I) deals with the Gods of chaos, part (II) deals with the Gods of order and arrangement in creation, and part (III) deals with the Primate of the Gods, through whose Logos creation was accomplished. In part (I) pre-creation or chaos is represented by (i) Ptah, the Primate of the Gods, emerging from the primeval waters Nun in the form of a Hill, Ta-tjenen, i.e., The Risen Land (ii) Atum, i.e., Atom, the sun God, immediately joining Ptah, by emerging also from the chaotic waters Nun, and sitting upon him (the Hill).

(iii) A description of the other qualities within the chaos follows:—There are four pairs of male and female Gods in the form of frogs and serpents. Their names are (a) Nun and Naunet, the primeval ocean and primeval matter; (b) Huh and Hauhet, the Illimitable and the Boundless, (c) Kuk and Kauket, Darkness and Obscurity; and (d) Amon and Amaunet, the Hidden and concealed ones. (Memphite Theology in Ancient Egyptian Religion by Frankfort, p. 10, p. 21; Frankfort's Intellectual Adventure of Man, p. 10, 21, 52).

In part (II) the Gods of order and arrangement are represented as follows:—

The same first pair of pre-creation Gods are together present, i.e., Ptah, the primeval Hill, who is the thought and word of all the Gods, together with Atum, who rests upon Ptah.

Atum, i.e., Atom, having absorbed the thought and creative power of Ptah, then proceeds with the work of Creation. He names four pairs of parts of his own body, which become Gods, and in this way, eight Gods are created, who together with himself become nine Gods in one family or Godhead, called the Ennead.

N.B.

Magic is the key to the interpretation of ancient religions and philosophy.

(a) Part (III) tells of the specific powers of Ptah, which Atum absorbs, but does not tell us how He absorbs them.

(b) Part (I) tells us how, for it describes the movement of Atum, as emerging from the primeval waters, and sitting upon Ptah (the risen land or hill). It however does not give us the reason for Atum's movement: a behavior which can be understood, only when we apply to its interpretation, the key of magical principles.

(c) The Magical Principle

Now, what is the magical principle involved in Atum's behavior? It is this:—

"The qualities or attributes of entities, human or divine, are distributed throughout their various parts, and contact with such entities, releases those qualities."

(d) It is now clear that by making contact with Ptah, Atum immediately received the attributes of Ptah's creative thought and speech and omnipotence and became the instrument and the Logos and the Demiurge, through whom the task of creation was undertaken and completed.

(Dr. Frazer's Golden Bough).

(e) It is also clear that according to the Memphite Theology, the doctrines of a Demiurge and created Gods originated from the Egyptian religion and Mystery System, and not from Plato who lived from 427 to 347 B.C.

(Ancient Egyptian Religion: Memphite Theology by Frankfort, p. 20 and 23).

(Intellectual Adventure of Ancient Man, by Frankfort, p. 21, and 51–60).

(The Egyptian Book of the Dead, c. 17).

(The Golden Bough, by Dr. Frazer—on Magic).

(The Mediterranean World, by Sandford, p. 182).

(History of Philosophy, by Weber, p. 21–22).

(The Cure of the woman who touched the hem of Christ's garment: Mark, chapter 5, verses 25–34).

(The cure of several people who held the kerchiefs of St. Paul: Acts, chapter 19, verse 12).

N.B.

The Memphite Theology will be dealt with in a separate chapter to show the origin of Greek Philosophy.

IV. The doctrines of (A) the highest good (B) virtue and (C) the cardinal virtues.

N.B.

This is really the earliest theory of salvation and it originated from the Egyptian Mysteries but not from Plato.

(A) The main purpose of the Egyptian Mysteries was the salvation of the human soul. The Egyptians believed the human body to be a prison house, where the soul is chained by ten fetters. This condition not only kept man separated from God, but made him subject to the wheel of re-birth or re-incarnation.

In order to escape from the effects of his condition, two requirements had to be fulfilled by the Neophyte:—

(i) He must keep the Ten Commandments taught by the Mysteries, for by such a discipline, he would gain conquest over the fetters of the soul, and liberate it, so as to make its development possible, and

(ii) he now being well qualified and duly prepared, must undergo a series of initiations, in order to develop his soul from the human stage to that of a God. Such a transformation was known as salvation. It placed the Neophyte in harmony with nature, man and God. It deified him, i.e., made him become godlike; and this attainment was known as the highest good.

According to this theory of salvation, man is expected to work out his own salvation, without a mediator between himself and his God.

(B) Plato defines virtue as the order or discipline of the soul. This meaning we accept, since it agrees with the purpose of the ten commandments of the Mysteries.

The doctrines of the ten virtues and the ten fetters are as old as the Egyptian history itself. Each commandment or discipline represented a principle of virtue, and the function of each virtue was to remove a fetter. Hence a life of virtue was antecedent and preparatory to those further experiences, i.e., the initiations which led to gradual perfection and the divinity of the Neophyte.

(C) Plato is also credited with having reduced all virtues to four cardinal virtues, and with assigning the highest place among them to wisdom, as follows:—wisdom, fortitude, temperance and justice.

We are also informed through the history of philosophy, that Socrates, the alleged teacher of Plato, taught that wisdom was the equivalent of all virtue. This divergence of opinion between pupil and teacher is significant, since it points to the fact that both of them simply speculated about a system of Ethics which was current in the ancient world, and which neither of them had produced.

This system of Ethics as has already been mentioned belonged to the Mystery System of Egypt, which required Neophytes in preparation for initiation, to keep the following ten commandments, underlying which were ten principles of virtue:—

The Neophyte must (I) control his thoughts (II) control his actions (III) have devotion of purpose (IV) have faith in the ability of his master to teach him the truth (V) have faith in himself to assimilate the truth (VI) have faith in himself to wield the truth (VII) be free from resentment under the experience of persecution (VIII) be free from resentment under experience of wrong, (IX) cultivate the ability to distinguish between right and wrong and (X) cultivate the ability to distinguish between the real and the unreal (he must have a sense of values).

If we now compare the order in the above outline with the order in which the cardinal virtues are said to be arranged, we shall immediately see that the first place which wisdom occupies among the virtues was given to it by the Egyptian Mysteries, and not by Plato. Consequently in (I) and (II) from the control of thoughts and actions, we derive the virtue of wisdom; in (VI) from freedom of resentment under persecution, we derive the virtue of fortitude; in (IX) and (X) from an ability to distinguish between right and wrong, and between the real and unreal, we derive the virtues of justice and temperance.

(Plato's Republic, c. IV, 44, and 443).

(Ancient Mysteries by C. H. Vail, p. 25 also 109–112).

(Wm. Turner's History of Philosophy, p. 115).

and the other at Cyprus in 449 B.C., when the island was captured by the Persians.

N.B.

Chariots were not used in any of these engagements.

B. Internal wars, i.e., the Peloponnesian wars, 460–445 B.C., and 431–421 B.C. respectively.

These wars were fought between the different Greek states, and their major engagements were maritime.

In 432 B.C. Athens blockaded Potidaea and Megara was excluded from Greek markets. In 431 B.C. Thebes attacked Plataea, and while a Peloponnesian army occupied Attica, an Athenian fleet raided Peloponnesus.

Pericles conducted the evacuation of Attica, the oligarchs at Corcyra were massacred, and after the seizure of Amphipolis: Nicias sued for peace 422 B.C.

N.B.

It is evident that Greek culture and tradition did not furnish Plato with the idea of the charioteer and winged steeds, for nowhere in their brief military history, (i.e., up to the time of Plato) do we find the use of such a war machine by the Greeks as a chariot. The only nearby nation who specialized in the manufacture of chariots and horse breeding was the Egyptians, as already mentioned.

And since the Judgment Drama in the Egyptian Book of the Dead depicts the allegory of the charioteer and winged steeds, credit for its authorship cannot be given to Plato, but to the Egyptians.

(Sandford: Mediterranean World, c. 12, p. 197: 202; 203; 205: c. 13, p. 220–221).

(Genesis, c. 45, 27; c. 47, 17; Deut. c. 17, 16).

(I Kings, c. 10, 28).

(Homer II. i, 381; Diodorus; Roger's Hist. of Phil., p. 8384).

(John Kendrick: Ancient Egypt, Vol. I, p. 166).

(The Egyptian Book of the Dead).

3. Aristotle: (i) (a) Early Life and Training and (b) His Own List of Books (c) Other Lists of Books (ii) Doctrines (iii) Summary of Conclusions: A. His Doctrines B. (i) The Library of Alexandria B. (ii) True Source of his Unusual Number of Books C. The Discrepancies and Doubts in His Life. (i) (a) Birth and early life and training.

According to the textbooks on the history of Greek philosophy, Aristotle was born in 384 B.C. at Stagira, a town in Thrace. His father, Neomachus is said to have been a physician to Amyntas, King of Macedonia. Nothing is mentioned in books about his early education, only that he became an orphan and at the age of 19 he went to Athens, where he spent twenty years as a pupil of Plato.

We are also informed that after the death of Plato, his nephew, became the master of his school, and that Aristotle left immediately for Mysia, where he met and married the niece of Hermeias.

Likewise, that after the death of Amyntas of Macedon, his son Phillip having become king, appointed Aristotle as Tutor of his son Alexander a boy of 13 years (later to be called the Great in consequence of his conquest of Egypt).

After Phillip's assassination in 336 B.C. Alexander became king, and we are informed that he immediately planned an Asiatic campaign and included Egypt, during which time Aristotle is said to have returned to Athens and founded a school in a gymnasium called the Lyceum. We are further informed that Aristotle conducted this school for only twelve years, that Alexander the Great advanced him the funds to purchase a large number of books, that his pupils were called Peripatetics, and that owing to an indictment for impiety, brought against him by a priest named Eurymedon, he fled from Athens to Chalcis in Euboea, where he remained in exile until his death in 322 B.C.

(Roger's Student's History of Phil. p. 104).

(Zeller's History of Philosophy, p. 171–172).

(Fuller's History of Philosophy, Aristotle's Life).

(B. D. Alexander's Hist. of Phil. p. 91–92).

(Diogenes Laertius Bk. V. p. 449).

(b) His own list of books.

(Zeller's History of Philosophy, p. 155–157).

V. (A) The doctrine of the Ideal State.

Concerning the authorship and source of this doctrine, there are two conclusions: First, Plato was not the author of the Republic and second, the allegory of the charioteer and winged steeds, is not a product of Plato, but is derived from the Egyptian Book of the Dead, in the Judgment Drama.

Concerning the first conclusion it is only necessary to reaffirm what has already been stated in connection with the writings of Plato, and that is that they are disputed not only by such modern scholars as Grote and Schaarsmidt, but also by ancient historians: Diogenes Laertius, Aristoxenus and Favorinus (80–150 A.D.), who declare that the subject matter of the Republic was found in the controversies written by Protagoras (481–411 B.C.) at the time of whose death Plato was but a boy.

Furthermore, the authorship of Plato rests only upon the opinions of Aristotle and Theophrastus, both of whose aims were the compilation of a Greek philosophy with Egyptian material.

(Diogenes Laertius, p. 311 and 327; Aristotle Metaphysics Bk. I).

(Zeller's History of Philosophy; Introduction, p. 8 and 13; Wm. Turner's History of Philosophy, p. 95).

Concerning the second conclusion, it must be pointed out that the allegory of the "Charioteer and the winged steeds" is a description of the quality and destiny of the soul as it appears at the bar of justice, in the Judgment Drama of the Egyptian Book of the Dead. In this Drama, the Great Chief Justice and President of the Unseen World, Pethempamenthes, i.e., Osiris is seated on a throne, and is attended by the Goddesses Isis and Nephthys, while 42 assistant judges are seated around.

Near Osiris there are four genii of Amenthe, the Unseen World, represented as short vases, called canopi, in which the different viscera, symbolizing the moral qualities of the individual, are kept embalmed. The intestines hive a very important connection with the moral qualities of the individual since they are blamed for any sin which the individual commits. At the opposite end the deceased is introduced by Horus, while in the centre stands the Scale of Justice which has been erected by Anubis. On one side of it, there appears a heart-shaped vase containing the moral qualities of the deceased, while on the other side, there is a figure of the Goddess of Truth. Toth, the scribe, holding a roll of papyrus, stands by and makes a record of the weighing. After this is completed, Horus receives the record from Toth and advances to Osiris to make known the results. Osiris listens and at the end of the report, pronountes sentence of reward or punishment. In the meantime, fearful monsters lurk around the scene to destroy the soul, if the verdict is against it.

Let us observe that

(1) the motion of the scale in the Judgment Drama corresponds with the up and down motion of the winged steeds of the allegory

(2) the opposite qualities weighed on the scale correspond with the opposite qualities possessed by the noble and ignoble steeds of the allegory

(3) the idea of justice symbolized by the scale of Judgment Drama, corresponds with the idea of justice expressed in the allegory.

(4) The winged steeds corresponds with the monsters of the judgment drama.

(B) The Authorship of the Republic.

According to Diogenes Laertius book III and pages 311 and 327, it is stated both by Aristoxenus and Favorinus, that nearly the whole of the subject matter of Plato's Republic was found in the Controversies, written by Protagoras. Furthermore, according to Roger's Students History of Philosophy p. 78, it is stated that although Plato might have drawn heavily upon the reminiscences of Socrates, whose lectures he attended: yet the subject matter of the Republic is a more carefully reasoned system of philosophy, than can be easily attributed to Socrates. 'That the whole volume is a cumulative argument into which there are subtly interwoven opinions on almost every subject of philosophical importance.

It is obvious that modern scholarship doubts that Plato drew the subject matter of the Republic from Socrates, and is inclined to attribute authorship to Plato himself. If however, we take into consideration the fact that the subject matter of the Republic was in circulation long before the time of Plato: for Protagoras is supposed to have lived from 481–411 B.C. and Plato, from 427–347 B.C., reason forbids the assignment of the authorship to Plato.

But the important question remains: From what source did Protagoras draw the ideas of the Republic which were circulated in the Controversies?

Text books on Greek philosophy tell us that Protagoras was a pupil of Democritus; but when we turn to the writings of Democritus we are unable to discover any connection between them and the (a) educational system and the (b) paternal government which are advocated in the Republic.

This fact forces us to the conclusion that the subject matter of Plato's Republic was neither produced by Plato, nor any Greek philosopher.

(C) The Authorship of Timaeus.

According also to Diogenes Laertius Book VIII p. 399–401, when Plato visited Dionysius at Sicily, he paid Philolaus, a Pythagorean, 40 Alexandrian Minae of silver, for a book, from which he copied the whole contents of the Timaeus.

Under these circumstances it is clear that Plato wrote neither the Republic nor the Timaeus, whose subject matter identifies them with the purpose of the Mysteries of Egypt.

(Roger's Students Hist. of Philosophy p. 76; 78; and 104).

(Zeller's Hist. of Philosophy: Introduction p. 13 and 103).

(Wm. Turner's Hist. of Philosophy p. 79 and 95).

(Plato; Apology, Crito, and Phaedo).

(Xenophon: Memorabilia; Strabo; Ancient Mysteries by C. H. Vail).

(Clement: Stromata Bk. V. C. 7 and 9).

VI. The Chariot was not a culture pattern of the Greeks, at the time of Plato, nor was it used by them in warfare:—

Greek culture and traditions did not furnish Plato with the idea of the chariot and winged steeds, for nowhere in their brief military history, (i.e., up to the time of Plato) do we find the use of such a war machine by the Greeks.

The only nearby nation who specialized in the manufacture of chariots and the breeding of horses was the Egyptians. When

Joseph was Governor in Egypt, the horse and war chariot were in use; and when the Israelites fled from the country, Pharaoh pursued them to the Red Sea in chariots. Even Homer and Diodorus who visited Egypt, testify that they saw a great multitude of war chariots and numerous stables along the banks of the Nile, from Memphis to Thebes.

And since the Judgment Drama in the Egyptian Book of the Dead reveals the entire philosophy contained in the allegory, Plato cannot be credited as its author.

The following sketch of the military history of the Greeks shows that the chariot was not used by them, nor was it their culture pattern:—

A. External wars or wars with the Persians.

(a) The Ionian revolt against Persian rule, 499–494 B.C. This climaxed in a naval engagement at Lade, where the Ionian fleet was defeated.

(b) The battle of Marathon, 490 B.C.

During the summer of 490 B.C., the Greeks met the Persians at the bay of Marathon, and after a brief fight with bows and arrows, both belligerents withdrew to prepare for more decisive engagements.

(c) The battle of Thermopylae, 480 B.C.

Ten years after Marathon, the Persians and Greeks met again to settle their grievances. The Persians anchored in the Gulf of Pagasae, while the Greeks anchored off Cape Artimesium. A battle followed and Thermopylae was captured by the Persians.

(d) The battle of Salamis, 479 B.C.

Both Persians and Greeks met again at Salamis in 479 B.C., and a naval engagement followed, with considerable loss of ships on both sides. Both belligerents withdrew without any decision.

(e) The confederacy of Delos and their wars with the Persians, 478–448 B.C.

The purpose of the confederacy was defense against Persian aggression, and two naval battles were fought: one at the river Eurymedon in 467 B.C., when the Greeks gained a minor victory,

Aristotle is credited with classifying his own writings as follows:—

(i) The Theoretic, whose object is truth, and which included (a) Mathematics (b) Physics and (c) Theology.

(ii) The Practical, whose object is the useful, and which included (a) Ethics (b) Economics and (c) Politics.

(iii) The Productive or Poetic whose object is the beautiful, and which included (a) Poetry (b) Art and (c) Rhetoric.

N.B.

Neither Logic nor Metaphysics was in this list. (History of Philosophy, B. D. Alexander, p. 92).

(c) Other lists of books.

There are two lists of books which have come down to modern times from Alexandrine and Arabian sources.

(i) The older list, derived from the Alexandrine Hermippus (200 B.C.), who estimated the books of Aristotle at 400, which, according to Zeller's suggestion, must have been in the Alexandrine Library, at the time of the compilation of the list, since works which are now considered to be Aristotle's are not found in the list.

(ii) The later, derived from Arabian sources, was compiled by Ptolemus, of the First or Second Century A.D. This list mentions most of the works in the modern collection, and has a total of one thousand books.

(Zeller's History of Philosophy, p. 172–173; B. D. Alexander's History of Philosophy, p. 92–93).

(ii) DOCTRINES OF ARISTOTLE

I. Metaphysics: or The Principles of Being, in the Metaphysical realm.

1. Aristotle defines Metaphysics as the science of Being as Being.

2. He names the Attributes of Being as

(a) actuality (entelecheia) i.e., perfection and

(b) potentiality i.e., the capacity for perfection. (dynamis).

3. He states that all created beings are composed of actuality and potentiality.

These two principles are present and are mixed in all created beings except one, whose being is actuality, and includes the composition of (a) matter and form (b) substance and accident (c) soul and its faculties (d) active and passive intellect.

II. Principles of being in the physical realm.

There are four principles of being in the physical realm which are called Causes:—

(1) Matter (hyle) the material cause, is the potentiality or capacity of existence (hyle prole). It is that out of which being is made.

(2) Form or Essence (morphe) i.e., the formal cause is that which gives actuality to existence. It is that into which a thing is made. When matter is united with form the result is organized or realized being that has come to existence in the processes of nature (synolon, ousia prote).

(3) Final Cause, is that for which everything exists. Everything has a purpose and that purpose is the final cause. A final cause always implies intelligence: but this is not always true in the case of the efficient Cause.

Consequently in the realm of nature, every being or living organism is the complex effect of four causes:—

(1) The substance out of which it is made (i.e., material cause).

(2) The type or idea, according to which the embryo tends to develop (i.e., formal cause).

(3) The act of creation or generation (i.e., efficient cause).

(4) The purpose or end for which the organism is created (i.e., final cause). In other words, matter, type, creation and purpose are the four principles which underlie all existing things.

(B. D. Alexander's History of Philosophy, p. 97–100: Aristotle, Meta. I, 3; Wm. Turner's History of Philosophy, p. 136140. Alfred Weber's Hist. of Phil., p. 80–84).

III. Doctrines concerning the existence of God.

(1) Although motion is eternal, there cannot be an indefinite series of movers and the moved, therefore there must be One, the first in the series which is unmoved (proton kinoun akineton) i.e., The Unmoved Mover.

(2) The actual is antecedent to the potential for although last in appearance, is really first in nature. Therefore before all matter and the composition of actual and potential, pure actuality must have existed. Therefore actuality is the cause of all things that exist and since it is pure actuality, its life is essentially free from all material conditions. It is the thought of thought, the absolute spirit, who dwells in eternal peace and self enjoyment, who knows himself and the absolute truth, and is in need of neither action nor virtue.

(3) God is one, for matter is the principle of plurality, and the First Intelligence is free from material conditions. His life is contemplative thought: neither providence nor will is comparable with the eternal repose in which He dwells. God is not concerned with the world.

IV. The doctrine of the origin of the world.

The world is eternal, because matter, motion and time are eternal.

V. The doctrine concerning Nature.

Nature is everything which has the principle of motion and rest. It is spontaneous and self determining from within. Nature does nothing in vain, but according to definite law. It is always striving for the best according to a plan of development, which is obstructed only by matter. The striving of nature is through the less perfect to the more perfect.

VI. The doctrine concerning the Universe.

The world is globe shaped, circular and most perfect in form. The heaven, which is composed of ether, stands in immediate contact with the First Cause. The stars, which are eternal come next in order, the earth-ball is in the middle, and is the furthest from the prime mover, and least participant of divinity.

(Eth. Wic 10, 8; 1178b. 20) (Op. cit. 10: 8, 9; 1179).

(Wm. Turner's History of Philosophy, p. 141–143; B D. Alexander, History of Phil. p. 102–103; Zeller's History of Philosophy. p.

221; Roger's History of Philosophy, p. 109).

(Aristotle's Physics II, I, 192b 14) (De Caelo, I, 4, 271a, 33).

(De Part. An. IV, 2, 677a 15)

(Aristotle's Physics II, 8, 199).

(B. D. Alexander's Hist. of Phil. p. 104).

(De Generatione Animalium, IV, 4, 7706, 9).

VII. The doctrine of the soul.

The soul is not merely a harmony of the body or the blending of opposites. It is neither the four elements nor their compound, for it transcends all material conditions.

The soul and body are not two distinct things: but one in two different aspects, i.e., just as form is related to matter.

The soul is the power which a living body possesses, and it is the end for which the body exists, i.e., the final cause of its existence.

While the soul which is the radical principle of life, is one, yet it has several faculties. Those faculties are:—(1) Sensitive (2) Rational (3) Nutritive (4) Appetitive (5) Locomotive.

Of these, the sensitive and the rational are the most important: sensation being the faculty by means of which the forms of sen'sible things are received, just as impression is made as by a seal; and intelligent knowledge being the faculty by means of which intellectual knowledge is acquired.

It is the seat of ideas only, it does not create them, since knowledge comes through the senses.

(B. D. Alexander's History of Philosophy, p. 105–106).

(Wm. Turner's History of Philosophy, p. 147–153).

(Zeller's History of Philosophy, p 201–204).

(iii) SUMMARY OF CONCLUSIONS.

A. His Doctrines.

1. The doctrine of Being (To on).

Stolen Legacy

By declaring the attributes of Being as (a) actuality or the determining principle, and (b) potentiality or the indeterminate principle: Aristotle attempted to explain Reality in terms of the principle of opposites.

But this principle was used not only by the Pythagoreans, Parmenides, and Democritus in a similar manner but also by Socrates in his attempt to prove the immortality of the soul, and by Plato who saw reality as the concept of things as distinguished from the things themselves: as the noumena as distinct from phenomena, and as the real, distinct from the unreal.

But the principle of opposites originated from the Egyptian Mystery System, whose Gods were male and female, and whose temples carried in front of them two pillars as symbols of the principle of opposites. It is obvious that Aristotle was not the author of this doctrine, but the Egyptians.

(Aristotle's Metaphysics I, 5, 985b, 24; Aristotle's Metaphysics I, 5, 98b, 31).

(Aristotle's Metaphysics I, 6, 987b, 9; Wm. Turner's Hist. of Phil., p. 41; 47; 48).

(Plato's Phaedo, c. 15; c. 16 and c. 49; Parmenides 132D). (Memphite Theology, King-ship and the Gods, by Frankfort, c. 3, p. 25, 26, 35).

(Egyptian Religion by Frankfort, p. 64, 73, 88).

2. The existence of God.

(a) The teleological concept has not only been embraced by Socrates, Plato and Aristotle, but also by the peoples of the remotest antiquity. In the accounts found in the first chapter of Genesis and in the Memphite Theology, found in chapters 20 and 23 of Frankfort's Ancient Egyptian Religion, creation proceeds from chaos to order, by definite and gradual steps, showing design and purpose in nature, and suggesting that it must be the work of a divine Intelligence. The dates of these sources carry us far back into antiquity, many centuries before the time of Aristotle, between 2000 and 5000 B.C.

We are also told that in addition to the teleological concept, Aristotle introduced the concept of the "Unmoved Mover" in order to prove the existence of God. But the "Unmoved Mover" is none other than the Atum of the Memphite Theology of the Egyptians, the Demiurge, through whose command (logos) four pairs of Gods were created out of different parts of his body and who accordingly moved out of him. This act of creation took place while Atum remained unmoved; as he embraced Ptah. Thus the family of Nine Gods was created, and has been named the Ennead. It is quite clear that the concept of the "Unmoved Mover" is derived from the Egyptian theological or mystery system, and not from Aristotle, as the modern world has been made to believe.

N.B.

Incidentally, but no less important, it might be mentioned here that in this story of the created Gods by Atum the Sun God into a family of nine, i.e., the Ennead, we have the original source of two important scientific hypotheses of modern times:—

(1) There are nine major planets and (2) The Sun is the parent of the other planets (This latter being supported by the Nebular Hypothesis). Let us remember also that

(a) the worship of the planets began in Egypt and

(b) the Egyptian temples were the first observatories of history.

(c) In attempting to prove the existence of God or a First Cause by reference to actuality and potentiality, Aristotle simply followed the traditional custom of the Ancients, who used the principle of Opposites in order to explain the functions of nature.

(d) Plato used it, through the theory of Ideas, to explain the real and unreal in the phenomena of nature.

(e) Socrates used it in order to establish the fact of immortality by showing that the death of one form of life of existing things, is but the beginning of another form of life of these things. In other words life is perpetual, it only changes its form in its course of progress.

Democritus applied the principle of opposites in their interpretation of a particular phase of reality. We cannot therefore consider Aristotle's use of the terms, actuality and potentiality in the problem of the existence of God as a new method of interpretation.

Furthermore, Aristotle's review of the doctrines of all previous philosophers including Plato, together with his exposure of their

Stolen Legacy

errors, and inconsistencies, shows that he had become confident not only of the fact that he was in possession of a new and correct knowledge one that had not before been made available to the Greeks, but also that he could then speak with great authority. Right here I must say that I am convinced that Aristotle represents a culture gap of 5000 years or more between his innovation and the Greek level of civilization; because it is impossible to escape the conviction that he obtained his education and books from a nation outside of Greece, the Egyptians who were far in advance of the culture of Greeks of his day.

(Memphite Theology in Kingship & The Gods by Frankfort c. 3. p. 25, 26, 35).

(Herodotus I, 6–26) (Egyptian Religion by Frankfort p. 64, 73, 88).

(Plato's Phaedo c. 15, 16, 49) (Zeller's History of Philosophy p. 61).

(Aristotle's Eth., Nic. 10, 8; 1178b, 20) (Op. cit. 10: 8, 9; 1179).

(Zeller's History of Philosophy p. 221) (Roger's History of Philosophy p. 109).

(William Turner's History of Philosophy p. 141–143).

(B. D. Alexander's History of Philosophy, p. 102, 103).

(B D. Alexander's History of Philosophy p. 92. 93; Roger's Student History of Philosophy p. 104).

(William Turner's History of Philosophy p. 126–127, 135).

(Zeller's History of Philosophy p. 171–173) (Plutarch's Alexander) (Aristotle's Metaphysics) (William Turner's History of Philosophy, p. 128 footnote also Noct. Mt. 20: 5).

(Strabo).

3. The doctrine of the origin of the world.

According to the doctrine that has been ascribed to Aristotle: "because matter, motion and time are eternal, therefore the world is also eternal", he plainly accepts and repeats a doctrine which has also been ascribed to Democritus (400 B.C.), whose dictum we are all quite familiar with: ex nihillo nihil fit (nothing comes out of nothing), and consequently matter or the world must always have existed.

But the antiquity of the doctrine of the eternal nature of matter, takes us back to the creation story of the Memphite Theology of the Egyptians, in which Chaos is represented by the Primeval Ocean Nun, out of which there arose the Primeval Hill Ta-tjenen. Under these circumstances we cannot give Aristotle credit for the authorship of this doctrine.

In addition to the false authorship that has been attributed to Aristotle, he contradicts himself in his physics VIII 1. 25; when he also speaks of the world as caused. A thing cannot be eternal and infinite, and at the same time finite.

(Memphite Theology in Egyptian Religion by Frankfort p. 20).

(Intellectual Adventure of Man by Frankfort p. 10, 21, 52).

4. The doctrine of the attributes of nature.

Aristotle defines nature as that which possesses the principle of motion and rest and also adds that the motion is an effort to move from the less perfect to the more perfect by a definite law: supposedly what we would today call evolution.

As we examine this definition, we find that Aristotle has only applied the principle of opposites to explain one of the modes by which nature has revealed herself just as he has done in his attempt to explain Being in the dual terms of actuality and potentiality.

But change and motion, permanence and rest, were by no means new problems at the time of Aristotle; since they appear to have been investigated not only by Parmenides, Zeno and Melissus, but also by Democritus, who stressed the notion of permanence in his famous dictum: ex nihillo nihil fit (out of nothing, nothing comes) implying thereby that nature is permanent and eternal.

Similarly, his reference to nature's movement from the less perfect to the more perfect, was by no means a new discovery of a principle of nature.

The creation account found in the first chapter of Genesis speaks of the gradual development of life, in which the Demiurge or Logos was engaged at work during six stages and rested on the seventh. Similarly, the creation account of the Egyptians pound in the Memphite Theology, also speaks of nature's movement from

Chaos to order.

These accounts by many thousand years antedate Aristotle's time for the former is about 2000 B.C. while the latter 4000 B.C., and since the principle of opposites has already been shown to originate from the Egyptians, as well as that of the gradual development of life, it is clear that this doctrine on the attributes of nature did not originate from Aristotle.

(Zeller's History of Philosophy, p. 60–65;) (William Turner's History of Philosophy p. 44–52).

(Genesis c. 1).

(Roger's History of Philosophy p. 28–32).

(Intellectual Adventure of Man by Frankfort, p. 21, 51–60).

(Ancient Egyptian Religion by Frankfort, p. 20, 23).

5. The Soul.

According to Aristotle the soul possesses the following attributes (1) Identity with body, as form with matter (2) The power which a living body possesses, i.e., the radical principle of life, manifesting itself in the following attributes:—

(a) sensitive

(b) rational

(c) nutritive

(d) appetitive

(e) locomotive.

This description of the soul by Aristotle, seems to vary somewhat from the more familiar and current ideas held by the Atomists, on the one hand and Socrates, Plato and the Pythagoreans on the other; for while the former believed that the soul is material and is composed of fire atoms; the latter regarded it as a harmony of the body and a blending of opposites.

(William Turner's History of Philosophy, p. 42, 67–68).

(Plato Phaedo, c. 15) (Zeller's History of Philosophy, p. 61).

(De Respiratione, 4, 30, 47a).

George G. M. James

Naturally we are now forced to ask the question: Did this doctrine of the soul originate from Aristotle? It is clear that he did not get it from his teacher Plato, nor from the Pythagoreans and Atomists; but from some other source outside of Greece.

As we turn our attention to ancient history, we happily discover that there are two such sources outside of Greece (1) The Creation story in Genesis first chapter and (2) The Egyptian Book of the Dead, which does not only contain attributes of the soul, identical with those mentioned by Aristotle, but far more in an elaborate system of philosophy in which human nature is explained as a unity of nine inseparable parts consisting of different bodies and souls interdependent one upon another, the physical body being one of them. (The Egyptian Book of the Dead by Sir E. A. Budge. Introduction, p. 29–64).

In the Genesis story, it is asserted that God made man out of matter (i.e., the dust of the earth), and breathed into his nostrils, the breath of life, and "man became a living soul". Here we have a clear statement of the identity of "body and soul", taken from a document (Genesis) which antedates Aristotle by many centuries.

In the Egyptian Book of the Dead, we also find that the human soul is composed of the following nine inseparable parts:—

(1) The Ka, which is an abstract personality of the man to whom it belongs possessing the form and attributes of a man with power of locomotion, omnipresence and ability to receive nourishment like a man. It is equivalent to (Eidolon), i.e., image.

(2) The Khat, i.e., the concrete personality, the physical body, which is mortal.

(3) The Ba, i.e., the heart-soul, which dwells in the Ka and sometimes alongside it, in order to supply it with air and food. It has the power of metamorphosis and changes its form at will.

(4) The Ab, i.e., the Heart, the animal life in man, and is rational, spiritual and ethical. It is associated with the Ba (heart-soul) and in the Egyptian Judgment Drama it undergoes examination in the presence of Osiris, the great Judge of the Unseen World.

(5) The Kaibit, i.e., shadow. It is associated with Ba (heart-soul) from whom like the Ka, it receives its nourishment. It has the power of locomotion and omnipresence.

(6) The Khu, i.e., spiritual soul, which is immortal. It is also closely associated with the Ba (heart-soul), and is an Ethereal Being.

(7) The Sahu, i.e., spiritual body, in which the Khu or spiritual soul dwells. In it all the mental and spiritual attributes of the natural body are united to the new powers of its own nature.

(8) The Sekhem, i.e., power or the spiritual personification of the vital force in a man. Its dwelling place is in the heavens with spirits or Khus.

(9) The Ren, i.e., the name, or the essential attribute for the preservation of a Being. The Egyptians believed that in the. absence of a name, an individual ceased to exist.

N.B.

It must be noted that according to the Egyptian concept

(1) The soul has nine parts, whose unity is so complete, that even the Ren, i.e., the name, is an essential attribute, since without it, it cannot exist.

(2) The Ba (or heart-soul), is connected with the Ka, Kaibit and Ab (Abstract personality or Shadow and Animal life) on the one hand, and also with Khu and Sekhem (spiritual Soul and spiritual personification of vital force) on the other hand, as the power of Nourishment.

(3) The Sahu is a spiritual body which is used both by Khu and Sekhem.

(4) The Khat, i.e., the physical body, is essential to the soul while manifesting itself upon the physical plane.

(5) The soul has the additional following attributes:—

(a) omnipresence

(b) metamorphosis

(c) locomotion

(d) nutritive

(e) mortality (in case of one khat)

(f) immortality

(g) rationality

(h) spirituality

(i) morality

(j) ethereal

(k) shadowy

(6) It is clear therefore from such a comparison as this, that the Aristotelian doctrine of the soul is identical and coincides with only a very small portion of the Egyptian philosophy of the soul, which therefore stands in relation to it as a whole to its part. Consequently we must conclude that Aristotle obtained his doctrine of the soul from the Egyptian Book of the Dead, directly or indirectly.

B (i) The Library of Alexandria was the true source of Aristotle's large numbers of books:

It is to be expected that the library of Alexandria was immediately ransacked and looted by Alexander and his party, no doubt made up of Aristotle and others, who did not only carry off large quantities of scientific books: but also frequently returned to Alexandria for the purpose of research. Just as these books were captured in Egypt by the army of Alexander and fell into the hands of Aristotle, so after Aristotle's death, these very books were destined to be captured by a Roman army and conveyed to Rome according to the following story taken from the histories of Strabo and Plutarch:—

The books of Aristotle fell into the hands of Theophrastus who succeeded him as Head of his School. At the death of Theophrastus, they were bequeathed to Neleus of Scepsis. After the death of Neleus, the books were hidden in a cellar, where they remained for almost two centuries.

When Athens was captured by the Romans in 84 B.C., the books were captured by Sulla and carried to Rome, where Tyrannio a grammarian secured copies and enabled Andronicus of Rhodes to publish them.

(Strabo; Plutarch; Wm. Turner's Hist. of Phil., p. 128 footnote).

(Noct., Mt. 20; 5)

Stolen Legacy

The fragmentary character of Aristotle's writings and their lack of unity, reveal the fact that he himself made notes hurriedly from books while doing his research at the great Egyptian Library. The ancient teaching method was oral; not by lecture and note taking.

Right here I must repeat that I am convinced that Aristotle represents a culture gap of 5000 years between his innovation and the Greek level of civilization; because it is impossible to escape the conviction that he obtained his education and books from a nation outside of Greece, who was far ahead of the culture of the Greeks of his day, and that was the Egyptians.

(B. D. Alexander's History of Philosophy, p. 92 and 93).

(Roger's Student History of Philosophy, p. 104).

(Alfred Weber's History of Philosophy, p. 77 and 78).

(Wm. Turner's History of Philosophy, p. 126, 127, 135).

(Zeller's History of Philosophy, p. 171-173).

(Plutarch's Alexander, c. 8).

(Aristotle's Metaphysics) (Wm. Turner's History of Phil., p. 128 footnote also Noct., Mt., 20; 5).

(Strabo).

The so-called books of Aristotle deal with scientific knowledge which was not in circulation among the Greeks, and consequently, it was impossible, as has already been stated, for him to have purchased them from other so-called Greek philosophers.

It is for the purpose of concealing the true source of his books and of his education, that history tells the very strange stories about Aristotle (a) that he spent 20 years, as a pupil under Plato, whom we know was incompetent to teach him; and (b) that Alexander the Great also gave him money to buy the large number of books to which his name has been attached; but at the same time, fails to tell us when, where and from whom Aristotle bought the books.

Furthermore, as already pointed out, Aristotle's review of the doctrines of all previous philosophers including Plato, together with his exposure of their errors and inconsistencies, shows that he had become confident not only of the fact that he was in possession of correct knowledge, one that had not before been made available to the Greeks; but also that he could then speak with great authority.

B (ii) The lack of uniformity between the lists of books points to doubtful authorship.

1. There are at least three lists of books. One list is said co be Aristotle's own classification of his writings, and naturally it must be dated within the period of his own life time 384–322 B.C. In this list Aristotle has told the world that he wrote texts on (a) Mathematics, Physics and Theology, (b) Ethics, Economics and Politics and (c) Poetry, Art and Rhetoric.

Now, in order to write these texts one must have received his education and training in the subjects on which they are written. We are told in the history of Greek philosophy, that Socrates taught Plato and that Plato taught Aristotle. But there is no evidence that Socrates ever taught mathematics or economics or politics.

Consequently, it was impossible for him to teach Plato these subjects, and also impossible for Plato to teach Aristotle these subjects, under the Egyptian Mystery System which was graded, and which required proof of efficiency before promotion.

We are therefore unable to accept the claim of Aristotle to have been the author of those books.

2. Two lists are derived from different sources and the two together differ widely in (a) number (b) subject matter and (c) date.

The list of Hermippus the Alexandrine (200 B.C.) contains 400 books. The list compiled by Ptolemus, between First and Second Centuries A.D. contains 1000 books. The very fact that there is no uniformity in the lists points to a doubtful authorship. Also, if Aristotle in 200 B.C. had only 400 books, by what miracle did they increase to 1000 in the Second Century A.D.? Or was it forgery?

C. The discrepancies and doubts in his life.

(i) He wastes 20 years as a pupil under Plato:—

It is said that he went to Plato at the age of 19 and spent 20 years with him as a pupil. But this is doubtful and unreasonable. Doubtful because Plato is regarded as a Philosopher, while Aristotle as a Scientist, who has been credited with all the scientific

Stolen Legacy

knowledge of the Ancient World, and it is impossible for a master to teach a pupil what he himself does not know.

It is also unreasonable to expect a man who has been credited with Aristotle's knowledge, to waste 20 of the best years of his life, under a master who was incompetent to teach him.

(B. D. Alexander, Hist. of Phil., p. 92; Roger's Student History of Philosophy, p. 104).

(ii) The truth of how he got such a large number of books is misrepresented:—

He is said to have received financial aid from Alexander the Great, and was able to purchase a large number of books in order to advance his studies.

(Zeller's Hist. of Phil., p. 171; Wm. Turner's History of Phil. p. 127).

But this sounds more like a fable than the truth, for up to the time of Aristotle, Greek education was represented by the Sophists who taught Rhetoric and dialectics; while the study of elementary science was confined to a few unknown philosophers. This was the standard of Greek education, for the Sophists were the only authorized teachers.

Yet Aristotle is credited with producing a thousand different books dealing with all branches of the scientific knowledge of antiquity. Certainly he could not have obtained them from the Greeks, for that vast body of knowledge, which bears his name and which was presented as new, would really have been the traditional common possession of all who were members of the Greek schools of philosophy for they would have been the only persons inside Greece permitted to own such books; for knowledge was protected as secret.

Under these circumstances it is evident that the vast body of scientific knowledge ascribed to Aristotle, was neither in the possession of the Greeks of his time, nor was there any one in Greece competent to teach him Science and, least of all, on so vast a scale.

(iii) He got the books by looting the Library of Alexandria:—

The question must now be asked: How did Aristotle, a single individual, come to possess such a vast number of scientific works, a body of knowledge which took the Ancient World five thousand years or more to accumulate? It is evident that Aristotle's fame as a scholar has been grossly exaggerated: for such an accomplishment would have been both a physical and mental impossibility. Throughout the intellectual advancement of man, the world has witnessed many a genius; but those have always been specialists in particular fields, not specialists in every branch of science.

And the modern world is no exception, for our great men of science are not specialists in every branch of science, but only in a particular one. That appears to be nature's way.

As a matter of fact, the many discrepancies and doubts in the life and activities of Aristotle lead us to the only reasonable solution of the problem that instead of the tales (a) that Alexander the Great gave him money to buy books (b) that he spent 20 years of his life as a pupil with Plato and (c) that he left the Palace of Alexander for Athens, when Alexander started on his Egyptian invasion, he, on the contrary, must have spent a large part of those 20 years under the tutorship of the Egyptian Priests, and also must have accompanied Alexander on the Egyptian invasion, which gave him the opportunity, not only to carry away from the Alexandrian Library, the vast number of books which are now said to be his, but also to copy notes from a large number of volumes. Indeed modern scholarship has shown that the writings of Aristotle bear all the marks of hurriedly copied notes which of course suggests that Aristotle himself copied these notes from the books of the Alexandrian Library. The historical account of Aristotle's life is incredible.

(iv) It was the custom of ancient armies to capture books as valuable war booty:—

When a victorious army takes possession of a country, it is customary for special companies to search for and seize war booty, i.e., to help themselves to everything that is considered valuable. The Greeks, among all the surrounding nations, were the most anxious to obtain the valuable secrets of the Egyptians, in the Ancient Sciences, and it would appear that the greatest opportunity came to them to accomplish the desire when Alexander the Great invaded Egypt. As stated elsewhere, ancient invading armies looted libraries, because of the great value attached to books; and temples were also looted, not only for books, but also for the gold and silver, out of which the gods and ceremonial vessels were made.

CHAPTER VII

The Curriculum of the Egyptian Mystery System

1. The Education of the Egyptian Priests According to Their Orders. From Diodorus, Herodotus and Clement of Alexandria, we learn that there were six Orders of Egyptian Priests, and that each Order had to master a certain number of the books of Hermes. Clement has described a procession of the Priests, calling them by their Order, and stating their qualifications, as follows:

First comes the Singer Odus, bearing an instrument of music. He has to know by heart two of the books of Hermes; one containing the hymns of the Gods, and the other, the allotment of the king's life. Next comes the Horoscopus, carrying in his hand a horologium or sun-dial, and a palm branch; the symbols of Astronomy. He has to know four of the books of Hermes, which deal with Astronomy.

Next comes the Hierogrammat, with feathers on his head, and a book in his hand, and a rectangular case with writing materials, i.e., the writing ink and the reed. He has to know the hieroglyphics, cosmography, geography, astronomy, the topography of Egypt, the sacred utensils and measures, the temple furniture and the lands.

Next comes the Stolistes, carrying the cubit of justice, and the libation vessels. He has to know the books of Hermes that deal with the slaughter of animals.

Next comes the Prophetes carrying the vessel of water, followed by those who carry the loaves.

The Prophetes is the President of the temple and has to know the ten books which are called hieratic, and contain the laws and doctrines concerning the Gods (secret-theology) and the whole education of the Priests. The books of Hermes are 42 in number and are absolutely necessary. 36 of them have to be known by the Orders which precede, and contain the whole philosophy of the Egyptians.

The remaining six books must be known by the Order of Pastophori. These are medical books and deal with physiology, male and female diseases, anatomy, drugs and instruments. The books of Hermes were well known to the ancient world and were known to Clement of Alexandria, who lived at the beginning of the third century A.D.

In addition to the education contained in the 42 Books of Hermes, the Priests gained considerable knowledge from the selection and examination of sacrificial victims, and the strict bodily purity which their priestly office imposed.

In addition to the Hierogrammat and Horoscopus, who were skilled in theology and hieroglyphics, a Priest was also a Judge and an interpreter of the law. This led to a select tribunal, which made the Egyptian Priest the custodian of every kind of literature. We are also told that the Science of Statistics was cultivated to the greatest perfection among the Egyptian Priests.

(Diodorus I, 80; Clement of Alexandria; Stromata 6, 4,

p. 756; John Kendrick's Ancient Egypt Bk. I, p. 378–379; Bk. II, 85–87; Aelian, Var. Hist. 14, 34; Clement of Alexandria: Stromata 6, 4, p 758: John Kendrick's Ancient Egypt Bk. II p. 31–33).

2. The Education of the Egyptian Priests in—A. The Seven Liberal Arts. B. Secret Systems of Languages and Mathematical Symbolism. C. Magic. A. The education of the Egyptian Priests in the Seven Liberal Arts.

As has already been pointed out, in connection with Plato and the Cardinal Virtues, the Egyptian Mysteries were the centre of organized culture, and the recognized source of education in the ancient world. Neophytes were graded according to their moral efficiency and intellectual competence, and had to submit to many years of tests and ordeals, in order that their eligibility for advancement might be determined. Their education included the Seven Liberal Arts, and the virtues. The virtues were not mere abstractions or ethical sentiments; but positive valours and the virility of the soul. Beyond these, the Priests entered upon a course of specialization.

B. The education of the Egyptian Priests consisted also in the specialization in secret systems of language and mathematical symbolism.

(i) It would appear that there were two forms of writing in use among the Egyptians: (a) The demotic, believed to have been introduced by Pharaoh Psammitichus, for trade and commercial purposes; and (b) The hieroglyphics of which there were two forms, i.e., the hieroglyphics proper, and the hieratic a linear form, both of which were used only by the Priests, in order to conceal the secret and mystical meaning of their doctrines. (Clement of Alexandria:

Stromata Bk. V. c. 4 p. 657; Plutarch, De Iside et Osiride Bk. II, p. 374; John Kendrick; Ancient Egypt, Bk. II, p. 84; 119, 336, and 245).

(ii) We are also informed that the mystery system of Egypt employed modes of spoken language which could be understood, only by the initiated. These consisted not only of myths and parables; but also of a secret language called Senzar.

(Ancient Mysteries: C. H. Vail, p. 23).

(iii) We also understand that the Egyptians attached numerical values both to letters of words and to geometrical figures, with the same intention as with their use of hieroglyphics. i.e., to conceal their teachings. It is further understood that the Egyptian numerical and geometrical symbolism were contained in the 42 Books of Hermes, whose system was the oldest and most elaborate repository of mathematical symbolism. Here again we are reminded of the source of the number philosophy of Pythagoras.

(Ancient Mysteries: C. H. Vail, p. 22–23; Clement of Alexandria: Stromata Book V, c. 7 and 9).

C. The education of the Egyptian Priests consisted also in the specialization in magic.

According to Herodotus, the Egyptian Priests possessed supernatural powers, for they had been trained in the esoteric philosophy of the Greater Mysteries, and were experts in Magic. They had the power of controlling the minds of men (hypnosis), the power of predicting the future (prophecy) and the power over nature, (i.e., the power of Gods) by giving commands in the name of the Divinity and accomplishing great deeds. Herodotus also tells us that the most celebrated Oracles of the ancient world were located in Egypt: Hercules at Canopis; Apollo at Apollinopolis Magna; Minerva at Sais; Diana at Bubastis; Mars at Papremis; and Jupiter at Thebes and Ammonium; and that the Greek Oracles were Egyptian imitations.

Here it might be well to mention that the Egyptian Priests were the first genuine Priests of history, who exercised control over the laws of nature. Here it might also be well to mention that the Egyptian Book of the Dead is a book of magical formulae and instructions, intended to direct the fate of the departed soul. It was the Prayer Book of the Mystery System of Egypt, and the Egyptian Priest received training in post mortem conditions and the methods of their verification. It must also be noted that Magic was applied religion, or primitive scientific method.

(The Egyptian Book of the Dead; Herodotus Bk. II 109, 177; Sandford's Mediterranean World, p. 27; 507; Definition of Magic, Frazier's Golden Bough).

3. A Comparison of the Curriculum of the Egyptian Mystery System with the Lists of Books Attributed to Aristotle. p. 135

A. The Curriculum

The Curriculum of the Egyptian Mystery System consisted of the following subjects:

(i) The Seven Liberal Arts, which formed the foundation training for all Neophytes and included: grammar, Arithmetic, Rhetoric and Dialectic (i.e., the Quadrivium) and Geometry, Astronomy and Music (i.e., the Trivium).

(ii) The Sciences of the 42 Books of Hermes

In addition to the foundation training prescribed for all Neophytes, those who sought Holy Orders, had to be versed in the books of Hermes and according to Clement of Alexandria, their orders and subjects were as follows:—

(a) The Singer or Odus, who must know two books of Hermes dealing with Music i.e., the hymns of the Gods.

(b) The Horoscopus, who must know four books of Hermes dealing with Astronomy.

(c) The Hierogrammat, who must know the hieroglyphics, cosmography, geography, astronomy and the topography of Egypt and Land Surveying.

(d) The Stolistes, who must know the books of Hermes that deal with slaughter of animals and the process of embalming.

(e) The Prophetes, who is the President of the temple, and must know ten books of Hermes dealing with higher esoteric theology and the whole education of priests.

(f) The Pastophori, who must know six books of Hermes, which are medical books, dealing with physiology, the diseases of male and female, anatomy, drugs and instruments.

(iii) The Sciences of the Monuments (Pyramids, Temples, Libraries, Obelisks, Phinxes, Idols):—

Architecture, masonry, carpentry, engineering, sculpture, metallurgy, agriculture, mining and forestry. Art (drawing and painting).

(iv) The Secret Sciences

Numerical symbolism, geometrical symbolism, magic, the book of the Dead, myths and parables.

(v) The Social Order and Its Protection

The Priests of Egypt were also Lawyers, Judges, officials of government, Business Men and Sailors and Captains. Hence, they must have been trained in Economics, Civics, Law, Government, Statistics, census taking, navigation, ship building, military science, the manufacture of chariots and horse breeding.

If we compare 3A with 3B which immediately follows, we would discover that the curriculum of the Egyptian Mystery System covered a much wider range of scientific subjects than those of Aristotle's list, which it includes.

N.B.

Note also that The Seven Liberal Arts: The Quadrivium and Trivium originated from the Egyptian Mysteries.

(The Mechanical Triumphs of the Ancient Egyptians by F. M. Barber).

(The Book of the Foundation of Temples by Moret).

(A short history of Mathematics by W. W. R. Ball).

(The Problem of Obelisks by R. Engelbach).

(The Great Pyramid Its Divine Message by D. Davidson).

(History of Mathematics by Florian Cajori).

B. Aristotle's list of books, prepared by himself.

(1) Aristotle is said to have prepared a list of books in the following order (B. D. Alexander's Hist. of Phil. p. 97; Wm. Turner's Hist. of Phil. p. 129).

(i) Theoretic whose purpose was truth, and which included (a) Mathematics (b) Physics and (c) Theology.

(ii) Practical, whose purpose was usefulness, and which included (a) Ethics (b) Economics (c) Politics and

(iii) Poetic or Productive, whose purpose was beauty, and which included (a) Poetry (b) Art and (c) Rhetoric. An examination and comparison of 3 A. with 3 B. show that (a) The Curriculum of the Egyptian Mystery System included all the scientific and philosophic subjects credited to the authorship of Aristotle. (b) The books attributed to Aristotle's authorship cannot be dissociated from Egyptian origin, as elsewhere referred to, both through the plunder of the Royal Library of Alexandria and through research carried on at the centre by Aristotle himself. As has been mentioned elsewhere, the writings of Aristotle are disputed by modern scholarship (Wm. Turner's Hist. of Phil. p. 127) and I feel more justified in making the comparison between the curriculum of the Mystery System and the list said to be drawn up by Aristotle himself; rather than with the notorious list of one thousand books, whose subjects are nevertheless included under the curriculum of the Egyptian Mystery System.

(Zeller's Hist. of Phil. p. 173).

CHAPTER VIII

The Memphite Theology is the Basis of all Important Doctrines in Greek Philosophy.

History and Description:

The Memphite Theology is an inscription on a stone, now kept in the British Museum. It contains the theological, cosmological and philosophical views of the Egyptians. It has already been referred to in my treatment of Plato's doctrines; but it must be repeated here to show its full importance as the basis of the entire field of Greek philosophy. It is dated 700 B.C., and bears the name of an Egyptian Pharaoh who stated that he had copied an inscription of his ancestors. This statement is verified by language and typical arrangement of the text, and therefore assigns the original date of the Memphite Theology to a very early period of Egyptian history, i.e., the time when the first Dynasties had made their new capital at Memphis: the city of the God Ptah, i.e., between 4000 and 3500 B.C. (Intellectual Adventure of Man by Frankfort, p. 55).

The Text:

This consists of three supplementary parts, each of which will be treated separately: both as regards its teachings and the identity in Greek philosophy.

Part I presents the Gods of Chaos. Part II presents the Gods of Order and arrangement in creation; and Part III presents the Primate of the Gods, or the God of Gods, through whose (Logos) creation was accomplished.

In Part I pre-creation or chaos is represented as follows:—

A. Text of Part I:

The Primate of the Gods Ptah, conceived in his heart, everything that exists and by His utterance created them all. He is first to emerge from the primeval waters of Nun in the form of a Primeval Hill. Closely following the Hill, the God Atom also emerges from the waters and sits upon Ptah (the Hill). There remain in the waters four pairs of male and female gods (the Ogdoad, or unity of Eight-Gods), bearing the following names:—

(1) Nun and Naunet, i.e., the Primeval waters and the counter heaven.

(2) Huh and Hauhet, i.e., the boundless and its opposite:

(3) Kuk and Kauket, i.e., darkness and its opposite; and

(4) Amun, i.e., (Amon) and Amaunet, i.e., the hidden and its opposite.

(Egyptian Religion by Frankfort, p. 20; 23. Intellectual Adventure of Ancient Man by Frankfort, p. 21).

B. The Philosophy of Part I:

(1) Ptah has the following attributes: (a) The Primate of the Gods, i.e., The God of Gods (b) The Logos. Thought and creative utterance and power (Egyptian Religion by Frankfort, p. 23). (c) The God of Order and form (d) The Divine Artificer and Potter (Fire Philosophy by Swinburne Clymer; Jamblichus; Ancient Egypt by John Kendrick, Bk. I, p. 318; 339).

It must be noted that while the Sun God Atom sits upon Ptah the Primeval Hill He accomplishes the work of creation. But the Memphite Theology dates back to 4000 B.C., when it is believed the Greeks were unknown (Frankfort's Intellectual Adventure of Man, p. 5; 53; 55. The Book of the Dead, p. 17).

This arrangement in the Memphite Theology could only mean that the ingredients of the Primeval Chaos contained ten principles: four pairs of opposite principles, together with two other gods: Ptah representing Mind, Thought, and creative Utterance; while Atom joins himself to Ptah and acts as Demiurge and executes the work of creation. From such an arrangement in the cosmos we are in position to infer the following philosophies:—

(a) Water is the source of all things.

(b) Creation was accomplished by the unity of two creative principles: Ptah and Atom, i.e., the unity of Mind (nous) with Logos (creative Utterance).

(c) Atom was the Demiurge or Intermediate God in creation. He was also Sun God or Fire God.

(d) Opposite Principles control the life of the universe.

(e) The elements in creation were Fire (Atom), Water (Nun), Earth (Ptah or Ta-tjenen) and Air.

Part I of the Memphite Theology is the correct Source of these

Stolen Legacy

philosophies: but strangely the Greeks have claimed them as their production, although without any right whatever.

C. Individual Greek Philosophers to whom portions of the philosophy of the Memphite Theology has been assigned:

Of these doctrines, "water as the source of all things" has been assigned to Thales (Zeller: Hist. of Phil. p. 38); that of the "Boundless or Unlimited", has been assigned to Anaximander (Zeller: Hist. of Phil. p. 40); while that of "Air as the basis of life" has been assigned to Anaximenes (Zeller: Hist. of Phil. p. 42). Furthermore, the doctrine "that Fire underlies the life of the universe", has been assigned not only to Pythagoras, who spoke of the functions of the central and peripheral Fires; but also to Heraclitus who spoke of the transmutation of Fire into the other elements, and their transmutation back into Fire. Also Democritus who spoke of Fire Atoms, as filling space as the Mind or Soul of the World; and Plato who spoke of a World-Soul, which is composed of Fire Atoms. (Wm. Turner's Hist. of Phil. p. 42; 5; Zeller's Hist. of Phil. p. 53; 149; Plato's Timaeus, 30A; B. D. Alexander's Hist. of Phil., p. 40).

Likewise the doctrine of opposites has been assigned not only to Pythagoras, who spoke of the elements of the unit as odd and even; but also to (a) Heraclitus who spoke of "the unity of warring opposites"; (b) Parmenides who spoke of the distinction between Being and Not-Being; (c) Socrates, who spoke of things as being generated from their opposites; and

(d) Plato who spoke of Ideas and Noumena as real and perfect; but phenomena as unreal and imperfect. (The Phaedrus of Plato 250; Parmenides 132D; Aristotle Metaphysics I, 6; 987b, 9; Plato Phaedo 70E; Zeller's Hist. of Phil. p. 51; 61, 68; The Timaeus, p. 28).

Furthermore, the doctrines of the Nous (or Mind) or an Intelligent Agency as responsible for creation, has been assigned not only to Anaxagoras, but also to Socrates who spoke of the existence of useful things as the work of an Intelligence: To Plato who spoke of a World-Soul or Mind, as the cause of life and knowledge in the universe and to Democritus, who attached a similar meaning. (Zeller's Hist. of Phil. p. 80; p. 85; Wm. Turner's Hist. of Phil. p. 82; p. 109). The doctrine of the Logos has been assigned to Heraclitus who spoke of Fire as the Logos or creative principle in nature; while the doctrine of the Demiurge, or an Intermediate God who created the world, has been assigned to Plato (Wm. Turner's Hist.

of Phil. p. 55, p. 108).

A. Text of Part II

The Gods of Order and arrangement in the cosmos are represented by nine gods, in one God-head, called the Ennead. Here Atum (Atom), the source of the Ogdoad, is also retained as the source of the Gods of Order and arrangement. Atum (Atom) names four pairs of parts of his own body, and thus creates eight Gods, who together with himself become nine. These Eight Gods are the created Gods, the first creatures of this world; and Atum (Atom), the Creator God, the Demiurge, of whom Plato spoke. The Gods whom Atum (Atom) projected from his body were

(i) Shu (Air)

(ii) Tefnut (Moisture)

(iii) Geb (Earth) and

(iv) Nut (Sky);

who are said to have given birth to four other Gods:

(v) Osiris (the God of omnipotence and omniscience)

(vi) Isis (wife of Osiris, Female Principle)

(vii) Seth (the opposite of good)

(viii) Nephthys (Female Principle in the Unseen World).

(Plutarch: Isis et Osiris, 355A; 364C; 371B; Frankfurt; Intellectual Adventure of Ancient Man, p. 66–67).

B. The Philosophy of Part II.

As we read the text of Part II, we find that the Sun God Atum (Atom) who was present in the Chaos was also present at the development of orderly arrangement in the cosmos. At this stage Atum (Atom) assumes the role of creator of all Gods except Ptah, the God of Gods. He next proceeds to accomplish this special type of creation in the following manner: He commands Eight Gods to proceed from His own body according to the names of those eight parts.

The result of this creation presents us with what has been called (a) the "Ennead" or the unity of "nine Gods in one Godhead" (b) the doctrine of the Demiurge as in Part I, (c) the doctrine of the

Stolen Legacy

created Gods and (d) the doctrine of the Unmoved Mover; also (e) the doctrine of opposites and (f) Omnipotence and Omniscience. Of these doctrines, that of the "Ennead" will be dealt with elsewhere, and since the doctrine of the Demiurge has already been treated, together with (c) the created Gods, I shall now discuss the doctrine of the Unmoved Mover, as based upon the same act of creation. According to the Memphite Theology of the Egyptians, Atum created Eight Gods who proceeded from eight parts of His own body. He was seated upon Ptah the Hill and was unmoved. In this act of creation Atum (Atom) became the Unmoved Mover. In spite of the Memphite Theology being the direct source of these doctrines, yet Plato has been given credit for the doctrine of the created Gods: while Aristotle has received credit for that of the "Unmoved Mover". Certainly the world has never been more misled.

Here it must be made quite clear, that the doctrine of a Demiurge in creation includes two other doctrines: that of the created Gods and that of the Unmoved Mover.

It was the function of the Demiurge to create the universe; and in doing so, his first act was the creation of the Gods, who accordingly became the first creatures.

But the manner in which the Demiurge created the Gods was the process of projecting them from His own body.

This method of creation clearly makes the Demiurge the Unmoved Mover.

However the history of Greek philosophy has assigned the authorship of the doctrines of the Demiurge and the created Gods to Plato, and the authorship of the doctrine of the Unmoved Mover to Aristotle.

But this so-called Platonic doctrine is one, made up of three inseparable parts (a) the Demiurge (b) the function of the Demiurge and (c) the method of the function: a unity which contradicts Aristotle's authorship of what is really only an inference from the supposed original doctrine of Plato.

(The Myth of Creation in Plato Timaeus: Wm. Turner: Hist. of Phil., p. 109–110; Zeller's Hist. of Phil. p. 192; Wm. Turner's Hist. of Phil. p. 142).

The doctrine of opposites has already been discussed, however, in Part I of the Memphite Theology. One of the pairs of created

Gods, Osiris and Isis was used to represent the male and female principles of nature. In addition to this, Osiris had other qualities attached to Him, which might be understood from the following derivatives (a) osh meaning many, and (b) iri meaning to do and also (c) meaning an Eye. Consequently Osiris came to mean not only many eyed or omniscient, but also omnipotent or all powerful. Here again, as in all instances already mentioned, in spite of the fact that the Memphite Theology is the source of Greek philosophy, yet the doctrines of "an Intelligent Cause", a Nous as responsible for the life and conduct of the world, has been assigned to Anaxagoras,

Socrates and also Plato, whose World Soul, consisted of fire atoms, like the World Soul of Democritus. (Plato Timaeus 30, 35. Xenophon Memorabilia I, 4, 2; Wm. Turner's Hist. of Phil. 63).

A. Text of Part III

In this third part of the Memphite Theology, the Primate of the Gods is represented as Ptah: Thought, Logos and Creative Power, which are exercised over all creatures. He transmits power and spirit to all Gods, and controls the lives of all things, animals and men through His thought and commands. In other words it is in Him that all things live move and have their eternal being.

B. The Philosophy of Part III

From Part III we infer the following doctrines:—(a) all things were created by the thought and command of Ptah, the God of Gods. (b) Through the thought and command of Ptah, we all live, move and have our eternal Being. (c) Ptah is Creator and Preserver as has already been pointed out elsewhere; Ptah's powers were transmitted by magical means to Atum who performed the work of creation. (Intellectual Adventures of Man by Frankfort, p. 52–60).

II. Memphite Theology is the Source of Modern Scientific Knowledge.

A. The Ennead and the Nebular Hypothesis.

B. The identity between the Sun God Atom, and the atom of science.

A. The Ennead and the Nebular Hypothesis coincide.

Just as the Memphite Theology is the source of Greek philosophy or primitive science, so it is also the basis of modern scientific belief. The Gods of Order and arrangement in the cosmos are represented by nine Gods in the Godhead, called the Ennead. Atum, (Atom), the Sun God, i.e., Fire God, creates eight other Gods, by naming four pairs of parts of his own body, from which they came forth. Here the names of the created Gods were given as Shu and Tefnut (Air and Moisture), Geb and Nut (Earth and Sky); and two other pairs of opposites: Osiris and Isis; and Seth and Nephthys, who are supposed to be the first creatures of this world (Frankfort's Intellectual Adventures of Man, p. 54).

Now if we compare this Egyptian cosmology with the Nebular hypothesis of Laplace, we would find very striking similarities in the two contexts. According to the Nebular hypothesis our present solar system was once a molten gaseous nebula. This nebula rotated at an enormous speed, and as the mass cooled down it also contracted and developed greater speed. The result was a bulging at the equator and a gradual breaking off of gaseous rings, which formed themselves into planets. These planets in turn threw off gaseous rings, which formed themselves into smaller bodies, until at last, the sun was left as the remnant of the original parent Nebula. From this context it is clear that the original parent nebula was fire or the Sun, and that by throwing off parts of itself, it created some planets, which in turn threw off parts of themselves and created others. According to the context of the Memphite Theology, the creator God was the Sun God or fire God Atum (Atom), who named four pairs of parts of his own body, from which Gods came forth.

But Atum (Atom) together with the Eight Created Gods composed the Ennead or Godhead of nine: a very striking similarity with modern science which teaches that there are nine major planets. We may now summarise these similarities:—(a) The creator God in both the Egyptian and Modern Cosmologies is the Sun or Fire. (b) The creator God in both cosmologies creates Gods from parts of Himself. (c) The number of Gods are nine and correspond with the nine major planets. These similarities make it evident that Laplace obtained his hypothesis from the Memphite Theology or other Egyptian sources.

Of course the Memphite Theology, according to Frankfort in his Intellectual Adventure of Ancient Man, p. 54 does not mention the creation of planets. Nevertheless, since it was the method of the Egyptian to conceal the truth by the use of myths, parables magical principles (primitive scientific method), number philosophy and hieroglyphics, we can easily see what methods might be involved before we could arrive at a better translation of the Memphite Theology.

At any rate, the entire setting of the Memphite Theology is astronomical, and what could be more natural, than to expect an astronomical interpretation? It seems well within reason, to regard the Ennead as the heliocentric system of history. Atom the sun God, creating eight other Gods or planets from his own body, as the Unmoved Mover a teaching which has been falsely attributed to Aristotle.

B. The identity between the Egyptian Sun God Atum (Atom) and the atom of Modern Science:

There are two things which I desire to point out in connexion with the relationship between Atum (Atom) the Egyptian Sun God and the atom of modern science. These things are (i) the similarity of attributes and (ii) the similarity of names. (i) The Egyptian God Atum (Atom) means self-created; everything and nothing: a combination of positive and negative principles:—all-inclusiveness and emptiness; a Demiurge, possessing creative powers; the Creator Sun. (p. 53, Frankfort's Intellectual Adventure of Ancient Man; p. 182, Frankfort's Kingship and the Gods).

Atum (Atom) also means "the all and the not yet Being"; (p. 168 Frankfort's Kingship of the Gods). As a God Atum (Atom) represents the principles of opposites. The atom, as the substratum of matter, according to Greek philosophy, is defined by Democritus as "movement of that which is" (To on) within "that which is not" (To mē on). It therefore represents the principle of opposites, and shows the identity between the Egyptian Sun God and the substratum of matter. Furthermore, the atom is defined as "the full and void; being and not-being (Zeller's Hist. of Phil., p. 38) and these definitions coincide with the everything and nothing, and the "all-inclusiveness" and emptiness of the Egyptian Sun God.

(ii) The similarity of names shared by the Egyptian Sun God and the atom of science:

Now, with reference to the similarity of these two names, the first thing we should bear in mind is the fact that they both possess identical attributes, as has been already pointed out in section i; and consequently we are compelled to conclude that the atom of science is the identical name of the Egyptian Sun God: the most an-

Stolen Legacy

cient of Gods except Ptah, who was present with Atom at creation. The second thing we should bear in mind is the fact that the name of the God Atom (sometimes spelt Atum) belongs to the cosmology of the Memphite Theology, whose date goes back to 4000 B.C. when the Greeks were not even known. Consequently we are compelled to conclude that the Greeks obtained both the original name and the attributes of the Sun God Atom from the Egyptians.

Furthermore, the Greeks were unacquainted with the Egyptian language, during the period of the so-called Greek philosophy, dating from the sixth century B.C. and as a consequence transliterated Egyptian words into Greek without regard to their Coptic derivatives. The following Homeric stories verify the practice of the Greeks in the transliteration of Egyptian words and the plagiarism of their legends. (a) According to Homer, Proteus was a Maritime Divinity feeding his phocae on the coast of Egypt. He was endowed with the gift of prophecy which was exercised only upon compulsion. Proteus, however was an Egyptian Pharaoh who succeeded to the throne on the death of Pheron, the son of Sesostris. Proteus was also worshipped at Memphis. The Greeks did not only transliterate the name of this Egyptian King, but also plagiarized on the legend. (Herodotus II, 112).

(b) Likewise the story of Io the Argive Princess, who was changed into a heifer, and after long wanderings, reached Egypt, where she gave birth to a God, and where she herself was worshipped as the Goddess Isis, points clearly to the introduction of the worship of Isis or Athor, under the symbol of the heifer, at an early period into Argos. Here it must be pointed out that Io is the Coptic name for Moon, and the same word was preserved as the dialect of Argos, without any affinity with any Greek root. It was a habit of the Greeks to Hellenize Egyptian words by transliterating them and adding them to the Greek vocabulary.

(c) This practice of borrowing words from nearby nations continued until New Testament times. In Acts of Apostles of the Greek Testament, Chapter 13th and verse 1, the word Niger (i.e., black man) in the name Simeon the Negro is a Roman or Latin word (niger, nigra, nigrum) meaning black. Simeon, of course, was an Egyptian Professor attached to the Church at Rome.

The atom of science is really the name of the Egyptian Sun God that has come down to modern times, through the so-called Greek philosophy, and carries identical attributes, with the Sun God. (Diodorus I, 29; John Kendrick's Ancient Egypt, vol. II 5–52;

Eust. ad Dionys: Perieg: V).

N.B.

It must be remembered that what we erroneously call Greek philosophy, was the beginning of science or the investigation of nature; and consequently we cannot separate modern science from Greek philosophy.

III. Memphite Theology Opens Great Possibilities for Modern Scientific Research. A. Greek Concept of the Atom; erroneous.

The Greeks derived the meaning of the atom from (i) (alpha) i.e. a negative prefix meaning not; and (ii) (temnein) i.e. the present infinitive active of (temno) to cut. The two derivatives together meaning "that which cannot be cut". For centuries the world has been misled by this misconception of the Greeks: a fact which no doubt, had impeded the progress of atomic research by Western scholars, who had believed in the so-called Greek origin of philosophy or primitive science.

Today, however, the Greek conception of the atom is no longer tenable, since modern science has successfully split the atom.

B. Great scientific secrets in the Memphite Theology, yet to be discovered.

I believe that the time has come, within which man will be able to unlock most of the secrets of nature hitherto hidden and unknown. I have shown that the Nebular Hypothesis of modern times coincides with the teachings of the Memphite Theology, in which the Sun God Atom is said to have created eight other Gods, which together with himself constitute the Ennead of the Egyptians, which correspond to the nine major planets of modern scientific teaching.

We also know that out of Cosmic Chaos there arose from the primeval waters a pair of Gods i.e. the Primeval Hill and Atom the Sun God, and that through the contact of Atom with the Hill, He received power to create the other eight major planets. This seems to imply that

(i) Atomic energy originates from water and earth, since water H_2O, and uranium, an indispensable ingredient in atomic energy, is found in the bowels of the earth. Note that both Atom and the Hill came out of the primeval Waters.

(ii) Four pairs of Gods, representing positive and negative principles still remain in water, in the form of male and female frogs and snakes, and constitute four fifths of the secrets of creation, which man has yet to fathom.

(iii) Successful scientific research in the principles and secrets of nature lies in the study of the Memphite Theology, whose symbology requires the key of magical principles for its interpretation. With this approach our men of science should be able to unlock the doors of the secrets of nature and become the custodians of unlimited knowledge.

This is the legacy of the African Continent to the nations of the world. She has laid the cultural foundations of modern progress and therefore she and her people deserve the honour and praise which for centuries have been falsely given to the Greeks. And likewise, it is the purpose of this book to make this revelation the beginning of a universal reformation in race relations, which I believe would be the beginning of the solution of the problem of universal unrest.

George G. M. James

PART II

CHAPTER IX

Social Reformation through the New Philosophy of African Redemption. Now that it has been shown that philosophy, and the arts and sciences were bequeathed to civilization by the people of North Africa and not by the people of Greece; the pendulum of praise and honour is due to shift from the people of Greece to the people of the African continent who are the rightful heirs of such praise and honour.

This is going to mean a tremendous change in world opinion, and attitude, for all people and races who accept the new philosophy of African redemption, i.e. the truth that the Greeks were not the authors of Greek philosophy: but the people of North Africa; would change their opinion from one of disrespect to one of respect for the Black people throughout the world and treat them accordingly.

It is also going to mean a most important change in the mentality of the Black people: a change from an inferiority complex, to the realization and consciousness of their equality with all the other great peoples of the world, who have built great civilizations. With this change in the mentality of the Black and White people, great changes are also expected in their respective attitudes towards each other, and in society as a whole.

In the drama of Greek philosophy there are three actors, who have played distinct parts, namely Alexander the Great, who by an act of aggression invaded Egypt in 333 B.C., and ransacked and looted the Royal Library at Alexandria and together with his companions carried off a booty of scientific, philosophic and religious books. Egypt was then stolen and annexed as a portion of Alexander's empire; but the invasion plan included far more than mere territorial expansion; for it prepared the way and made it possible for the capture of the culture of the African Continent. This brings us to the second actor, that is the School of Aristotle whose students moved from Athens to Egypt and converted the royal library, first into a research centre, and secondly into a University and thirdly compiled that vast body of scientific knowledge which they had gained from research, together with the oral instructions which Greek students had received from the Egyptian priests, into what they have called the history of Greek Philosophy.

In this way, the Greeks stole the Legacy of the African Continent and called it their own. And as has already been pointed out, the result of this dishonesty has been the creation of an erroneous world opinion; that the African continent has made no contribution to civilization, because her people are backward and low in intelligence and culture.

This erroneous opinion about the Black people has seriously injured them through the centuries up to modern times in which it appears to have reached a climax in the history of human relations. And now we come to the third actor, and that is Ancient Rome, who through the edicts of her Emperors Theodosius in the 4th century A.D. and Justinian in the 6th century A.D. abolished the Mysteries of the African Continent; that is the ancient culture system of the world. The higher metaphysical doctrines of those Mysteries could not be comprehended; the spiritual powers of the priests were unsurpassed; the magic of the rites and ceremonies filled the people with awe; Egypt was the holy land of the ancient world and the Mysteries were the one, ancient and holy Catholic religion, whose power was supreme. This lofty culture system of the Black people filled Rome with envy, and consequently she legalized Christianity which she had persecuted for five long centuries, and set it up as a state religion and as a rival of Mysteries, its own mother. This is why the Mysteries have been despised; this is why other ancient religions of the Black people are despised; because they are all offspring of the African Mysteries, which have never been clearly understood by Europeans, and consequently have provoked their prejudice and condemnation. In keeping with the plan of Emperors Theodosius and Justinian to exterminate and forever suppress the culture system of the African continents the Christian church established its missionary enterprise to fight against what it has called paganism. Consequently missionaries and educators have gone to the mission field with a superiority complex, born of miseducation and disrespect: a prejudice which has made it impossible for them to accomplish the blessings which missionary enterprise might otherwise have accomplished. For this reason Missionary enterprise has been responsible for a positive injury against the African people, which consists of the perpetual caricature of African culture in literature and exhibitions which provoke laughter and disrespect. This then is only a brief summary of the parts played by the persons of the drama of Greek philosophy and the resultant effects upon the Black people. This drama might be called the Causa Causarum of the social plight of the peoples of African descent, because it has made the White and Black races not only common victims of a false racial tradition about the African Continent but also partners in the solution of the problem of racial reformation.

I believe that a reformation of this kind is possible, if the best minds of both racial groups co-operate in its accomplishment. Both groups have been the common victims of miseducation arising from a false tradition about the African Continent and it has caused them to develop attitudes according to their common belief: The White people, a superiority complex: and the Black people, the corresponding inferiority complex; and if we are to accomplish a reformation in race relations it is obvious that both racial groups must combine their efforts in the abandonment and destruction of that mentality which has plunged the Black people into their social plight.

This I suggest should be done by a world wide dissemination of the truth, through a system of re-education, in order to stimulate and encourage a change in the attitude of races toward each other In combining their efforts, both races must not only preach and teach the truth that the Mystery system of the African Continent gave the world philosophy and religion, and the arts and sciences, but they must see to it that all false praise of the Greeks be removed from the textbooks of our schools and colleges: for this is the practice that has blind-folded the world, and has laid the foundations for the deplorable race relations of the modern world. (a) The name of Pythagoras, for instance, should be deleted from our mathematical textbooks: in Geometry, where the theorem of the square on the hypotenuse of a right angled triangle is called the Pythagorean theorem, because this is not true. (b) we must point out to the world the deception in attaching the authorship of Socrates to the precept 'man know thyself'; and in attaching the authorship of Plato to the four cardinal virtues; since Socrates obtained the self-knowledge precept from the Egyptian temples where it was used as an inscription: and Plato reduced the ten virtues of the North African Mystery system to four (c) we must also prove to the world that the doctrines of the so-called Greek philosophers originated from the ancient Mystery System of North Africa.

This proof has been set forth in chapters five to eight of 'Stolen Legacy,' and in order to carry out our world-wide crusade we must recommend 'Stolen Legacy,' for adoption and study in the schools and colleges of both racial groups and in our fraternities, sororities and inter-racial groups, in order that young and old of our present generation might all get to know the truth and be able to pass it on to future generations.

This I believe would be a very helpful method by which this process of re-education would become universal and effective in the creation of a much needed racial reformation. The White people of 'our modern age cannot be regarded as wholly responsible for social conditions which are the result of false racial tradition. It is this that makes race relations a challenge to the best minds of both racial groups to combine their efforts in its solution.

But our disturbed race relations have also another cause. This I would say is both supplementary and intensive; for the false tradition about the backwardness of the African Continent, created by Alexander the Great and Aristotle's School has been dramatized by missionary literature and exhibitions, as the will of Roman Emperors and as a source of laughter and disrespect. There is no doubt that this policy has created bitterness and dissatisfaction in the minds of natives, who have been compelled to question the sincerity of the missionary. In the meantime missionary enterprise gains the sympathy and support of a miseducated world, in order to carry on its programme.

What can we do to eradicate this second and more subtle evil: the dramatization of a false tradition so as to make it appear as true? I suggest that since the missionary dramatizes false tradition because he himself also believes it, we should combine our efforts, first of all in re-educating him so that he might know the truth and change his superiority complex which is responsible for his mistaken policy. His re-education should not only consist of a thorough study of the ideas and arguments contained in my book 'Stolen Legacy'; but he must also be given special training in the language, customs and ideals of Africans, in order to make him cultivate an attitude of respect for the culture of the African Continent, seemingly the oldest specimen to have been developed by mankind; because that continent is the birth place and the cradle of the Ancient Mysteries. With a world enlightened as to the real truth about the place of the African Continent in the history of civilization, false tradition and belief should cease to be effective, disrespect and prejudice should tend to disappear, and race relations should tend to be normal and peaceful. This brings us to the final problem, the problem of African redemption. The aims of 'Stolen Legacy' are not only to stimulate a reformation in race relations and scientific research; but also to cultivate race pride in the Black people themselves and to offer them a New Philosophy of African Redemption as the Modus Operandi of achieving racial reformation.

This New Philosophy of Redemption consists of a simple proposition as follows:

'The Greeks were not the authors of Greek philosophy, but the Black people of North Africa, The Egyptians.'

Now, in order to explain the value of this proposition, three questions must be asked and answered.

(a) As a simple proposition, what is its significance?

Its significance lies in the fact that it is a statement of an important truth, which is the exposure of Greek dishonesty.

(b) Why is this proposition called a philosophy?

A philosophy is an accepted belief, and this proposition is a philosophy because it is offered as a belief, worthy of acceptance.

(c) What is a philosophy of redemption?

A philosophy of redemption is not merely an accepted belief; but a belief that is also lived in order to enjoy the benefits of its teaching.

This proposition will become a philosophy of redemption to all Black people, when they accept it as a belief and live up to it. This brings us to our final question and that is, how to live up to this philosophy of redemption? In other words, how shall the Black people work out their own salvation?

From the outset my readers and co-workers in the solution of a common problem, must be reminded that our philosophy of redemption is a psychological process, involving a change in belief or mentality to be followed by a corresponding change in behaviour. It really signifies a mental emancipation, in which the Black people will be liberated from the chain of traditional falsehood, which for centuries has incarcerated them in the prison of inferiority complex and world humiliation and insult. This mental emancipation or redemption, it must be remembered, has two functions. It is general, when, on the one hand, the phenomenon of our unwholesome race relations is regarded as a general problem needing a general emancipation of both races in order to effect a solution. In this general sense emancipation transcends the limitations and boundaries of race, and therefore includes the whole world, White and Black people, since we are all victims of the same chain of the traditional falsehood, that has incarcerated the modern world. On the other hand, emancipation or redemption is specific, when we refer to the effects of the phenomenon of unwholesome race relations upon the Black people. It is freedom from such conditions that constitutes the specific function of emancipation or redemption.

We digressed somewhat in order to explain the terms philosophy and philosophy of redemption, believing it to be necessary before proceeding to answer the next question: how to live up to this New Philosophy of Redemption? How must it be worked out?

Being liberated from inferiority complex by their New Philosophy of Redemption, which is destined to destroy the chain of false tradition which has incarcerated them, the Black people must face and interpret the world according to their new vision and philosophy. Throughout the centuries up to our modern times, world conditions have been influenced by two phenomena which have affected human relations.

(i) The giving of false praise to the Greeks: a custom which appears to be an educational policy conducted by educational institutions. This has led to the false worship of Socrates, Plato, and Aristotle, as intellectual gods in all the leading universities of the world, and in support of this intellectual worship, these institutions have also organized what are known as Greek lettered fraternities and sororities, as the symbols of the superiority of Greek intellect and culture.

(ii) The second phenomenon is Missionary enterprise whereby the Black people's culture has been caricatured in literature and exhibitions, in such specimens as provoke disrespect and laughter. Never let us forget that the Roman Emperors Theodosius and Justinian were responsible for the abolition of the Egyptian Mysteries that is the culture system of the Black people, and also for the establishment of Christianity for its perpetual suppression.

Likewise, never let us forget when we are reviewing this bit of history that the Greeks called the Egyptians Hoi Aiguptoi which meant Black people.

In living up to their New Philosophy of Redemption, the life of the Black people will have to be one of counteraction against these two sets of conditions. In the first place the Black people must adopt a negative attitude towards this type of phenomena, because they have become fully aware that these phenomena are the result of a false tradition, and therefore also partake of the nature of falsehood and insincerity.

In this negative attitude the Black people of the world must shun the false tradition and must teach the truth, which is their New Philosophy of Redemption. This must be done in the home to young children; in the colleges and schools to students; from the pulpits and platforms to audiences; and in the fraternities and sororities to young men and women. This New Philosophy of Redemption, being a revelation of truth in the history of Black people's civilization must become a necessary portion of their education, and must be taught for generations and centuries to come: in order to fill them with inspiration and pride and liberate them from mental servitude.

In the second place, in this negative attitude the Black people must demonstrate their disbelief in the false worship of Greek intellect. This should be done in the following three ways:—

(i) They must discontinue the practice of quoting Socrates, Plato and Aristotle in their speeches as intellectual models; because we know that their philosophy was stolen (ii) They must relinquish membership from all Greek lettered fraternities and sororities and (iii) They must abolish all Greek lettered fraternities and sororities from all colored colleges because they have been a source of the promotion of inferiority complex and of educating the Black people against themselves. We come now to the counteraction of the second set of phenomena, the missionary activities in defamatory literature and exhibitions which provoke disrespect for and laughter at the Black people.

Just as in the first set of phenomena, so is it in the second, the Black people must adopt a negative attitude in their attempt to live up to their philosophy of redemption. Of course, they are perfectly well aware that the activities of missionaries are the result of their own miseducation through the medium of a false tradition about Black people; but since their problem is also one of emancipation from certain social evils, the Black people feel that they are entitled to a change in Missionary policy. For these reasons I suggest that the negative attitude of the Black people should consist first of a boycott of missionary literature and exhibitions, and secondly, of a perpetual protest against these forms of missionary policy, until a change is brought about. For as long as Missionary enterprise maintains its policy of militancy against African culture, the Black people will be disrespected. This is the least that the Black people are entitled to: respectful treatment, because they are the representatives of the oldest civilization in the world, from which all other cultures have borrowed. I have frequently seen in the parish magazines of some European churches, pictures of the following description:—An African Chief, dressed in a new silk hat, a long shirt, but no trousers, a frock coat and barefeet; probably to provide amusement for the parishioners and to excite their pity. This is what the Black people must protest against and this is how they must live up to their philosophy of redemption and work it out.

In conclusion, let us remember that the unfortunate position of the modern church in being associated with the drama of Greek philosophy is excusable; because her missionary function has been due to the erroneous mandates and edicts of secular Princes and Emperors, who ruled the church, when it was only a department of state. This bit of ecclesiastical history should be well known to the early branches of the Christian church and consequently, they are the ones whom our enlightened age expects to initiate a change in missionary policy, which would free themselves from the error and superstition of human relations.

This lead of the various branches of Catholicism should be followed by Protestantism, so that the entire church of Christ on earth should be united in this racial reformation, and carry to the mission field a practical gospel of happiness; that is happiness that must begin while we are here on earth: a gospel that is interested in the total welfare of the people. A gospel which ignores the social and economic rights of natives and emphasizes only happiness in an unknown world is onesided, misleading, and contrary to Christian tenets and practice. It was early Christianity that established a diaconate for the express purpose of solving the economic problems of its adherents; so that they might begin in their earthly life to experience what happiness really meant.

It is evident that the benefits of religion are intended to be coextensive with human needs and unless the Christian religion changes its missionary policy with respect to the Culture of the Black people, it would be difficult for them to obtain complete emancipation from the social injuries created by Ancient Rome.

APPENDIX

The purpose of this appendix is to present a brief analysis and summary of the arguments, conclusions and inferences which relate to the subject matter which has already been treated. It is also hoped that it will serve the secondary purpose of simplification.

Argument I. Greek philosophy was stolen Egyptian philosophy.

Because history tells us that (i) The teachings of the Egyptian Mystery System travelled from Egypt to the island Samos, and from Samos to Croton and Elea in Italy, and lastly from Italy to Athens in Greece through the medium of Pythagoras and the Eleatic and late Ionic philosophers. Accordingly, Egypt was the true source of the Mystery teachings and therefore any claim to such origin by the ancient Greeks is not only erroneous but must have been based upon dishonest motives.

(ii) History also represents the early life and education of Greek philosophers as a blank and their chronology as a matter of speculation. Consequently it has given the world the opinion that the Greek philosophers, with the exception of the three Athenians, might never have existed and might never have taught the doctrines alleged to them. In other words History represents the Pre-Socratic philosophers as questionable in existence and under those circumstances they could neither produce philosophy nor claim its authorship, except by questionable and dishonest methods.

(iii) The compilation of Greek philosophy appears to have been the idea of Aristotle, but the work of the alumni of his school. The movement was unauthorized by the Greek Government which always hated and persecuted philosophy, because it was Egyptian and foreign. The organization, control and operation of the Mysteries gave the Egyptians the right of ownership to philosophy, and therefore any claims by the ancient Greeks to philosophy must be considered as illegal and dishonest.

Argument II. So-called Greek philosophy was alien to the Greeks.

Because (i) the period of Greek philosophy (Thales to Aristotle) was a period of internal wars among the city states themselves and external wars with their common enemy, the Persians. The Greeks were victims of perpetual internal strife and perpetual fear of annihilation by their common enemy. They had no time which they could devote to the study of nature, for this required the riches and wealth of the leisure classes: but they were too poor to engage in such a pursuit. This is one of the reasons why the Greek philosophers were so few and why the Greeks were unacquainted with philosophy.

(ii) The Greeks did not possess the native ability essential to the development of philosophy. The death of Aristotle, who had inherited a vast quantity of books from the library of Alexandria through his friendship with Alexander the Great, was also followed by the death of Greek philosophy which soon degenerated into a system of borrowed ideas known as eclecticism. This system contained nothing new in spite of the great treasure of knowledge which they had obtained through Alexander's friendship with Aristotle and his conquest of Egypt.

(iii) The Greeks rejected and persecuted philosophy owing to the fact that it came from an outside and foreign source and contained strange ideas with which they were unacquainted. This prejudice led to the policy of persecution. Hence Anaxagoras was indicted and escaped from prison and fled to Ionia in exile. Socrates was executed; Plato fled to Megara to the rescue of Euclid; and Aristotle was indicted and escaped into exile. This policy of the Greeks would be meaningless, if it did not indicate that philosophy was alien to Greek mentality.

Argument III. Greek philosophy was the offspring of the Egyptian Mystery System.

Because complete identity had been found to exist between the Egyptian Mystery System and Greek philosophy with the only exception of age in relation of parent to child. The Egyptian Mystery System antedated that of Greece by many thousands of years. The following are the circumstances and conditions of identity:—

(i) Complete agreement between the Egyptian, theory of salvation and the purpose of Greek philosophy, i.e., to make man become Godlike by virtue and educational disciplines.

(ii) Complete agreement of the conditions of initiation into both systems, i.e., preparation (in gradual stages of virtue) before every initiation.

(iii) Complete agreement in tenets and practice.

Stolen Legacy

(iv) History tells us that the remains of the Ancient Grand Temple of Luxor have been traced to the banks of the Nile in the ancient city of Thebes, a short distance from Danderah, now called upper Egypt. It also tells us that this Grand Temple was constructed by Pharaoh Amenothis III who began it, and Rameses II who completed it. At the time of Greek philosophy, the Mystery System of Egypt was the only such system in the ancient world, and therefore its Grand Lodge was the only such Grand Lodge in existence. It was the seat of government, having organized the ancient world into a universal or catholic brotherhood with jurisdiction over all minor lodges and schools wherever they were. And whether we call it the Mysteries or Greek philosophy or Free Masonry, the system was one and all branches came out of that one and were subordinate to it.

(v) The identity between the Egyptian Mysteries and Greek philosophy is also established by the fact that when the Roman Emperors Theodosius and Justinian issued their edicts closing down the Egyptian Mysteries, the effect was the same upon the philosophical schools in Greece, for they had to be closed. Things which are affected equally by the same cause are themselves equal.

Argument IV. The Egyptians educated the Greeks.

Because History supports the following facts:—

(i) The effects of the Persian conquest upon Egypt

(a) Removed immigration restrictions against the Greeks.

(b) Opened up Egypt to Greek research and (c) encouraged students from Ionia and elsewhere to visit Egypt for the purpose of their education.

(ii) The effects of the conquest of Alexander the Great upon Egypt

(a) It was the custom of ancient armies when invading countries to search for treasures in libraries and temples. Accordingly it is believed that Alexander and his friends who accompanied him ransacked the Library of Alexandria and other libraries and helped themselves with books. It is also believed that this was how Aristotle got the vast quantity of books alleged to his authorship and how he acquired exaggerated fame.

(b) The Library of Alexandria was taken over by the Alumni

of Aristotle's school and converted into a research centre and University, for the education of the Greeks who were compelled to use Egyptian Professors, on account of linguistic difficulties and other reasons.

(c) Apart from the looting of libraries and the conversion of the Library of Alexandria into a University for their education, the Greeks had another way of adopting the culture of the Egyptians. The Ptolemies used to commandeer useful information from the Egyptian High Priests, and we are told that Ptolemy I Soter commanded the High Priest Manetho to write a history of religion and philosophy of the Egyptians and this was done and the volumes became the chief text books in the University of Alexandria.

(iii) The Egyptians were the first to civilize the Greeks

History tells us that the Greeks received the influence of civilization from three sources: colonizers first from Egypt, colonizers secondly from Phoenicia and colonizers thirdly from Thrace. It also tells us that these colonies were under the government of wise men who subdued the ferocity of the ignorant populace, not only by means of civil institutions, but also by the strong chain of religion and the fear of the Gods. Those colonizers were Cecrops from Egypt, Cadmus from Phoenicia and Orpheus from Thrace.

Argument V. The doctrines of Greek philosophers are the doctrines of the Egyptian Mystery System.

The proof of this proposition is really one of the main purposes of this book and hence chapters five and six have been devoted to this purpose. The Egyptian teachings were expressed in symbols of various types and therefore their origin can be established by reference to the particular symbol in question. In these chapters therefore mention has been made not only of the names of Greek philosophers and the doctrines which have been ascribed to them; but also the necessary references to the particular types of symbology, in proof of their Egyptian origin. These have been given in the Summary of Conclusions as follow:—

1. The early Ionic philosophers have been credited with the doctrines that (a) all things originated from water (b) all things originated from the boundless or primitive chaos and (c) all things originated from air. But these doctrines could not have been those of the Ionic philosophers; since we find the same ideas expressed in the first chapter of Genesis, where we are told that at the be-

ginning the world was in a state of chaos, without form and void (boundless); and how the spirit of God (air) moved upon the waters and separated them from dry land and earth from sky; and how step by step, living things came out of the waters and how finally, through the breath of life (air) man came into existence. Genesis is the first book of the Pentateuch whose date has been placed to the Eighth Century B.C.: a time when the early Ionic philosophers did not even exist and who therefore could not have been the authors of these doctrines. Similarly, the authorship of Genesis has been ascribed to Moses, who Philo tells us was an Egyptian Priest, a Hierogrammat, and learned in all the wisdom of the Egyptians. But the age in which Moses lived must be associated with the Exodus of the Israelites which he conducted in the 21st Egyptian Dynasty: 1100 B.C. in the reign of Bocchoris. But the creation story of Genesis coincides with the creation story of the Memphite Theology of the Egyptians, which takes us back to between 4 and 5 thousand B.C. This means that the doctrines of the early Ionians arose neither at their time (the fifth century B.C.), nor at the time of Pentateuch (the eighth century B.C.), nor yet at the time of Moses (the eleventh century B.C.), but at the time of the Memphite Theology (between 4 and 5 thousand B.C.) and therefore definitely point to Egyptian origin.

2. The Eleatic philosophers have been named as (i) Zenophanes who was a satirist (ii) Zeno whose treatment of space and time led to a reductio ad absurdum and (iii) Parmenides who alone deserves notice. He has been credited with the definitions of Being and non-Being, which he expressed as 'that which is' and 'that which is not'. In other words, nature or reality consists of two properties, i.e., a positive and a negative. But Parmenides introduced no new doctrine, when he defined the principle of opposites. This principle was used by Pythagoras in his theory of numbers; by Socrates in his proof of the immortality of the Soul; by Plato in his Theory of Ideas and the distinction between phenomena and noumena; and by Aristotle in his definition of the attributes of Being. In all these instances it has been shown that the doctrine of opposites originated from the Egyptian Mystery System, in connection with which Gods were represented as male and female, and temples carried double pillars in front of them to indicate positive and negative principles of nature.

3. The late Ionic philosophers have been named as (i) Heracleitus who taught that the world was produced by fire, through a process of transmutation; and that since all things originate from

Fire, then Fire is the Logos.

(ii) Anaxagoras, who taught that Mind or Nous is the source of life in the Universe and

(iii) Democritus, who taught that atoms underlie all material things; that life and death are merely changes brought about by variation in the mixture of atoms, which do not die because they are immortal. Now, taking these doctrines in the order in which they come, their Egyptian origin has been fully established.

(a) The doctrine of Fire has been traced to the Egyptians, whose Mystery System was a Fire Philosophy and who worshipped the God of Fire in their pyramids. The word pyramid is a Greek word, whose derivative pyr means fire. This doctrine takes us back to the pyramid age in Egypt 33 hundred B.C. when, of course, the Greeks were unknown.

(b) It must be noted that the doctrine of the Logos has been identified by Heraclitus with the doctrine of Fire. This is as it should be, because (c) in the doctrine of the created Gods which has been ascribed to Plato, Atom the Sun God or Fire performs the function of Demiurge in creating the Gods.

(d) Similarly in the doctrine of the Unmoved Mover ascribed to Aristotle, the Fire God Atom while unmoved and sitting upon the Primeval Hill, creates the Gods by commanding them to proceed from various parts of His own body. In this way Atom also became the Unmoved Mover. This makes it clear that the Logos of Heraclitus is identical with the Demiurge of Plato and the Unmoved Mover of Aristotle. The function of Atom as Demiurge and the method of His creation are found in the Memphite Theology of the Egyptians. Here

I would like to suggest that students who are interested in tracing the influence of Egyptian philosophy upon Christian thought, should read this portion of my book together with the first chapter of St. John's gospel. The problem of permanence and change is also traced in the Creation story of the Memphite Theology in which eternal matter is represented by chaos, and change by the gradual formation of order.

(e) The doctrine of Mind or Nous, has been ascribed not only to Anaxagoras, but also to Democritus who spoke of it as being composed of fire atoms distributed throughout the universe and Socrates who has been credited with the teleological premise: that whatsoever exists for a useful purpose is the work of an Intelligence. This doctrine has been traced to the Egyptian Mystery System, in which the God Osiris was represented by an Open Eye; signifying not only omniscience, but also omnipotence. All Masonic lodges carry this symbol with the same meaning today.

(f) The doctrine of the atom has been ascribed to Democritus, who does not define but describes its properties. It is the basis of life; it is immortal and does not die; and when many of them are mixed in certain ways the result is a radical change. These properties coincide with the properties of Atom the Sun God and the Demiurge in creation, who created other Gods from various parts of himself. He was the basis of life and giver of life. But Atom the Sun God occurs in the creation story of the Memphite Theology and shows the Egyptian origin of the atom.

4. The system of Pythagoras seems to have been so comprehensive that nearly all subsequent philosophers have copied ideas from his teachings. Interpreting nature in the form of mathematics, Pythagoras is credited with teaching the following doctrines:

(a) The properties of Number include opposite elements: odd and even, finite and infinite, and positive and negative. This principle of opposites was copied by and used in the teachings of Heracleitus, Parmenides, Democritus, Socrates, Plato and Aristotle.

(b) The doctrine of Harmony, defined as the union of opposites. This idea was copied by and used in the teachings of Heracleitus, Socrates, Plato and Aristotle.

(c) Fire (central and peripheral) was taught to be the basis of creation. This doctrine was also used by and in the teachings of Heracleitus, Anaxagoras, Democritus, Socrates and Plato.

(d) The immortality of the soul and The Summum Bonum. This was taught by Pythagoras in the form of a transmigration of the soul. It was also taught by Socrates as the purpose of philosophy through which, the soul feeding upon the truth congenial to its divine nature, was enabled to escape the wheel of rebirth and to attain the final consummation of unity with God. All the doctrines of Pythagoras have been shown to originate from the Egyptian Mystery System. Number possesses opposite elements and the principle of opposites belongs to the Egyptian Mystery System in which it was represented by male and female Gods. Harmony being a blending of opposites, needs no further reference, and Fire likewise takes us back to the Egyptian Mystery System which was a Fire Philosophy and its Initiates Fire worshippers. Finally, the purpose of philosophy was the salvation of the soul. This was accomplished by methods of purification offered by the Egyptian Mysteries, which lifted man from the mortal to the immortal level. This was the Summum Bonum, The Greatest Good.

5. Socrates (A) His life and (B) His doctrines (C) His indictment, condemnation and death (D) His farewell conversations.

A. In his life he voluntarily adopted secrecy and poverty, in order that he might avoid the temptation of riches and be enabled to cultivate the virtues required by the Mysteries.

B. All his doctrines likewise associate him with the Egyptian Mysteries.

(i) His doctrine of the Mind or Nous as Intelligence which underlies creation, was represented in Egyptian temples, just as in modern Masonic temples, by the "Open Eye of Osiris", indicating omniscience and omnipotence.

(ii) His doctrine of self knowledge: "Man know thyself" was copied directly or indirectly from among the inscriptions which appeared on the outside of the Mystery temples in Egypt.

(iii) His doctrines of Opposites and Harmony were a testimony of the custom of the Mysteries to demonstrate the principle of opposites in nature by pairs of male and female Gods and also by double pillars in front of temples.

(iv) His doctrines of Immortality, Salvation of the Soul and The Summum Bonum were a summary of the theory of salvation as was taught by the Mysteries. Socrates himself explained it. The purpose of philosophy was the salvation of the soul by a process of purification which lifted man from the mortal level and raised him to the immortal. This was an attainment, this was the Summum Bonum or Greatest Good.

C. His indictment, condemnation and death are circumstances which also show his association with the Mysteries. He was indicted for the introduction of foreign Gods and the corruption of Athenian Youth and was condemned and put to death. The foreign Gods were the Gods of the Mysteries and his submission to martyrdom was due on the one hand to the prejudice of the Athenian authorities, while on the other hand, to his virtue of courage, required by the Mysteries.

D. His farewell conversations also show his membership with the great Egyptian Order. There are two accounts of these conversations: one by Crito and the other by Phaedo. Crito describes the brotherly behaviour of a band of faithful friends and Neophytes who visited him daily while he was in prison awaiting his execution. The purpose of these visits was to secure the escape of a brother; but their efforts were in vain, for he refused to yield to their entreaties. Phaedo mentions that the theme of the other conversation was the immortality of the soul in which Socrates endeavoured to give them some proofs by his application of the principles of opposites. We are also told that towards the end of the conversations, and just before he drank the poison, Socrates requested Crito to pay for him a certain debt which he owed. These conversations reveal the following facts:—

(a) The brotherly love of the visiting Neophytes in their attempt to secure the escape of their brother Socrates.

(b) A final class was conducted by Socrates on the doctrine of immortality: the central doctrine of the Egyptian Mysteries and

(c) A final request of Socrates to have a debt paid for him and

(d) These conversations constitute the earliest specimen of Masonic literature. All four of which facts point to membership in the Egyptian Mystery System. It was a Universal Brotherhood and required the cultivation of brotherly love. Its central teaching was the immortality of the soul, and it also required all Initiates to practice the virtues of justice and honesty and therefore to pay their debts.

E. It is believed that Socrates did not commit his teachings to writings. This was also in obedience to the secrecy of the Mysteries.

6. Plato

(A) His early life and education as in the case of all other philosophers are unknown to history, which represents him as fleeing from Athens after the death of Socrates and after twelve years during which time he visited Euclid at Megara. the Pythagoreans in Italy, Dionysius in Sicily and the Mystery System in Egypt, he returned to Athens and opened an Academy, where he taught for 20 years.

(B) His doctrines which are scattered over a wide area of literature consisting of 36 dialogues are disputed by modern scholarship. The pupils of Socrates especially Plato are supposed to have published his teachings, and it is not known how much of this vast literature belongs to Plato and how much to Socrates. The doctrines of Plato have all been traced to Egyptian origin.

(i) The Theory of Ideas, which he illustrated by reference to the phenomena of nature, is a distinction between the Ideas or noumena and their copies the phenomena; and between the real and unreal, by the application of the principle of opposites, which was manifested by the Egyptian Mystery System by male and female Gods and pairs of pillars carried in front of Egyptian temples.

(ii) The doctrine of the Mind or Nous has also been traced to the "Open Eye" used in Egyptian temples and modern Masonic lodges to symbolize the omniscience and omnipotence of the Egyptian God Osiris.

(iii) The doctrine of the Demiurge and created Gods have also been traced to Atom the Sun God in the creation story of the Memphite Theology of the Egyptians.

(iv) The doctrine of the Summum Bonum or Greatest Good has been shown to be identical with the theory of salvation of the Egyptian Mystery System. The salvation of the soul was the purpose of philosophy, whose methods of purification lifted the individual from the level of a mortal and advanced him to the level of a God. This goal was the Summum Bonum or Greatest Good.

(v) The doctrine of the Ideal State whose attributes have been compared with the attributes of the soul and justice which are contained in the allegory of the charioteer and winged steeds, points to Egyptian origin because the allegory has been traced to the Judgment Drama of the Egyptian Book of the Dead.

(vi) The doctrines of virtue and wisdom have been shown to have originated from the Egyptian Mystery System which required ten virtues in order to subjugate the ten bodily impediments.

7. Aristotle

1. The life of Aristotle is one of discrepancies and doubts.

(i) While like other philosophers, history does not know any thing about his early life and education, yet it tells the strange story that he spent 20 years as a pupil under Plato, that he never went to Egypt and that Alexander the Great gave him the money to secure the vast number of books which are attached to his name. But history also tells us that Plato was a philosopher and that Aristotle was a scientist and consequently we are forced to ask the question: why should a man like Aristotle waste 20 years of his life under a Teacher who was incompetent to teach him? These circumstances have led to the suspicion that Aristotle must have spent the greater part of those 20 years in advancing his education in Egypt and in accompanying Alexander the Great on his invasion of Egypt, when he got the opportunity to ransack the library at Alexandria and carry off all the books which he wanted. The story of history does not make much sense; but unfortunately throws a cloud of darkness over the life of Aristotle.

(ii) Another discrepancy is to be found in connection with three lists of books said to belong to him, but which differ in source, in date and in quantity, (a) His own list which must receive the date in which he lived: the 4th century B.C. This contains the smallest number of books. (b) A list from Hermippus of Alexandria two centuries later, i.e., 200 B.C. containing 400 books and (c) A list from Arabian sources, compiled at Alexandria, three centuries later, i.e., 1st century A.D. containing a thousand books. One is forced to ask the questions: Did Aristotle write a thousand books in his life time? How has his small list increased after his death to 400 after the lapse of two centuries, and to one thousand after the lapse of five centuries? These circumstances make the authorship of Aristotle very doubtful, for it is incredible that a single individual could write a thousand books on the various fields of science in a single life time.

2. The doctrines of Aristotle have all been shown to originate from the Egyptian Mystery System

(i) The doctrine of Being in the metaphysical realm has been explained as the relation between potentiality and actuality, which acts according to the principle of opposites. The Egyptians were the first scientists to discover the principle of duality in nature and therefore represented it by male and female Gods and by pairs of pillars in front of their temples. This is the source of this doctrine.

(ii) In the proof of the existence of God, Aristotle used two doctrines, (a) Teleology, showing purpose and design in nature as the work of an Intelligence and (b) the Unmoved Mover. Both doctrines have been traced to the creation story of the Memphite Theology of the Egyptians where it is shown that creation moved from chaos to order and indicated the work of an Intelligence: and also where Atom the Demiurge and Logos while sitting unmoved upon the Primeval Hill projected eight Gods from various parts of His body and thus became the Unmoved Mover.

(iii) The doctrine of the origin of the world, according to Aristotle, states that the world is eternal because matter, motion and time are eternal. This same view was expressed by Democritus in 400 B.C. in the dictum ex nihillo nihil fit (out of nothing, nothing comes), indicating that matter is permanent and eternal. The same view has been traced to the creation story of the Memphite Theology of the Egyptians in which chaos or primitive matter is represented by the Primeval Ocean Nun out of which arose the Primeval Hill. These are supposed to have always been in existence.

(iv) The doctrines of the attributes of nature, according to Aristotle, states that nature consists of motion and rest and that the motion moves from the less perfect to the more perfect by a definite law. I suppose the law of evolution. This teaching however did not originate from Aristotle for the problem of motion and rest permanence and change were not only investigated by the Eleatic and later Ionic philosophers, but by the Egyptians in whose creation story, the Memphite Theology, nature is shown to move from chaos by gradual steps to order. Certainly the doctrine of the attributes of nature came from the Egyptians.

(v) The doctrine of the soul, according to Aristotle, states that the soul is a radical principle of life which is identical with the body, and possesses five attributes, being sensitive, rational, nutritive, appetitive and locomotive. Other philosophers have defined the soul (a) as material and composed of fire atoms (b) as a harmony of the body through the blending of opposites, and (c) as the breath of life in the creation story of Genesis. The true source of Aristotle's doctrine of the soul has however been traced to the philosophy of the soul found in the Egyptian Book of the Dead. There we find the soul explained as a unity of nine inseparable souls in one just like the Ennead a God Head of Nine in One, with necessary bodies. In this Egyptian philosophy, the attributes of the soul of the physical body have been found to coincide with those described by Aristotle, and it therefore shows the Egyptian source of Aristotle's doctrine, which relates to a small fragment of the Egyptian philosophy of the soul.

Argument VI. The Education of the Egyptian Priests and the

Curriculum of the Mystery System show that Egypt was the source of Higher Education in the ancient world, not Greece.

The first idea that we get from chapter seven is the fact that the Institution of Holy Orders originated from the Egyptian Mystery System, where African Priests were organized into various Orders and trained according to their rank. This made the priesthood the custodians of learning until the dawn of the modern age and pointed to Africans as the first professors in Higher Education. The second idea that we get is that the Seven Liberal Arts also originated from the Egyptian Mystery System, because these subjects formed the basis of the education of the Priests, who in addition, had to be versed in the 42 Books of Hermes and to specialize in Magic, Hieroglyphics, secret language and mathematical symbolism. The third idea that we get is that the Curriculum of the Egyptian Mystery System was coextensive with the needs of the highest civilization of the ancient world. Its text books consisted of:—

(i) The 42 Books of Hermes.

(ii) The therapeutic use of the Seven Liberal Arts, for the cure of man's soul.

(iii) The applied Sciences and Arts as revealed by the monuments such as sculpture, painting, drawing, architecture, engineering.

(iv) The social Sciences appropriate for trade and commerce, such as geography, economics and ship-building.

Argument VII. The Memphite Theology contains the theology, philosophy and cosmology of the Egyptians and is therefore an authoritative source of doctrinal origin.

Chapter VIII attempts to show that the Memphite Theology of the Egyptians is the source of (i) Greek philosophy by showing that the separate doctrines of philosophers are portions of the teachings contained in it and also the source of (ii) modern scientific hypotheses by showing that (a) the Nebular Hypothesis and (b) the assumption that there are nine major planets of the solar system have originated from Atom the Egyptian Sun God or Fire God who has been shown to be identical with the atom of modern science. It is because of this great revelation, i.e., the identity of Atom the Sun God of the Egyptians with the atom of modern science that I have recommended the Memphite Theology as a new field of scientific research, and magic the scientific method of the Mysteries as the key to its interpretation. My second reason is the fact that the Memphite Theology is the first Heliocentric theory of the universe, and my third reason is the fact that the history of philosophy is the history of science.

IX. The New Philosophy of African Redemption

Chapter IX deals with the New Philosophy of African Redemption, the aim of which is mental and social redemption, by converting the world to the New Philosophy that the Black people of North Africa gave philosophy to the world, but not the Greeks; and by refusing not only to worship Greek intellect, because it is a process of miseducation, but also refusing to submit any longer to missionary policy. The New Philosophy of African Redemption is a necessary escape of the Black people from their social plight caused by a false tradition concerning them which has been set in motion by (a) Alexander the Great (b) Aristotle and his school and (c) Emperors Theodosius and Justinian whose edicts abolished the Egyptian Mysteries: the Greatest Educational and Ecclesiastical System that the world has ever known and established Christianity as its perpetual rival.

NOTES CHAPTER I (1) The Teachings of the Egyptians. This was called Sophia by the Greeks and meant Wisdom Teaching. It included (a) Philosophy and the Arts and Sciences (b) religion and magic and (c) secret methods of communication both linguistic and mathematical. Read The Stromata of Clement of Alexandria, Bk. 6, p. 756 and 758; also Diodorus I, 80; also Ancient Mysteries by C. H. Vail, p. 22–23; The Stromata of Clement of Alexandria, Bk. 5, c. 7 and 9.

(2) The Peri Physeos

This was the name given to one of the earliest books on science apart from the manuscripts of the Egyptians. The name means "Concerning nature". Read Ancient Mysteries by C. H. Vail, p. 16.

CHAPTER II The period of Greek philosophy was unsuitable for the production of Greek philosophers. Because (a) Persian domination did not only enslave the Greeks but kept them in a constant state of fear (b) It also kept them busy organizing Leagues in constant self-defense against aggression and (c) The city states could not agree, and the Peloponnesian wars kept them in constant warfare with each other. Read Sandford's Mediterranean World, c. 12, p. 203, 205; c. 13 and 15, p. 225, 255; also c. 18, p. 317, 319; also

The Tutorial History of Greece, c. 27, 28 and 29.

CHAPTER III (1) The Summum Bonum. This means (a) The Greatest Good (b) the lifting of man from the level of a mortal and advancing him to the level of a God (c) the salvation of the soul (d) the purpose of philosophy (e) the goal of the Egyptian theory of salvation. Read C. H. Vail's Ancient Mysteries, p. 25.

(2) The Grand Lodge of Luxor

The ruins of the ancient Grand Lodge of Luxor are found today on the banks of the Nile in Upper Egypt in the ancient city of Thebes. It was built by Pharaoh Amenothis III. It was the only Grand Lodge of the ancient world. It had branches or minor lodges throughout the ancient world; in Europe, Asia, Africa, North America, South America and probably in Australia. These were some of the places:—(a) Palestine at Mt. Carmel (b) Syria at Mt. Herman in Lebanon (c) Babylon (d) Media, near the Red Sea (e) India, on the banks of the Ganges (f) Burma (g) Athens (h) Rome (i) Croton (j) Rhodes (k) Delphi (l) Miletus (m) Cyprus (n) Corinth (o) Crete (p) Central and South America, especially Peru (q) Among the American Indians and among the Mayas, Aztecs and Incas of Mexico. Read Encyclopaedia of Religion and Ethics by Jas. Hastings; Lives of Eminent Philosophers by Diogenes Laertius; and History of Philosophy by Thomas Stanley. The discovery of the ruins of Luxor on the banks of the Nile and the organization of the Egyptian Mysteries into a Grand Lodge with minor lodges throughout the ancient world are evidence that Egypt was the cradle of the Mysteries and of the Masonic Brotherhood.

(3) The rebuilding of the temple of Delphi

This temple was burnt down in 548 B.C. by the Greeks who were always hostile towards the Egyptian Mysteries. The Brethren tried at first to raise funds from the native Greeks but failed in their attempt. They then decided to approach the Grand Master Amasis King of Egypt, who unhesitatingly donated three times as much as was needed for the purpose. This act of King Amasis shows the universality of the brotherhood of the Egyptian Mysteries and of Free Masonry. Read Sandford's Mediterranean World, p. 135 and 139; also John Kendrick's Ancient Egypt, Bk. II, p. 363.

(4) The abolition of Greek philosophy together with the Egyptian Mysteries

Identical effects proceed from identical causes. Therefore the edicts of Theodosius in the 4th century A.D. and of Justinian in the 6th century A.D., which closed down the Egyptian Mysteries, simultaneously had the same effect upon Greek philosophy, and proved the identity between them. Read The Ecclesiastical edicts of the Theodosian Code by W. K. Boyd; also Mythology of Egypt by Max Muller, c. 13, p. 241-245; also Sandford's Mediterranean World, p. 508, 548, 552-568.

(5) The Statue of the Egyptian Goddess Isis with Her Child Horns in Her arms

This was the first Madonna and Child of human history. It was a Black Madonna and Child. Read Max Muller's Mythology of Egypt, c. 13, p. 241-245; also Sandford's Mediterranean World, p. 552-568. Remember that the name Egyptian is a Greek word Aiguptos which means Black, and that primitive man visualized God in terms of his own attributes and this included colour.

(6) All the great religious leaders from Moses to Christ were Initiates of the Egyptian Mysteries

This is an inference from the nature of the Egyptian Mysteries and prevailing custom.

(a) The Egyptian Mystery System was the One Holy Catholic Religion of the remotest antiquity.

(b) It was the one and only Masonic Order of Antiquity, and as such,

(c) It built the Grand Lodge of Luxor in Egypt and encompassed the ancient world with its branch lodges.

(d) It was the first University of history and it made knowledge a secret, so that all who desired to become Priests and Teachers had to obtain their training from the Mystery System, either locally at a branch lodge or by travelling to Egypt.

We know that Moses became an Egyptian Priest, a Hierogrammat, and that Christ after attending the lodge at Mt. Cannel went to Egypt for Final Initiation, which took place in the Great Pyramid of Cheops. Other religious leaders obtained their preparation from lodges most convenient to them.

(e) This explains why all religions, seemingly different, have a common nucleus of similarity; belief in a God; belief in immortality and a code of ethics. Read Ancient Mysteries by C. H. Vail, p. 61;

Mystical Life of Jesus by H. Spencer Lewis; Esoteric Christianity by Annie Besant, p. 107, 128–129; Philo; also read note (2) Chapter III for branch lodges of the ancient world.

CHAPTER IV (1) The Genesis of Greek Enlightenment

In the reign of King Amasis, the Persians through Cambyses invaded Egypt 525 B.C. and as a result (a) Immigration regulations against the Greeks were removed (b) They were allowed to settle at Naucratis and do their research (c) This contact enabled the Greeks to begin to borrow Egyptian Culture and to become enlightened. Read Herodotus, Bk. II, p. 113; Plutarch, p. 380; Diogenes, Bk. IX 49; Ovid Fasti III 338.

(2) Cheops and Cecrops

Those were Greek names for the Egyptian Khufu who belonged to the 4th Dynasty of the Egyptians. It was during the Pyramid Age, and Cheops was also the name of the Great Pyramid where Christ received His Final Initiation into the Egyptian Mysteries. Read Brucker's Critical History of Philosophy; also Mystical Life of Jesus by H. Spencer Lewis.

CHAPTER V (1) The Diagram of the Four Qualities and Four Elements

This is important evidence that the teachings of the supposed early Ionic philosophers and of Heracleitus originated from the Egyptian Mysteries. Read the Diagram and also Ancient Mysteries by C. H. Vail, p. 61; and the Creation Story of the Memphite Theology by Frankfort; also Rosicrucian Digest, May 1952, p. 175.

(2) The Pythagorean Theorem

Pythagoras travelled to Egypt and was taught geometry by the Egyptian Priests and made to sacrifice to the Gods, before they showed him the proof of the theorem of the square on the hypotenuse of a right angled triangle. Pythagoras did not discover this proof, and it is misleading to name the theorem after him. Read Herodotus, Bk. III, p. 124; Diogenes, Bk. VIII, p. 3; Pliny, N. H., 36, 9; also Plutarch and Demetrius.

CHAPTER VI (1) The doctrine of self-knowledge: Man know thyself (Seauton gnothi)

This doctrine has been falsely ascribed to Socrates. It was an inscription that was placed on the Egyptian temples, and Socrates copied it directly or indirectly. Read Zeller's History of Philosophy, p. 105; S. Clymer's Fire Philosophy and Max Muller's Egyptian Mythology.

(2) The Farewell Conversation of Socrates with his pupils and friends

These conversations are significant in the following respects:—

(a) Socrates is identified as a member of the Egyptian Mysteries or Masonic Order.

(b) Masonic behavior is manifested through these conversations.

(c) The books containing these conversations; Plato's Crito, Phaedo, Euthyphro, Apology and Timaeus, are the earliest specimen of Masonic literature apart from the secret writings of the Egyptians.

(d) Of the three Athenian philosophers Socrates stood highest in the rank of a Free Mason. He was not afraid of death, he did not publish the knowledge imparted to him and he was an honest man. Read Crito and Phaedo of Plato.

(3) Plato's Theory of Ideas

After the Egyptian Priests discovered the fundamental principle of opposites as underlying life in the universe, they applied it in their interpretation of natural phenomena. Consequently this mode of interpretation has been reflected in the teachings of the socalled Greek philosophers who had obtained their education from the Egyptian Mystery System. Read the doctrines of Parmenides who in the problem of existence distinguishes between Being and non-Being; also of Heracleitus in the problem of flux and change through the process of transmutation; also of Socrates in the proof of immortality, and Plato in his supposed Theory of Ideas, in which he distinguished between (a) the real and unreal (b) the idea of a thing and the thing itself (c) the noumena and phenomena. In all these instances the principle of opposites has been used as a method of interpretation. This method is Egyptian not Platonic.

(4) The Republic of Plato: The Ideal State

Plato's authorship of the Republic is disputed for the following reasons:—

Stolen Legacy

(a) The attributes of an Ideal State are expressed in the allegory of the charioteer and winged steeds which is dramatized in the Judgment Drama of the Egyptian Book of the Dead and therefore proves its Egyptian origin.

(b) The chariot was neither a culture pattern nor war machine of the Greeks at the time of Plato. The wars of the Greeks with the Persians and the Peloponnesian wars were all maritime.

(c) At this time the Egyptians were specialists in the manufacture of chariots and horse breeding Gen., c. 45, v. 27; c. 47, v. 17; Deut., c. 17, v. 16; I Kings, c. 10, v. 28.

(d) The historians Diogenes Laertius, Aristoxenus and Favorinus have declared that the subject matter of the Republic was found in the controversies written by Protagoris (481–411) when Plato was but a boy. Read Diogenes Laertius, p. 311 and 327; also The Egyptian Book of the Dead, c. 17: also Republic III 415; V 478; and VI 490 sqq.

(5) The Timaeus of Plato

Plato's authorship of the Timaeus is also disputed for the following reasons:—

(a) The historian Diogenes Laertius in Bk. VIII, p. 399–401 has declared that when Plato visited Dionysius in Sicily, he paid Philolaus a Pythagorean forty Alexandrian Minae of silver for a book, from which he copied the whole contents of the Timaeus.

(b) The subject matter of the Timaeus is eclectic. Read the Timaeus.

(6) Magic is the Key to the interpretation of ancient religion and natural philosophy

Through the application of the principle: that the qualities of entities, human or divine, are distributed throughout their various parts: and that contact with such entities releases those qualities, many religious phenomena and those of primitive science could be interpreted and understood.

(a) The cure of the woman who touched the hem of Christ's garment, Mark, c. 5, verses 25–34.

(b) The cure of several people, who held the handkerchiefs of St. Paul. Acts, c. 19, verse 12.

(c) In order to accomplish creation, Atom the Sun God sat upon Ptah, the God of Gods, in order to absorb His qualities of creative thought, speech and omnipotence. This act qualified Him as the Logos and Demiurge and He first created the Gods and finally mortals. Read Memphite Theology in Frankfort's Ancient Egyptian Religion and Dr. Frazer's Golden Bough.

(7) The doubts and discrepancies in the life and activities of Aristotle

It is somewhat unfortunate that history has represented the life and activities of Aristotle in a way so repugnant to reason, that the world has been compelled to doubt his accomplishments and fame. It tells us that

(a) he spent twenty years as a pupil under Plato whom we know was incompetent to teach him.

(b) It tells us that Alexander gave him money to buy his large number of books, but the Greeks had no libraries at the time, nor was it easy to purchase books which were not in circulation.

(c) It also tells us that three lists of books which bear his name differ froth one another, in source, date and quantity.

(d) The third list contains one thousand books: a quantity which is a mental and physical impossibility as the production of a single individual in a single lifetime.

(e) It is silent about Aristotle's visits to Egypt, although it was the custom in his days for Greek students to go to Egypt for the purpose of their education. Read Zeller's History of Philosophy, p. 172–173; Diogenes, Bk. V, p. 449; B. D. Alexander's History of Philosophy, p. 92–93.

(8) The Unmoved Mover: Proton Kinoun Akineton

A doctrine ascribed to Aristotle in his attempt to prove the existence of God. The God in this doctrine was Atom the Egyptian Sun God, who in the creation story of the Memphite Theology, sat upon the God of Gods Ptah and having absorbed His creative qualities, speech and omnipotence, became the Logos and accomplished the work of creation by projecting Gods from various parts of His own body. This doctrine did not originate from Aristotle, but has been traced to the creation story of the Memphite Theology of the Egyptians. Read Memphite Theology in Frankfort's Ancient Egyptian Religion, c. 20 and 23; also p. 25, 26 and 35; William Turner's History of Philosophy, p. 141–143; B. D. Alexander, p. 102–103.

(9) Aristotle's doctrine of the Soul

This doctrine has been found to be only a very small part of the elaborate philosophy of the soul found in the Egyptian Book of the Dead, which is the original source of Aristotle's supposed doctrine. Read the Egyptian Book of the Dead by Sir E. A. Budge, p. 29–64.

CHAPTER VII The Curriculum of the Egyptian Mysteries

Through the curriculum of the Egyptian Mysteries it is now known that the African Continent has given the following Legacy to the civilization of the world. It consists of the following culture patterns:—

(1) Holy Catholic Orders, together with a priesthood divided into ranks according to training.

(2) Holy Catholic Worship, consisting of rituals, ceremonies including processions and appropriate vestments of priests.

(3) Greek Philosophy and the Arts and Sciences, including the Seven Liberal Arts, that is, the Quadrivium and Trivium which were the foundation training of Neophytes. These were included in the forty-two Books of Hermes.

(4) The applied Sciences which produced the pyramids, tombs, libraries, obelisks, and Sphinxes, war chariots and ships, etc.

(5) The social sciences, appropriate for the highest civilization in ancient times. Read The Stromata of Clement of Alexandria, c. 6, p. 756, 758; also Diodorus I, 80. Read also The Mechanical Triumphs of the Ancient Egyptians by F. M. Barber; History of Mathematics by Florian Cajeri; History of Mathematics by W. W. R. Ball.

CHAPTER VIII The Memphite Theology

(1) Definition

The Memphite Theology is an inscription on a stone containing the cosmology, theology and philosophy of the Egyptians. Read Frankfort's Ancient Egyptian Religion, c. 20 and 23; also Frankfort's Intellectual Adventure of Man. It is located in the British Museum.

(2) Importance

Its importance lies in the fact that (a) it is an authoritative source of Egyptian Philosophy, Cosmology and Religion (b) it is proof of the Egyptian origin of Greek philosophy.

(3) The Source of Modern Scientific Knowledge

(a) Atom the Egyptian Sun God who is the Logos of Heracleitus, the Demiurge of Plato and the Unmoved Mover of Aristotle creates eight other Gods by projecting them from His own body, thus producing nine Gods or the Ennead. This is identical with the Nebular Hypothesis of Laplace, in which the original Sun creates eight other planets, by throwing off rings from itself, thus producing the nine major planets of modern scientific belief.

(b) It has been shown on pages 146 and 147 of this book, that the name of Atom the Egyptian Sun God is the same name used for the atom of science and also that the attributes of both are the same. Read Frankfort's Intellectual Adventure of Man, p. 53; Frankfort's Kingship and the Gods, p. 182; also Herodotus II, 112; Diodorus I, 29.

(4) It offers great possibilities for modern scientific research

What science knows about (a) the number of major planets (b) how these major planets were created by the Sun and (c) the attributes of the atom has been traced to the Cosmology of the Memphite Theology, which suggests that (d) science knows only 1/5 of the secrets of creation and therefore 4/5 of such secrets yet remains to be discovered (e) consequently The Memphite Theology offers great possibilities for modern scientific research.

CHAPTER IX The Drama of Greek Philosophy

(1) This consists of three actors (a) Alexander the Great who invaded Egypt and plundered the Royal Library at Alexandria (b) Aristotle and the alumni of his school, who took possession of the Royal Library and having first carried off large quantities of scientific books, subsequently converted it into a research Centre and University. (c) The Roman government, which through the edicts of Emperors Theodosius and Justinian closed down the Egyptian Mysteries together with its schools, the University of the Ancient World and System of the African Culture.

(2) The result of this was (a) the misrepresentation and errone

ous opinion that the African Continent and people are backward in culture and have made no contribution to civilization and (b) the establishment of Christianity as a rival against the Mysteries or African System of Culture, in order to perpetuate this erroneous opinion.

(3) A further result has been (a) the false worship of Greek intellect and (b) the activities of Missionary enterprise through which the culture of Black people is caricatured both in literature and in exhibitions.

(4) A further result has been (a) the general feeling among Black people throughout the world that they are in great need of freedom from their social plight, and (b) The offer by "Stolen Legacy" of a "New Philosophy of African Redemption" in order to meet this universal need of "Social Reformation".

(5) The nature and methods of this New Philosophy and Social Reformation

(a) The New Philosophy of African Redemption is simply the proposition that the "Greeks were not the authors of Greek philosophy: but the people of North Africa, the Egyptians". This must be preached and circulated for centuries to come.

(b) The effects of this New Philosophy should be as follows:—

(1) To change the mentality both of White and Black people and their attitude towards each other and bring about a Social Reformation.

(2) To stimulate the Black people to abandon their false worship of Greek intellect, and to reject the caricature of their culture by Missionary enterprise and to demand a change in Missionary policy.

The Willie Lynch Letter
&
The Making Of A Slave

Published By:

Lushena Books
607 Country Club Drive, Unit E
Bensenville, IL 60106

Tel: 630-238-8708
Fax: 630-238-8824
Email: Lushenabks@yahoo.com

Distributed By Lushena Books
607 Country club Drive, Unit E
Bensenville, IL 60106
Tel: 630-238-8708
Fax: 630-238-8824

Historical Documentary
Layout & Cover Graphic Design
by Kashif Malik Hassan-EL

Published February, 1999
Second Printing August, 1999

INTRODUCTION

The infamous **"Willie Lynch"** letter gives both African and Caucasian students and teachers some insight, concerning the brutal and inhumane psychology behind the African slave trade. The materialistic viewpoint of Southern plantation owners that slavery was a **"business"** and the victims of chattel slavery were merely pawns in an economic game of debauchery, cross-breeding, inter-racial rape and mental conditioning of a negroid race, they considered sub-human.

Equally important is the international nature of the European economic, political and cultural climate, that influenced the slave trade. Within the time scale of African History, it was a relatively short period, a mere one and a half centuries -- from the most intensive phase of the Atlantic slave trade to the advent of European administration and dominance. Long before that the Slave coast had been chartered by the Portuguese and the people off the area west of Benin, between the Volta River and Lagos, European traders traced a cultural history which linked them with the earliest Yoruba settlements to the north and eastern borders of Africa.[1]

There were considerable debates during the colonial periods in the United States, and the late 1700's, the attention of the national government was mainly directed to slavery and the rising numbers of slaves traded and imported into the South.

The first debate was held in Congress, in 1789, on the question of whether taxes should be paid on imported slaves.

During the debate on the slavery duty bill, which was introduced by Mr. Clymer's committee, Parker of Virginia moved that on May 13, 1789 a tax of ten dollars per capita be laid on slaves imported.[2] He plainly stated that the tax was designed to check the trade, and that he was sorry that the Constitution prevented Congress from prohibiting the importation altogether. The proposal was evidently unwelcome and caused extended debate. Smith of South Carolina wanted to postpone the matter " so big with the serious consequences to the State he represented ".

Roger Sherman of Connecticut "could not reconcile himself to the insertion of human beings as an article of duty, among goods, wares, and merchandise". Jackson of Georgia argued against any restriction, and thought such states as Virginia " ought to let their neighbors get supplied, before they imposed such a burden upon the importation ".

Some Congressmen argued during that Congress " should wipe off the stigma under which America laboured ". This brought Jackson again to his feet. He believed, in spite of the fashion of the day," that Negroes were better off as slaves than as freedmen, and that, as the tax was partial, it would be the most odious tax Congress could impose ".

Such sentiments were a distinct advance in pro-slavery doctrine, and called for a protest from Congressman Madison of Virginia.

There were both moral arguments and legal positions to the questions of slavery in the South. On one side, it began with the *"Rights of Man "*, and descended to stickling for it to have a decent appearance on the statute-book.

On the other side, it began with the uplifting of the heathen; and descended to a denial of the applicability of moral principles to the question; said Holland of North Carolina: " It is admitted that the condition of slaves in the Southern states is much superior to that of those in Africa ". (Holland's opinion) Who, then, will say that trade is immoral? But , in fact, morality has nothing to with this traffic, for Joseph Clay declared, " it must appear to every man of common sense, that the question could be considered in a commercial point of view only ".[2]

The other side declared that, " by laws of God and man these captured Negroes, are entitled to their freedom as clearly and as absolutely as we are." Nevertheless, some were willing to leave them to the tender mercies of the Slaves states, so long as the statue-book was not disgraced by no explicit recognition of slavery.

The moral questions were argued back and forth, but there were no question of the tremendous profitability using slavery in exchange for molasses, sugar, textiles, spices, and the massive free labour of cotton production on numerous plantations in the South. The system began with a conspiratorial battle of wits between the European traders and African chiefs. Slave traders were required to know not only the state of the trade, if they were to " see a profit ", but also to know the likely supply of the slaves available on one hand, and the likely supply of ships on the other.

Also the varying values of many different standards of payment. Coins were seldom or never used on the coast. Mostly the chiefs and slave traders dealt in rolls of tobacco, barrels of rum, and firearms and generally in lengths of iron or copper, or in pots and basins of brass. The slaver's books are full of all of this.[3]

Regardless of the economic prosperity enjoyed during the African slave trade, and the tedious burden placed on the backs of African people, most will agree the psychological damage, and atrocities inflicted on Black people during that point of time, and even today, are the most outrageous examples of injustice and downpression ever experienced by humanity.

February, 1999

Kashif Malik Hassan-EL

Bibliography

1). The Western Slave Coast and It's Rulers
-- Newbury
2.) The Suppression of the African Slave Trade to the United States of America: 1638-1870
-- W.E.B. DuBois
3.) The African Slave Trade, Pre-Colonial History 1450-1850
-- Basil Davidson

WILLIAM LYNCH

THE UNTOLD "STORY" 1712

This speech was delivered by a white slave owner, William Lynch on the bank of the James River in 1712.

And The Message is Still True...
TODAY

By William Lynch

Gentlemen, I greet you here on the banks of the James River in the year of our Lord one thousand seven hundred and twelve. First, I shall thank you, the gentlemen of the Colony of Virginia for bringing me here. I am here to help you solve some of your problems with slaves. Your invitation reached me on my modest plantation in the West Indies where I have experimented with some of the newest and still the oldest methods for control of slaves. Ancient Rome would envy us if my program is implemented. As our boat sailed south on the James River, named for our Illustrious King, whose version of the Bible we cherish. I saw enough to know that your problem is not unique. While Rome used cords of wood as crosses for standing human bodies along it's old highways in great numbers, you are here using the tree and the rope on occasion.

I caught the whiff of a dead slave hanging from a tree a couple of miles back. You are not only losing valuable stock by hangings, you are having uprisings, slaves are running away, your crops are sometimes left in the fields too long for maximum profit, you suffer occasional fires, your animals are killed. Gentlemen, you know what your problems are; I do not need to elaborate. I am not here to enumerate your problems; however, I am here to introduce you to method of solving them.

In my bag here, **_I have a foolproof method for controlling your Black slaves._** I guarantee every one of you that if installed correctly, **_it will control the slaves for at least 300 hundred years._** My method is simple. Any member of your family or your overseer can use it.

I have outlined a number of DIFFERENCES among the slaves, and I take these differences and make them bigger. I use FEAR, DISTRUST, and ENVY for control purposes. These methods have worked on my modest plantation in the West Indies and it will work throughout the South. Take this simple little list of differences, and think about them. On top of my list is **_"AGE" but it is there only because it starts with an "A"; the second is "COLOR" or SHADE, there is INTELLIGENCE, SIZE, SEX, SIZE PLANTATIONS, STATUS ON PLANTATION, ATTITUDE OF OWNERS, WHETHER THE SLAVES LIVE IN THE VALLEY, ON THE HILL, EAST, WEST, NORTH, SOUTH, HAVE FINE HAIR, COURSE HAIR, OR IS TALL OR SHORT._** Now that you have a list of differences, **_I shall give you an outline of action - but before that I shall assure you that DISTRUST is stronger than TRUST, and ENVY is stronger than ADULATION, RESPECT OR ADMIRATION._**

The Black slave after receiving this indoctrination shall carry on and will become self refueling and self generating for hundreds of years, maybe thousands.

Don,t forget **you must pitch the OLD BLACK MALE vs. THE YOUNG BLACK and the YOUNG BLACK MALE against the OLD BLACK MALE. You must use the Dark Skin Slaves vs. the Light Skin Slaves and the Light Skin Slaves vs. the Dark Skin Slaves. You must use the Female vs. the Male, and the Male vs. the Female. You must also have your white servants and overseers Distrust all Blacks, but it is necessary that your slaves trust and depend on us . They must love, respect and trust only us.**

Gentlemen, these kits are your keys to control. Use them. Have your wives and children use them, never miss an opportunity. If used intensively for one year, the slaves themselves will remain perpetually distrustful. Thank you, gentlemen.

Editor's repeat: This speech was delivered by a white slave owner, William Lynch, on the banks of the James River in 1712.

LET'S MAKE A SLAVE
by

The Black Arcade Liberation Library

1970

It was the interest and business of slave holders to study human nature, and the slave nature in particular, with a view to practical results, and many of them attained astonishing proficiently in this direction. They had to deal not with earth, wood, and stone, but with men, and they by every regard they had for their safety and prosperity they had need to know the material on which they were to work. Conscious of the injustice and wrong they were every hour perpetrating and knowing what they themselves would do were they the victims of such wrongs, they were constantly looking for the first signs of the dread retribution. They watched, therefore, with skilled and practiced eyes, and learned to read, with great accuracy, the state of mind and heart of the slave, through his sable face. Unusual sobriety, apparent abstraction, sullenness, and indifference-- indeed, any mood out of the common way afforded ground for suspicion and inquiry.

Frederick Douglas

LET'S MAKE A SLAVE is a study of the scientific process of man breaking and slave making. It describes the rationale and results of the Anglo Saxon's ideas and methods of insuring the master/slave relationship.

Travelling sailors disseminated news, rumor, and style among far-flung black people, contributing to the creation of a shared African identity and multiple black identities. Above is two Africans contesting in a head-butting contest as drawn in Venezuela. Sailors from the eastern seaboard of North America frequently mingled with the local people, and completed in African-inspired martial arts contests.

LET'S MAKE A SLAVE

The Origin and Development of a Social Being Called the Negro

Let us make a slave a slave. What do I need? First of all we need a black nigger man, a pregnant nigger woman and her baby nigger boy. Second, I will use the same basic principle that we use in the breaking a horse, combined with some more sustaining factors.

When we do it with horses we break them from one form of life to another; that is, we reduce them from their natural state in nature; whereas nature provides them with the natural capacity to take of their needs and the needs of their offspring, we break that natural string of independence from them and thereby create a dependency state so that we may be able to get from them useful production for our business and pleasure.

CARDINAL PRINCIPLES FOR MAKING A NEGRO

For fear that our future generations may not understand the principles of breaking both horses and man, we lay down the art. For, if we are to sustain our basic economy we must break and tie both of the beasts together, the nigger and the horse. We understand that short range planning in economics results in periodic economic chaos; so that, to avoid turmoil in the economy, it requires us to have breath and depth in long range comprehensive planning, articulating both skills and sharp perception.

We lay down the following principles for long range comprehensive economic planning:

1.) Both horse and nigger are no good to the economy in the wild or natural state.
2.) Both must be broken and tied together for orderly production.
3.) For the orderly futures, special and particular attention must be paid to the female and the young offspring.
4.) Both must be crossbred to produce a variety and division of labor.
5.) Both must be taught to respond to a particular new language.
6.) Psychological and physical instruction of containment must be created for both.

We hold the above six cardinal principles as trues to be self-evident, based on the following discourse concerning the economics of breaking and tying the horse and the nigger together -- all inclusive of the six principles laid down above.

NOTE: Neither principles alone will suffice for good economics. All principles must be employed for the orderly good of the nation.

Accordingly, both a wild horse and a wild or natural nigger is dangerous even if captured for they will have a tendency to seek their customary freedom, and, in doing so, might kill you in your sleep. You cannot rest. They sleep while you are awake and are awake while you asleep. They are dangerous near the family house and it requires too much labor to watch them away from the house. Above all you cannot get them to work in the natural state. Hence, both the horse and the nigger must be broken that is break them from one form of mental life to another-- keep the body and take the mind. In other words, break the will to resist. Now the breaking process is the same for both the horse and nigger, only slightly varying in degrees. But as we said before, there is an art in long range economic planning. You must keep your eye and thoughts on the female and the offspring of the horse and the nigger.

A brief discourse in offspring development will shed light on the key to sound economic principles. Pay little attention to the generation of original breaking but concentrate on future generations. Therefore, if you break the female mother, she will break the offspring in its early years of development and, when the offspring is old enough to work, she will deliver it up to you for her normal female protective tendencies will have been lost in the original breaking process.

For example, take the case of the wild stud horse, a female horse and an already infant horse and

compare the breaking process with two captured nigger males in their natural state, a pregnant nigger woman with her infant offspring. Take the stud horse, break him for limited containment.
Completely break the female horse until she becomes very gentle whereas you or anybody can ride her in comfort. Breed the mare and the stud until you have the desired offspring. Then you can turn the stud to freedom until you need him again. Train the female horse whereby she will eat out of your hand, and she will in turn train the infant horse to eat out of your hand also.

When it comes to breaking the uncivilized nigger, use the same process, but vary the degree and step up the pressure so as to do a complete reversal of the mind. Take the meanest and most restless nigger, strip him of his clothes in front of the remaining male niggers, the female, and the nigger infant, tar and feather him, tie each leg to a different horse in opposite directions, set him a fire and beat both horses to pull him apart in front of the remaining niggers. The next step is to take a bullwhip and beat the remaining nigger male to the point of death in front of the female and the infant. Don't kill him, but *put the fear of God in him, for he can be useful for future breeding.*

THE BREAKING PROCESS OF THE AFRICAN WOMAN

Then take the female run a series of tests on her to see if she will submit to your desires willingly. Test her in every way because she is the most important factor for good economics. If she shows any sign of resistance in submitting completely to your will, do not hesitate to use the bull whip on her to extract the last bit of bitch out of her. Take care not to kill her, for, in doing so, you spoil good economics. When in complete submission, she will train her offspring in the early years to submit to labor when they become of age.

Understanding is the best thing. Therefore, we shall go deeper into this area of the subject matter concerning what we have produced here in this breaking process of the female nigger. We have reversed the relationships. In her natural uncivilized state she would have a strong dependency on the uncivilized nigger male, and she would have a limited protective tendency toward her independent male offspring and would raise the female offspring to be dependent like her. Nature had provided for this type of balance. *<u>We reversed nature by burning and pulling one civilized nigger apart and bull whipping the other to the point of death -- all in her presence.</u>* By her being left alone, unprotected, with the male image destroyed, the ordeal caused her to move from her psychological dependent state to a <u>frozen independent state.</u> **In this frozen psychological state of**

independence she will raise her male and female offspring in reversed roles. For fear of the young male's life, she will psychologically train him to be mentally weak and dependent but physically strong.
Because she has become psychologically independent, she will train her female offspring's to be psychologically independent. *What have you got?* You've got the nigger woman out front and the man behind and scared. This is a perfect situation for sound sleep and economics.

Before the breaking process, we had to be alertly on guard at all times. Now we can sleep soundly, for out of Frozen fear, his woman stands guard for us. He cannot get past her infant slave process. *HE IS A GOOD TOOL, NOW READY TO BE TIED TO THE HORSE AT A TENDER AGE.*

By the time a nigger boy reaches the age of sixteen, he is soundly broken in and ready for life's sound and efficient work and the reproduction of a unit of good labor force.

Continually, though the breaking of uncivilized savage niggers, by throwing the nigger female savage into a frozen psychological state of independency, by killing of the protective male image by creating a submissive dependent mind of the nigger male savage, we have created an orbiting cycle that turns in its own axis forever, unless a phenomenon occurs and reshifts the positions of the female savages. We show what we mean by example. Take the case of the two economic slave units and examine them closely.

" I been drug and put through the shackles so bad I done forgot some of my children's names." Laura Clarke, age 87, near Livingston, Sumter County, Alabama. Born in North Carolina and brought to Alabama as a child.

THE NEGRO MARRIAGE UNIT:

We breed two nigger males with two nigger females. Then we take the nigger males from them and keep them moving and working. Say the one nigger female bear a nigger female and the other bears a nigger male. Both nigger females, being without the influence of the nigger image, frozen with an independent psychology, will raise their offspring into reverse positions. The one with the female offspring will teach her to be like herself, independent and negotiable (**we negotiate with her, through her, by her and negotiate her at will**). The one with the nigger male offspring, she being frozen with a subconscious fear for his life, will raise him to be mentally dependent and weak, but physically strong-- in other words, body over mind. Now in a few years when these two offsprings become fertile for early reproduction, we will mate and breed them and continue the cycle. That is good, sound, and long range comprehensive planning.

WARNING: POSSIBLE INTERLOPING NEGATIVES

Earlier, we talked about the non-economic good of the horses and the nigger in their wild or natural state: We talked out the principle of breaking and tying them together for orderly production. Furthermore, we talked about paying particular attention to the female savage and her offspring orderly future planning; then, more recently we stated that, by reversing the positions of the male and the female savages, we had created an orbiting cycle that turns on its own axis forever, until this phenomenon occurred and reshifted the positions of the male and female savages.

Our experts warned us about the possibility of this phenomenon occurring, for they say the mind has a strong drive to correct and recorrect itself over a period of time. If it can touch substantial original historical base; and they advised us that the best way to deal with the phenomenon is to shave off the brute's mental history and create a multiplicity of phenomena of illusions that each illusion will twirl in it's own orbit, something similar to floating balls in a vacuum.

This creation of a multiplicity of phenomena of illusions entails the principles of cross-breeding the nigger and the horse as we stated above, the purpose of which is to create a diversified division of labor thereby creating different levels of labor and different values of illusions at each connecting level of labor, the results of which is the severance of the points of original beginnings for each sphere illusion.

Since we feel that the subject matter may get more complicated as we proceed in laying down our economic plan concerning the purpose, reasons, and effect of cross-breeding horses and niggers, we shall lay down the following definitional terms for future generations:

1.) Orbiting cycle means a thing turning in a given path.

2.) Axis means upon which or around which a body turns.

3.) Phenomenon means something beyond ordinary conception and inspires awe and wonder.

4.) Multiplicity means a great number.

5.) Sphere means a globe.

6.) Cross-breeding a horse means taking a horse and breeding it with an ass longheaded mule that is not reproductive nor productive by itself.

7.) Cross-breeding niggers means taking as many drops of good white blood and putting them into as many nigger women as possible, varying the drops by various tones that you want, and then letting them breed with each other until circle of colors appear as you desire. What this means is this: Put the niggers and the horse in the breeding pot, mix some asses and some good white blood and what do you get?

You got a multiplicity of colors of ass backward, unusual niggers, running, tied to backward ass long-headed mules, the productive of itself, the other sterile _(THE ONE CONSTANT, THE OTHER DYING-- WE KEEP THE NIGGER CONSTANT FOR WE MAY REPLACE THE MULE FOR ANOTHER TOOL, BOTH MULE AND NIGGER TIED TO EACH OTHER, NEITHER KNOWING WHERE THE OTHER CAME FROM AND NEITHER PRODUCTIVE FOR ITSELF, NOR WITHOUT EACH OTHER.)_

CONTROLLED LANGUAGE

Cross-breeding completed, for further severance from their original beginning, *we must completely annihilate the mother tongue* to both the new nigger and the new mule and institute a new language that involves the new life's work of both. You know language is a peculiar institution. It leads to the heart of a people. The more a foreigner knows about the language of another country the more he is able to move through all levels of that society. Therefore, if the foreigner is an enemy of another country, to the extent that he knows the body of the language, to that extent is the country vulnerable to attack or invasion of a foreign culture. For example, you take a slave, if you teach him all about your language, he will know all your secrets, and he is then no more a slave, for you can't fool him any longer, and *being a fool is one of the basic ingredients of and incidents to the maintenance of the slavery system.*

For example if you told a slave that he must perform in getting out *"OUR CROPS"* and he knows the language well, he would know that *"OUR CROPS"* didn't mean *"OUR" CROPS*, and the slavery system would break down, for he would relate on the basis of what *"OUR CROPS"* really meant.

So you have to be careful in setting up the new language for the slave would soon be in your house, talking to you as *"MAN TO MAN"* and that is death to our economic system.

In addition, the definition of words or terms is only a minute part of the process. Values are created and transported by communication through the body of the language. A total society has many interconnected value systems. All these values in the society have bridges of language to connect them for orderly working in the society, but for these language bridges, these many value systems would shapely clash and cause internal strife or civil war, the degree of the conflict being determined by the magnitude of issues or relative opposing strength in whatever form. For example, if you put a slave in a hog pen and train him to life there and incorporate in him to value it as a way of life completely, the biggest problem you would have out of him is that he would worry you about provisions to keep the hog pen clean, or partially clean, or he might not worry you at all. On the other hand, if you put this same slave in the same hog pen and make a slip and incorporate something in his language whereby he comes to value a house more than he does his hog pen, you got a problem. He will soon be in your house.

" My mammy was a fine weaver; this is her spinning wheel." Lucindy Lawrence Jurdon, age 79, Lee County, Alabama. Born 1858, Macon County, Georgia. Slave in Georgia.

FOOD FOR THOUGHT FROM THE INTERNET

Dear Black Americans:

After all of these years and all we have been through together, we think it's appropriate for us to show our gratitude for all you have done for us.

We have chastised you, criticized you, punished you, and in some cases even apologized to you, but we have never formally nor publicly thanked you for your never-ending allegiance and support to our cause.

This is our open letter of thanks. We will always be in your debt to you for your labor. You built this country and were responsible for the great wealth we still enjoy today. Upon your backs, laden with the stripes we sometimes had to apply for disciplinary reasons, you carried our nation.

We thank you for your diligence and your tenacity. Even when we refused to allow you to even walk in our shadows, you followed close behind believing that someday we would accept you and treat you like men and women.

We publicly acknowledge Black people for raising our children, attending to our sick, and preparing our meals while we were occupied with the trappings of the good life.

Even during the time when we found pleasure in your women and enjoyment in seeing your men lynched, maimed and burned, some of you continued to watch over us and our belongings.

We simply cannot thank you enough.

Your bravery on the battlefield, despite being classified as three-fifths of a man, was and still is outstanding. We often watched in awe as you went about your prescribed chores and assignments, sometimes laboring in the hot sun for 12 hours, to assist in realizing our dreams of wealth and good fortune.

Now that we control at least 90 percent of all of the resources and wealth of this nation, we have Black people to thank the most. We can only think of the sacrifices you and your families made to make it all possible.

You were there when it all began, and you are still with us today, protecting us from those Black people who have the temerity to speak out against our past transgressions.

Thank you for continuing to bring 95 percent of what you earn to our businesses.

Thanks for buying our **Hilfigers, Karans, Nikes**, and all the other brands you so adore.

Your super-rich athletes, entertainers, intellectuals, and business persons (both legal and illegal) exchange most of their money for our cars, jewelry, homes, and clothing. What a windfall they have provided for us!

The less fortunate among you spend all they have at our neighborhood stores, enabling us to open even more stores. Sure, they complain about us, but they never do anything to hurt us economically.

Allow us to thank you for not bogging yourself down with the business of doing business with your own people. We can take care of that for you.

You just keep doing business with us. It's safer that way. Besides, everything you need, we make anyway, even Kente cloth. You just continue to dance, sing and distrust and hate one another.

"Thank you for not doing business with your own people. We can take care of that for you."

Have yourself a good time, and this time we'll take of you. It's the least we can do, considering all you've done for us. Heck you deserve it, Black people. For all your labor, which created our wealth, for your resisting the messages of trouble making Blacks like Washington, Delany, Garvey, Bethune, Tubman, and Truth, for fighting and dying on our battlefields, we thank you.

And we really thank you for not reading about the many Black warriors that participated in the development of our great country. We thank you for keeping it hidden from the younger generation. Thank you for not bringing such glorious deeds to our attention.

For allowing us to move into your neighborhoods, we will forever be grateful to you. For your unceasing desire to be near us and for hardly ever following through on your threats due to our lack of reciprocity and equity -- we thank you so much.

We also appreciate your acquiescence to our political agendas, for abdicating your own economic self-sufficiency, and for working so diligently for the economic well-being of our people. You are real troopers.

And, even though the 13th, 14th, and 15th Amendments were written for you and many of your relatives died for the rights described therein, you did not resist when we changed those Black rights to civil rights and allowed virtually every other group to take advantage of them as well.

Black people, you are something else! Your dependence upon us to do the right thing is beyond our imagination, irrespective of what we do to you and the many promises we have made and broken. But, this time we will make it right, we promise. Trust us.

Tell you what. You don't need your own hotels. You can continue to stay in ours. You have no need for supermarkets when you can shop at ours 24 hours a day. Why should you even think about owning more banks? You have plenty now. And don't waste your energies trying to break into manufacturing.
You worked hard enough in our fields.

Relax. Have a party. We'll sell you everything you need. And when you die, we'll even bury you at a discount. How's that for gratitude?

Finally, the best part. You went beyond the pale and turned over your children to us for their education. With what we have taught them, it's likely they will continue in a mode similar to the one you have followed for the past 45 years (since school desegregation).

When Mr. Lynch walked on the banks of the James River in 1712 and said he would make us a slave for 300 years, little did he realize the truth of his prediction. Just 13 more years and his promise will come to fruition. But with two generation of your children having gone through our education systems, we can look forward to at least another 50 years of prosperity. Things could not be better -- it's all because of you. For all you have done, we thank you from the bottom of our hearts, *Black Americans*. You're the best friends any group of people could ever have!

Sincerely,

All Other Americans

Few Americans, black or white, recognize the degree to which early African American history is a maritime history. W. Jeffrey Bolster shatters the myth that the black seafaring in the age of sail was limited to the Middle Passage. Seafaring was one of the most significant occupations among both enslaved and free black men between 1790 and 1865. Ten of thousands of black seamen sailed on lofty clippers and modest coasters. They sailed in whalers, warships and privateers. Some were slaves, forced to work at sea, but by 1800 most were free man, seeking liberation and economic opportunity aboard ship.

Black Jacks places sailors of color squarely at the center of the Atlantic maritime culture. W. Jeffrey Bolster deserves our thanks for recovering an exciting, essential chapter in African-American history, one that not only deepens our appreciation for the roles black men played (as both able seaman and buccaneers, but also vividly demonstrates the fluidity and multi-dimensional complexity of black identity."

**--CHARLES JOHNSON,
AUTHOR OF "MIDDLE PASSAGE"**

Lushena Books would like to thank W. Jeffrey Bolster, for his excellent book on Black American sailors, which shows an important , but often neglected aspect of American History. And for the use of pictures and written material, which were included within this book.